THE

ORATOR'S TOUCHSTONE;

OR,

ELOQUENCE SIMPLIFIED.

EMBRACING

A COMPREHENSIVE SYSTEM OF INSTRUCTION
FOR THE IMPROVEMENT OF THE VOICE,

AND

FOR ADVANCEMENT IN THE GENERAL ART OF
PUBLIC SPEAKING.

BY HUGH McQUEEN.

NEW YORK:
HARPER & BROTHERS, PUBLISHERS,
Nos. 329 AND 331 PEARL STREET,
FRANKLIN SQUARE.
1860.

TO THE

HON. JOHN McLEAN,

ONE OF THE JUDGES OF THE SUPREME COURT OF THE UNITED STATES,

The following pages are very respectfully inscribed, by one who has uniformly cherished an equal admiration for the beautiful morality which adorns his private character, and for the solid learning, sound integrity, and inflexible firmness, the union of which in his person, has contributed to reflect an enduring lustre on the most elevated seat of American jurisprudence.

PREFACE.

The Essays presented in this volume were commenced by the author without any view to publication, during a suspension of professional duties, occasioned by the pressure of ill health. The earlier numbers were written under the united influence of two very innocent desires. The one of which was to occupy the thoughts of the writer with some species of employment, and the other to embody in a tangible and specific form, some novel if not profitable views which had been long floating on the surface of the mind, and which had been directly derived from an observation of practical life.

The determination to hold these papers in reserve was changed by the persuasion of a few cultivated and judicious friends who had carefully perused them, and expressed the conviction that some good might probably be accomplished by investing them with a more enduring form than was originally contemplated.

It is highly probable that the ultimate results may

prove that the opinions which influenced the writer to change his early decision on this subject, were the dictate of a partial spirit of kindness, rather than of a severe judgment of what was best for the writer and the public interests. But the publication of the ensuing chapters has been induced by a sincere desire on the part of the writer to make some contribution, even should it prove to be a mere pittance, to the common treasury of his country's information. If a portion of the exercises presented in these essays shall be impressed with the stamp of novelty, a lively hope is cherished that they will prove practically beneficial to those who may adopt them. And if they should not ascend so high in the scale of public appreciation as to be commended for their utility, they will at least experience an immunity from censure for the infliction of any positive injury on the interests of society. And they are accordingly submitted to the world by the writer in a spirit of humble but fearless confidence in regard to the personal results of the adventure to himself.

The words "speaker," "pupil," and "student," have been alternately adopted in the following essays, as descriptive terms to indicate the person who may conceive it expedient to apply to his own interests and improvement any of the disciplinary exercises which are suggested in this Book. Neither the term "*speaker*,' "*pupil*," nor "*student*," as used in the ensuing pages, has the slightest shade of reference to the age of the person who shall subject himself to the discipline of the exercises which have been advised. Either of the preceding descriptive terms as used in this treatise may include a person in the maturity of life equally with one who may be buoyant with the spirit and bloom of youth—the octagenarian as well as the minor amongst those classes of persons who shall choose to make an experiment on the validity and soundness of the suggestions contained in this book.

It may possibly be objected that the preceding terms "*speaker*," "*pupil*," "*student*," have been introduced with a culpable degree of frequency. But, in paying a due share of homage to the interests of perspicuity, it was found impracticable to indulge in a more sparing use of the terms in question. For they have been used as descriptive of character, and that particular character too, which forms the principal subject of the essays contained in this book.

There is another feature which prominently marks the ensuing essays, which, without explanation, may be pronounced a glaring and incurable imperfection. The feature to which reference is now made, is the fact of first devoting a chapter specially to the consideration of a particular exercise, and then recurring to the exercise already described again, and repeating it in union with some distinct subject presented in a subsequent chapter. The act of bringing up again or repeating an exercise which may have been already considered, and of blending it to a brief extent with some subject included in a succeeding chapter, has been adopted for the purpose of calling the attention of the practitioner in a special manner, to the subject which may be thus repeated. The preceding course has been also pursued for the purpose of preserving the unity between two exercises, where the use of one would be utterly useless and unproductive, independent of the other as an adjunct or auxiliary.

In regard to the general arrangement of the chapters contained in this book, it may be affirmed that it was found utterly impossible to reduce them to that precise and symmetrical beauty of form and of system which marks the pages of the stricter and sterner sciences. All which has been attempted by the writer was to preserve a distinct and visible boundary between those exercises which have been suggested for the improvement of the voice, and those other appliances of a more varied and miscellaneous character which conduce to fill up and perfect the entire scope of oratory. The writer is animated by the faint hope that in the last-mentioned attempt he has not entirely failed.

ASTOR HOUSE, *New York, Nov. 25th*, 1853.

Contents.

CHAPTER VII.

CHAPTER VIII.

CHAPTER IX.

CHAPTER X.

CHAPTER XI.

CHAPTER XII.

CHAPTER XIII.

CHAPTER XIV.

CHAPTER XV.

CHAPTER XVI.

CHAPTER XVII.

CHAPTER XVIII.

CHAPTER XIX.

CHAPTER XX.

CHAPTER XXI.

CHAPTER XXII.

CHAPTER XXIII.

CHAPTER XXIV.

CHAPTER XXV.

CHAPTER XXVI.

CHAPTER XXVII.

CHAPTER XXVIII.

CHAPTER XXIX.

CHAPTER XXX.

CHAPTER XXXI.

CHAPTER XXXII.

CHAPTER XXXIII.

CHAPTER XXXIV.

CHAPTER XXXV.

CHAPTER XXXVI.

CHAPTER XXXVII.

CHAPTER XXXVIII.

CHAPTER XXXIX.

CHAPTER XL.

CHAPTER XLI.

CHAPTER XLII.

CHAPTER XLIII.

CHAPTER XLIV.

CHAPTER XLV.

CHAPTER XLVI.

CHAPTER XLVII.

CHAPTER XLVIII.

CHAPTER XLIX.

CHAPTER L.

CHAPTER LI.

CHAPTER LII.

CHAPTER LIII.

CHAPTER LIV.

CHAPTER LV.

CHAPTER LVI.

CHAPTER LVII.

CHAPTER LVIII.

CHAPTER LIX.

CHAPTER LX.

CHAPTER LXI.

CHAPTER LXII.

CHAPTER LXIII.

CHAPTER LXIV.

CHAPTER LXV.

CHAPTER LXVI.

CHAPTER LXVII.

CHAPTER LXVIII.

CHAPTER LXIX.

CHAPTER LXX.

CHAPTER LXXI.

CHAPTER LXXII.

CHAPTER LXXIII.

CHAPTER LXXIV.

CHAPTER LXXV.

CHAPTER LXXVI.

CHAPTER LXXVII.

CHAPTER LXXVIII.

CHAPTER LXXIX.

CHAPTER LXXX.

CHAPTER LXXXI.

CHAPTER LXXXII.

CHAPTER LXXXIII.

CHAPTER LXXXIV.

CHAPTER LXXXV.

CHAPTER LXXXVI.

CHAPTER LXXXVII.

CHAPTER LXXXVIII.

CHAPTER LXXXIX.

CHAPTER XC.

INTRODUCTION.

The commentaries presented in this book are based upon two very sincere convictions, which, if fortified by the deductions of an enlightened experience, are assuredly deserving of the most munificent and profound attention from every intelligent mind.

The first of these convictions is, that every human being who has been endowed by nature with reasoning powers of an ordinary grade of respectability, may be rendered an efficient and useful debater, by a persevering application of the appropriate disciplinary appliances, and that accomplished orators, by the influence of well-applied culture, may be drawn forth from the rough materials of intellectual nature, just as statues of exquisite mould and finish are extracted from the rugged marble by an application of the artist's chisel.

The second conviction is, that the accomplishment of public speaking, instead of waving as a proud and attractive plume in the coronet of any peculiar class or profession, will soon become an universal attribute of the American people.

Our faith in the justness of the first conviction, is founded on the fact that the instance is exceeding rare in which history, with her impartial pen, has recorded, or tradition, with its authentic voice, has reported, an example of any person failing to grasp the palm of eloquence, who aspired to it with a perseverance which never faltered, and who was endowed by nature with powers of a respectable grade.

The reason why the second conviction is believed to be

just, is because speakers are bursting in rapid succession upon the world, who were utterly unknown to themselves or their acquaintances in that character, until their powers received an impulse from some casual train of circumstances, which started them into life as public speakers. Tongues are growing nimble under the spreading influence of the spirit of liberty, which had formerly been as torpid as that of the toad or the serpent. The farmer who scatters grain upon the broad surface of the earth for our physical nutriment, during the day, raises his voice in our public meetings at night, to encourage his countrymen to sow broad-cast the seeds of education. The mechanic, who yielded his devotions with unrelenting patience to his tools by day, pleads in fervid strains for the cause of religion, science, literature, and temperance at night. Every village and neighborhood in the country plumes itself on its orators. And there is not an aspirant to the post of constable, or to an inferior clerkship throughout the land, but who has the confidence to ascend the hustings, and address his countrymen not only in intelligible, but frequently in very intelligent terms.

And why should it not be so? The plain and unpretending farmer converses as sensibly at the fireside, as the politician who is seeking his vote; and he frequently furnishes him with bullion, in the shape of ideas, which is coined up into arguments, and expended with prodigious power upon the hustings. The mechanic can state his case more intelligently and lucidly, perhaps, whilst sitting on his work-bench, than the attorney whose boot he mends. Why is it that these men, who abound in the most precious stores of wisdom and information for private conversation, should not be able to ascend the hustings, or take a position within the bar, and speak at large to the assembled multitude on topics of public interest? They are restrained from doing so by the same circumstance which deters children from making their first attempts to walk, by a distrust of their powers to execute with intelligence and propriety. When a child shall have perfected one step in walking, without tumbling down, he will venture to make another, and another, and others, in endless progression, until he shall acquire the pervasive but useful and graceful accomplishment of walking. It is thus with the sensible speaker in ordinary conversation, who may never have ventured to participate in public speaking. If he once stands erect upon the public stage, and utters one sensible idea intelligibly, he can proceed farther in the business, and state two appropriate views of a subject; and he can afterwards so perfect himself by practice, as to speak as long as he pleases. The accomplishment of speaking, like that of dancing, lies dormant in the system of a large number of persons, who may be charmed by the brilliant and attractive powers of others; and, similar to dancing, this faculty or power only requires the application of one vigorous and determined attempt to secure its permanent possession. For, when once acquired, the faculty of public speaking is never lost, unless an individual shall wantonly and capriciously throw it aside. Men of limited education, almost universally, and frequently men of the most enlightened understanding, who have not acquired any experience in regard to the process of speaking, by sharing in the labors it imposes, lie under a gross misapprehension respecting the difficulties which are connected with this engaging exercise. Persons destitute of a practical acquaintance with the matter, are almost inclined to believe that a superior degree of fluency of speech flows directly from divine inspiration, and that where a person may not be endowed with supernatural gifts in this department of human exertion, that it is aiming at an impracticable height, to reach after the palm of eloquence. And those who excel in the business of speaking, have encountered no Herculean labor to expel the delusion which has fastened itself on the minds of their silent brethren, relative to the difficulties connected with the acquisition of speaking talents.

Persons at the porch of human existence often express their astonishment at witnessing the capability which exists in some men of speaking several hours in succession without even a brief resignation of the floor, and they marvel how the thing can be effected. And yet, after the lapse of a few years from the period at which the admiration was expressed at the observation of this almost celestial accomplishment, the very same men will be often found speaking during the space of four or five hours in succession themselves. So great a revolution does a nearer approach to the maturity of intellect, and the application of appropriate exertion, produce in the sum of human accomplishments.

A broader illustration of the deep and impenetrable darkness in which persons are often steeped in regard to their own accomplishments, cannot be exhibited than that which is sometimes afforded by men who suddenly burst upon the world in a strain of fervid and impetuous eloquence, without having previously dreamed of possessing the faculty themselves, or having yielded any symptom of its existence to others. The breath of life is infused into their latent powers by some exciting and unexpected circumstance, and the magic powers which are thus started into life are seldom quenched except by the icy finger of death.

For every human being who possesses the power of reflection, is competent to fix in his memory the leading views or arguments which will be reasonably suggested by any subject which may deserve his attention or excite his interest in the business of life. And if he may be able to fix these views in his mind and memory, he will certainly be as competent to repeat them to the public in an intelligible discourse as ever a pupil in a country academy was to repeat a lesson to his preceptor, in the presence of his class, which he had learned by the study and reflection of the previous night. For the faculty of acquisition brings into action a power of much more elevated reach, than that of recitation. The first operation demands thought, which is the attribute of philosophers; the last calls for impudence, which is the property of fools. In relation to the possession of the gift of eloquence by a large number of our race, unknown to themselves, a beautiful and touching fragment, from one of the sweetest poets in the English tongue, is eminently applicable:

> "Some mute inglorious Milton here may rest,
> Some Cromwell guiltless of his country's blood."

If, then, every person who is capable of reasoning mentally can be qualified, by persevering practice, for the business of intelligibly conveying his reasoning through a medium of words to others, it is a matter of crowning importance in this noble enterprise, that he should prepare himself by the adoption of the essential preliminary measures, for performing this duty agreeably, gracefully, and efficiently. And Lord Chesterfield, in those letters to his son, which have acquired a celebrity commensurate with the diffusion of letters, has somewhere submitted some remarks on the blandishments of manner and the melodies of intonation, which might be appropriately recorded on a tablet of marble in characters of gold. He says to his son, in substance, "that there was a member of the popular branch of Parliament, who never arose to address the house without at once commanding the most breathless attention, and yet that this member never submitted any views of a question more instructive than those which were spoken by a large proportion of the members." And he asks his son, in continuation of his remarks, "What particular quality it was in this member that constituted the source of his fascination?" and he answers the question himself, by observing that, "it was his pleasing address." He then proceeds by stating to his son that "there was another who never opened his lips in addressing the house without shedding light on every question he touched, and yet that the homage of a very slender share of attention was paid to him whilst speaking." And he asks his son in continuation, "Why this was so?" He answers this interrogatory also, by remarking, "that it was owing to an imperfect delivery and a graceless manner." And we might explore the speaking world from one of its extremities to the other, and we would behold the proposition written in characters as bright and as intelligible as sunbeams, that music and grace impart to the business of speaking a charm equal in fascination, and infinitely more enduring in its influence, than these qualities ever lend to halls resounding with the sweetest and most cultivated music.

Whilst recurring to the charm exerted by a musical delivery and an engaging manner, it may not be considered a culpable degree of minuteness, on a subject of such vital concern to the best interests of humanity, to present a few illustrations of the matter, both from historical and traditional reports. It has been said of Burke, that with all his strength and solidity of reasoning and magnificence of phrase, that it was his custom, from the effect of an ungainly delivery, to send the members of the English House of Commons to their dinner whenever he addressed the house; whilst Lord Chatham, (however great his far-reaching and intuitive wisdom may have been,) who was greatly the inferior of Burke in solid argument and varied attainment, almost universally chained the members to their seats by his rich, sweet, and varied tones.

One of the most distinguished divines in this country, for the saintly sanctity of his life, as well as for the classic purity and elegance of his diction in speaking, once followed in preaching an exceedingly illiterate clergyman, who was yet favored in possessing a most melodious intonation of voice, in the process of delivery; and the cultivated preacher cleared the church, in a very brief interval, of a congregation which had been previously held in a state of deathlike silence for an hour or two by his illiterate predecessor on the stage. What was the occasion of this graceless and unbecoming desertion of their spiritual counsellor, on the part of the congregation? It was the cold and lifeless enunciation of the one speaker, following immediately in the train of the musical and fervid tones of another.

The voice may be legitimately regarded, then, as far as physical agencies are estimated in the business of speaking, as the exuberant spring of a speaker's fascination; for a voice of music not only insinuates its own incidental charm into the heart of an assembly, but it almost universally bears with it the blended charm of an engaging and graceful manner. For whilst it will prove utterly impracticable for a speaker, who possesses a voice deficient in fulness and flexibility, to execute graceful gestures, the occurrence will prove equally rare, of finding a speaker blessed with a full and melodious voice, who can indulge in any other than flexible gestures, unless he shall perversely, choose to do so, contrary to the organic structure of the human system, for in this particular the voice and the hands move in sympathetic unison together, as has been demonstrated in the sixteenth chapter of this book.

If the voice may be justly regarded as the principal source of that power which is wielded by a speaker over human opinion and action, no rational or innocent measure should be omitted which may promise to bring an accession of improvement to that important instrument of power. And the principle is here assumed, that the voice is equally as susceptible to improvement from the influence of sterner disciplinary exercises, as those which are imposed upon the organs of speech by ordinary conversation; as the mind is accessible to an augmentation of its vigor from the effect of severer exercises than those imposed upon it by the reading of any plain and simple author, or as the body is to be improved in its measure of energy and elasticity by the circumstance of being frequently brought in contact with more trying exercises than those involved in the ordinary motion of walking.

The proposition is advanced in the commentaries contained in this book, that the organs of speech, which constitute an integral portion of the human machine, are as greatly improved in the work of producing sweet and agreeable sounds, by being frequently subjected to the severe discipline of declamation or singing on a high key, as the limbs of the body are magnified in their power to execute swift, graceful, and energetic movements, by the application and training of the exercises imposed by a gymnasium. The most surprising corporeal feats or evolutions which can be displayed to an admiring assembly, by any member of our race, may be regarded as an effect produced by a specific agency. And it requires but a limited expenditure of words to demonstrate the proposition, that in proportion as the productive power of the agency is enhanced, in the same ratio the effect must be pushed forward towards that degree of perfection which it is capable of reaching. If the limbs shall be carried from humbler degrees of elasticity, to those of a more elevated grade, in almost endless progression, by the exacting exercises of a gymnasium, it is evident that those evolutions of the body which depend for their perfect execution upon the activity of the performer of them, must keep pace in their advances to perfection with the extension of the activity of the frame that is to execute them. The human voice may be denominated an effect of supervening agencies, as justly as the motions which are produced by the limbs of the body. It is a motion of the organs of speech, caused by an exertion of the human will, which produces the sounds of the human voice conveyed in music and in speech. And although the organs of speech are not as clearly revealed to the vision, from their want of that extension which pertains to the limbs of the body, yet their agency in producing the effect of sound is equally as positive as that which is exerted by the limbs of the body in the production of motion; and the sounds when produced by the organs of speech, are just as perceptible to the sense of hearing as the motions of the limbs are to the visual organs. It follows as a necessary sequence from the premises, that should the organs of speech be improved in their strength and flexibility, by the disciplinary training imposed by declamation and vocal music, that the sounds which are produced by agents thus improved, must correspond in their approaches to perfection with the agents themselves.

Another illustration of the immense improvement which may be imparted to the voice by the imposition of disciplinary exercises on the organs of speech, is presented in that intellectual development of our race, which is constantly going forward under the influence of the sterner sciences, and the ancient classics. There is a permanent share of activity and strength communicated to the human intellect by the discipline of mathematical science, which will broadly assert its presence to the world, and to the subject of the discipline himself, when he shall be summoned to perform the grave and important duties of life. But the votary of these sciences may obtain a satisfactory revelation of the benefits conferred by them upon his intellectual powers, long previous to the time when he shall be called to participate in the more solemn duties of life.

Immediately after a student shall have taxed the powers of his mind by the study and solution of an abstruse problem in fluxions, or in conic sections, let him open a volume of some historical work which has formerly been regarded by him as being as dry as the dust of the earth itself, and if the work is commended by any intrinsic value or interest, he will find it as charming as the legends of some beautiful fiction, from the facility with which he reads it in immediate contrast with the scientific exercises, which he has just laid aside. And after having taxed the corporeal functions, in running with considerable celerity up steep ascents, in jumping over elevated bars, or wide rivulets, or ditches, or in raising heavy bodies from the earth, a person will find, after a brief interval of repose, that the simple exercises of life, such as walking, jumping any ordinary distance, or performing any common operation which requires the application of the hands, will be performed with a large increase of ease. This transition is brought about not merely by the effect of contrast between the relative exercises, but the muscles of the body will have experienced a positive accession to their strength and elasticity, from the influence of the previous exercises. And where the disciplinary exercises are continued in a proper degree of moderation and regularity, the amount of strength and activity added to the limbs will become perpetual.

It is asserted in this treatise, that the organs of speech are fitted for the production of superior sounds to what they would have otherwise been adequate by the severe and acute exercise of singing and declaiming on the highest key of the voice, just in the same way that the mind is trained for the better and more skilful performance of the whole catalogue of human duties, by subjecting its faculties to the maximum severities of scientific training, and just as the limbs of the body are prepared for performing, with greater alacrity and ease, all the simple duties of life which tax the corporeal functions.

Immediately after a pupil shall have stretched his vocal functions to their utmost point of tension, by singing or declaiming on the highest pitch of the voice, when he shall have indulged himself in an interval of rest, he will find that he can read or speak with infinitely greater fulness and clearness than he was able to attain immediately before the exercises in question were indulged in. And should he subject his voice to that sort of severe training daily, or even occasionally through life, he will find that it will be permanently improved in its music, depth, flexibility, and power of modulation. And as the most elevated keys in singing and declamation, when the force of the voice shall be fully exerted on them, impose the greatest amount of labor on the organs of speech, so the lower keys, in a gradual descent to the natural, middle, or conversational pitch, impose proportionally a less amount of labor on the organs of speech, when singing or declamation shall be practiced on them. And it will be vastly beneficial to a pupil in elocution, to take this descending scale, and practice his voice on the different keys in declamation and singing, for each key higher than the conversational or middle key, affords some degree of expansion to the voice.

And it should never be forgotten that the pupil ought to subject himself to an exercise in declaiming and in reading on the conversational or middle key universally, when he can do so shortly after having practiced his voice on the higher key, for this branch of practice seems to be as essential to preserve the natural key of the voice in speaking, as walking is in exercises of the body to secure the equable tenor of its motions. And there is some danger to be apprehended, where the voice is frequently practiced on the higher keys, that the pupil will involuntarily slide into the adoption of those keys as a permanent habit in speaking, unless they should be followed immediately by exercises on the natural key of the voice. And it will not be possible for him ever to speak with perfect ease on the more elevated keys of the voice.

A very lucid illustration of the benefit which may be derived by the human voice from an adoption of the disciplinary exercises which are recommended in this treatise, may be drawn from a reference to several objects which are very familiar in the practical duties of life. Scarcely any observing mind is ignorant of the very perceptible improvement of its tones, which is imparted to an ordinary church-bell, by a long application of the clapper to it in the usual process of ringing. Every person who possesses even a limited conception of the nature and properties of musical instruments, is conscious of the vast improvement which is communicated to violins and flutes by constantly subjecting them in the hands of a careful performer to the process of being played on.

But the favorable change which is usually produced in the tones of the instruments just referred to, by the fact of being long used, seems to result from a clarification of the tones of these instruments, in wearing from their inner surfaces, by the constant attrition of sound upon them, any roughness or slight excrescences which invisibly to the naked eye may exist upon these surfaces. This effect bears a striking analogy to that clarification of the notes of the human voice, which is often temporarily produced by clearing it from a pre-existing hoarseness, by a short subjection to sharp exercises in declamation or music.

But there are other objects connected with the business and the pleasures of life which afford a very simple and clear illustration of the vastly-augmented expansion, depth and flexibility which are yielded to the human voice by the exercises of declamation and singing with the utmost strength of the lungs on a key of great elevation.

We will in the first place adopt, for the purpose of the illustration just suggested, the instance of an accordion, which, when its possessor first commences using it, may be stiff and difficult from the want of flexibility in the leather of which it is usually composed, to pull to that degree of extension from one side to the other, which may be essential to its complete inflation; and to the production of the proper sounds in music. But when the performer shall have frequently seized the sides of the accordion, and stretched it to its utmost power of tension in producing music from it, the instrument becomes so perfectly flexible as to open mechanically when used in playing, the proper extensions, curves, folds, and contractions, so as to render the matter of performing on it quite an easy task to one who may be at all acquainted with the nature of the operation.

The preceding illustration corresponds as nearly as any illustration drawn from material nature can accord with the beneficial changes which may be wrought in the human voice by an application of that training to the vocal functions, which is conveyed by a habitual resort to the exercises of singing and declamation.

But the shoes which cover our feet, and the gloves which we wear on our hands, exhibit in very strong relief the extension and the flexibility which is produced in the organs of speech by the preceding exercises. The leather which enters into the composition of a pair of shoes, may be so unyielding when they are first obtained by their owner, as to render them not only exceedingly difficult to get on, but when actually put on, to exert a very stringent and painful pressure on the feet. But when the operation of pulling them on shall be daily repeated, and they are worn for some time, they become as yielding and flexible as a bit of India rubber. A pair of gloves when first purchased, may demand a considerable degree of pains and exertion to fit them to the hands of the wearer. But when he shall have thrust his hands into them a few times, and subjected them to the wear of a few hours, they become adjusted to his hands just as if they had been made for him expressly.

The voice, under the influence of the exercises prescribed in this book, becomes just as flexible and just as controllable to its possessor as any of the articles or objects which we have just mentioned may be rendered by use in the hands of their owner.

In subjecting the vocal organs to the process of tension, by a perseverance in the use of the proper disciplinary exercises, they receive a degree of extension and flexibility which not only increases the strength of the voice, but which grafts on it the faculty of modulation to such an extent, that it may yield a measure of sound which may be regulated by the discretion of its possessor. It may be enabled to indulge in the deep tones, as well as the high and the sharp ones, the soft and sweet as well as the loud and vehement ones.

But in the prosecution of the object now in view, a very satisfactory class of illustrations may be derived from the practical philosophy of the human voice itself. We may be enabled almost constantly to observe the vast progression both in strength and melody, which occurs in the voices of those who frequently exercise the lungs in musical performances in union with the choirs of churches. We recognize the vast revolution which may be produced in the voices of those who are subjected to the task of hallooing in answer to calls which may be made upon them in the character of ferrymen at fords on rivers. The voices of such persons, by the fact of being frequently exercised in hallooing, acquire incidentally a great increase of compass and depth. Persons also who have long been subjected to the necessity of speaking loudly, amidst the noise of mills and factories and the din of workshops, exhibit a vast reinforcement to the original vigor of their voices. Those at all familiar with the habits and peculiarities of the African race, must have recognized, even with the aid of a very superficial observation, how much their voices are almost universally improved in compass, depth, and music of tone, by the daily habit of singing and hallooing about the farms of their owners. The world has been long apprized too of the immense energy which is added to voices naturally feeble, by the practice of daily speaking in the open air, or even within the walls of churches. The itinerating system of the Methodist denomination affords abundant examples of the improvement referred to. And to close in this connection the consideration of examples, it will occur to every member of the bar, how much the voice suffers, in both its music and flexibility, in consequence of that long suspension of its usual exercises which flows from a vacation between the courts. When the labors of a lawyer are resumed again, upon the close of one of these vacations, until his voice shall be disciplined afresh by the exercises of the bar, he will imagine that he has one of the most unmanageable voices on earth.

The instances of improvement recognized in the powers of the human voice which have been submitted in the preceding lines, were obtained merely as an incident to other avocations and duties. They came to the recipients of these improvements unsought, and involuntarily to them. They consulted no lights thrown upon the path of elocution and music by the beneficence of art. They only enjoyed the benefit of two exercises for the voice—those on the loud and the high keys; and they paid no attention to the application and adjustment of these. They adopted no discipline for the voice, tending to prepare it for the production of the softer and sweeter notes. They subjected the organs of speech to no exercises on the intermediate keys between the high and the low. The pupil in elocution may ask himself the question—If the voice of man may experience involuntarily, and merely as an incident to the performance of other duties, such an enlargement of its powers, what indefinite accessions to its improvement may it not receive from the use of the appliances which have been prescribed by the enlightened and approved experience of past times discreetly and artistically applied?

It must not be imagined, from the degree of earnestness with which exercises on the highest key of the voice have been enjoined in this treatise, that the sounds or notes produced by the voice when exercised on those keys, are intended to be conveyed into the business of practical speaking. They are generally too sharp and straining to interweave with the simple and prevailing uses of the voice. They are intended merely as exercises to give expansion, depth, and flexibility to the voice.

The sweet tones produced in the preliminary exercises—those which possess a glassy melody, and which convey a music similar to that produced by the waving sounds of the clearest notes of a bell—are those which the pupil has to transfer from his disciplinary training, to the business of grave and practical speaking.

And there is no proposition more true, than that a voice constantly habituated to the production of sweet and musical tones, in the exercises which are imposed for the purpose of discipline, can be made to transfer the same tones to the business of speaking. The production of such tones constantly in exercise will, in the course of time, ripen into a fixed habit, and will introduce itself into other exercises of the voice, and will blend itself with them. The nerves and muscles about the throat—the organs of speech—become influenced in such a way in the exertion of frequently producing such tones, that they at length receive an inclination, formation, or curve, adapted to the yielding of them. The act of producing them in the grave and important business of speaking on the active stage of life, after having habitually repeated them in exercises adopted merely for the purposes of training the voice, will be similar to the act of transferring by a sportsman that precise degree of accuracy which he may have acquired in the exercise of shooting at a mark, to the practical business of shooting at living objects. For the organs of speech, like other materials in nature which yield under the force of pressure which may be exerted upon them, are expanded and rendered flexible by the stress of the voice being frequently brought to bear upon them; and when a certain inflexion or curvature of the organs of speech is caused by the force applied in producing a melodious tone of voice, that same inflexion, curvature, or yielding of the organs of speech will occur again, whenever the same measure of force shall be brought to bear upon them, and consequently the sweet tone or sound will follow as the result, until it shall become as mechanical as any tune produced on the flute or violin.

The perplexing difficulty which meets a great proportion of speakers at the very threshold of their exertions in speaking, is what appears to be on some occasions a level surface, and on other occasions a convex surface about the root of the tongue, that prevents him, let him exert himself as he may, in sounding the voice, from producing deep, full, and swelling tones. At his early essays in speaking, the inevitable product of the student's voice, will be superficial notes.

The speaker, under the experience of the preceding difficulties, eagerly covets a hollow space, or concave surface in that portion of the throat, about the root of the tongue, which will afford room for creating and sending forth deep, mellow, and full tones, in the business of speaking. What will appear to a practitioner or pupil, to be a cavity or hollow about the root of the tongue, will be produced by a long perseverance in exercising his voice with its utmost strength, on the most elevated key in declamation, and in singing. Which exercises should be invariably followed by exercises on the middle and lower keys, in order to blend softness with depth and strength in the tones of the voice.

The pupil will find exercises on the high key of the voice, almost universally followed by an apparent deepening or concave curvation of the surface, about the root of the tongue. But this sense of hollowness will disappear, and will not become permanent in its duration, until it shall be habitually contracted from a long perseverance in practicing the voice on the highest key.

And whilst the subject of full and swelling sounds of the voice is under consideration, it may not prove a culpable expenditure of time, to suggest to the pupil, that the voice is qualified to produce full and melodious sounds in their greatest perfection, by frequently exercising it on the highest key. But sounds of this description are rarely if ever yielded in perfection by the voice, in the article of being trained on the high key. Full and swelling sounds are yielded in their best form, and in their utmost reach and extension, when the voice is pitched on the natural or middle key, and exerted on that key. The notes produced by the voice, when exerted on its highest key, are too sharp to admit of fulness or softness. Hence follows the necessity of practicing the voice frequently on the middle or natural key, in order to render the production of full and swelling sounds, a permanent accomplishment or property of the voice.

If the voice of a speaker should habitually yield feeble, effeminate, or treble notes in speaking, the practitioner or pupil may remedy this defect, and render the voice more masculine and energetic in its tones, by exercising it with frequency, on the high key in declamation and in song, by hallooing loudly when in the depths of the forest, or the retirement of the fields, and by putting in requisition the various exercises which have been prescribed in this work.

The question is often propounded, whether a voice naturally extended in its compass, and soft and musical in its tones, can be improved by an application of the rules of art. There is no proposition more true, than that a voice of this description may be improved by culture and discipline, and it is an affirmation equally true, that even a very superior voice requires the assistance of art, to perfect its powers. The voice, in this respect, is like the limbs of the body. One individual may throw another an immense distance behind him in a foot race, and yet in dancing, or in any other exercise of the limbs which might be perfected by the application of art and skill, the person thus distanced in a foot race, would perhaps surpass his elastic and nimble-footed neighbor, so far as to shame him into insignificance. So great is the efficacy of science, practice, and method, in regulating, and in disposing to advantage, the functions of the human frame. The result of discipline and cultivation, will be found as perceptible in relation to the finest human voice. Unregulated and uncultivated music, melody, and softness, in a human voice, may be appreciated for the agreeable intonations which the combination of these qualities in one voice will be likely to produce. And a sparkling eye, a crimson cheek, and regular features, planted by nature in a rustic face, will excite pleasing sensations in the breast of a beholder. But to invest such qualities in the human face with that just measure of power and influence which they are capable of yielding, they must receive their crowning graces and finishing touches from the hand of art. It is thus with the human voice. Its inherent possession of the properties of softness and melody, without the ability to give a specific application or direction to these advantages, according to the pleasure of their possessor, renders them, to some extent, vain and nugatory gifts. Even the wild birds of song may be enabled, under the influence of care and culture, to yield sweeter and more varied notes. What incalculably greater benefits must the voice of man derive from culture, when he, in his highest state of development, is the noblest and proudest monument of cultivation and art. A large proportion of those who contemplate devoting their lives to the business of speaking, appear to repose with a spirit of perfect contentment on the conviction that their accomplishments in elocution are fully developed and completed by the instructions on that subject which are incidentally imparted to students during an academic or collegiate career. This supposition is as shadowy as it would be to suppose that a student of divinity, law, or medicine, was perfected in either of these sciences, by the preliminary lessons which might be received under the roof of a preceptor. The discipline received in either of the professional sciences, from a preceptor, may be regarded in the light of a porch of entry to a temple, in which the most precious and occult mysteries were concealed. The instruction received by a student on the subject of elocution during a college course, is not designed by those who administer the instruction, to be final to any greater extent than that which is communicated in the various other branches of education. Elocution, as it is usually taught in colleges, is merely incidental. It is rarely taught as a distinct branch of education, in which a professor is to devote his whole time and talents to the cultivation of the style and manner of a pupil in delivering a speech. Most universities are liberally provided with the means of instruction in the department of rhetoric. But here the beauties of diction are cultivated to the almost entire exclusion of that ample and unremitted care which should be bestowed on the voice and action. It is not denied that the instructions given during a college course, possess their efficacy in giving the general principles of the art of speaking. But if the seeds are permitted to perish and decay in the ground, without subsequent and continued culture, the labors thus expended upon the pupil, are worse than thrown away. Unless he yields as devoted a share of attention to the voice and manner, amidst the active duties of life, as he does to his intellectual interests, he never will attain the maximum of his powers as a speaker.

The general course of remarks pursued in this introduction, might incline the reader to believe that the voice and the action of a speaker, the physical agencies employed in the business of speaking, had received an exclusive share of attention in the chapters which are comprehended in this work. This is so far from being the case, that we think it may be safely assumed that much the larger proportion of the ensuing pages have been devoted to a consideration of those branches of the business of speaking, which require the expenditure of thought and the application of what may be deemed pure intellection. It is true the voice has been extensively considered, but this important agent in the accomplishment of speaking, has been heretofore so much neglected both by public speakers themselves, and in the works devoted to the subject of elocution, that we could not consent to dispose of it with an exposition less elaborate and minute than has been displayed in our treatment of it here.

And in conclusion it may be truly said, that the student in elocution is lured by the brightest and holiest incentives to tread with an elastic and unfaultering step the path which leads to the steep but radiant summit of oratorical renown. He is stimulated by the growing demands of his country for speaking talent in every department of her service. He is stimulated to advancement by the fresh fields for the exertion and display of oratorical accomplishments, which are opening in rapid succession in every part of the world. He is prompted to a perfect development of his powers by a prospect of the incalculable benefits which may possibly flow from the future employment of his faculties in advocating the interests of religion, of peace, of science, literature, and all the varied and endearing objects which are inscribed on the extended catalogue of human interests. He is encouraged to persevere in the race of improvement, by the precious rewards which will gather on his path from the commencement of his career until he shall attain the goal of glory. He is encouraged to press forward in his approaches to the heights of celebrity, by the example of those names which shine as conspicuously as the brightness of a star on the long and shadowy expanse of past ages, and who trampled in the dust of the earth, with a proud and triumphant spirit the most startling difficulties which accosted them in their march. And he is invited to persevering exertion by the cheering light of those noble and ethereal spirits, who, on the American continent, have encountered the force of every billow, the anger of every surge, and the fury of every tempest, in passing over the sea of difficulty to reach the bright landscape of promise which they finally enjoyed as orators and statesmen, and whose memory now stands revealed to the contemplation of the American people, like the roses in the sky, after the parting beams of the sun have disappeared.

CHAPTER I.

THE MANAGEMENT OF THE VOICE ONE OF THE PRINCIPAL ELEMENTS IN SUCCESSFUL SPEAKING.

IF a person is endowed by nature with a voice of full compass and melody, the usual exercises in declamation which pertain to the system of collegiate and academic discipline prevalent in this country, will exert a highly-improving influence on the speaker. But the great mass of human beings require an attention to the voice vastly greater than that which is afforded by the field of collegiate culture. The voice of but few persons, unaided by continued attention, will ever arrest the attention of the listener on account of the special beauty and melody of its tones. Many voices are what we would classify as indifferent, having no peculiarity either of excellence or deficiency. The voice, too, in some instances, is decidedly disagreeable, either on account of the monotony of its tones, the screeching character of its enunciation, its hoarseness, or its utter incapacity for cadence or modulation of sounds.

In every instance where the voice of the speaker is either indifferent or disagreeable, it does not execute the functions for which it was designed by nature; and it requires in such cases a degree of culture as sedulous to develop its inherent capabilities as the human mind itself. On this subject, perhaps, there is a more pervasive degree of ignorance prevailing, than on any other which is so intimately associated with the best interests of the human race. Those to whose professions and duties public speaking may pertain in life, are inclined to believe that nature itself has done all for the voice which is necessary to its uses, and that it will serve as an intelligible medium through which their ideas may be conveyed to the world, and that nothing more can be done, or is required to be done. And it is by the happening of a combination of circumstances apparently fortuitous in their character, or by the providential interposition of some friend who possesses an enlightened experience on the subject of the human voice, that a person is usually awakened to a just perception of the vast, we may affirm indefinite, susceptibilities of the human voice to improvement from continued culture.

Every person who has enjoyed an ordinary share of experience in the practice of speaking, will apprehend the justness of the preceding remarks, in the comparative influence and effect exerted by his own efforts at different times. He will at times anticipate a rich and brilliant harvest of admiration and plaudits from the immensity of his preparations and the plenitude of the resources which he knows he will be enabled to bring to bear on the subject before him. His mortification will be frequently proportioned in its intensity to the vividness of his previous expectations, at the perfection of his disappointment. What was intended and expected to be the music of eloquence, falls in lifeless and futile accents from the lips of the speaker. Not a syllable of commendation is uttered—the audience has not been wooėd into a breathless silence by the speaker; and perhaps the current of expectation, which flowed with so much fervor a few minutes before, is frozen in its channel, by commentaries on the length of the speech, on the introduction of topics which had nothing to do with the question discussed, or the culpable omission of others which were vitally essential to its fair exposition. The same person has been perhaps regaled with miracles of achievement and raptures of applause where he cherished but little interest in the disposition of the subject debated, and where his preparation had been culpably superficial. The solution of this apparent capriciousness in the admiration and taste of the public, may be infallibly traced to the varying powers of execution in the speaker himself. Where his mental preparation was commensurate with the occasion, his vocal functions did not act in unison with the powers of thought. When his treasury of thought had been lightly taxed, his machinery of utterance had invested poverty of language and feebleness of argument with the deceptive glare of artificial beauty. The same peculiarity is recognized in the varied effects attendant on efforts in the department of music. The skilful votary of science turns over leaf after leaf in the volume of his printed melodies, and plays off his piece with the glibness of well-oiled machinery, without having omitted the minutest dot, cross, or bar which enters into the composition of the piece. The universal exclamation is, alas! how insipid. Another performer takes up the same piece of music who is vastly inferior in point of science to the first, but who is competent to draw forth the latent treasures of sound from the instrument, and he discourses his audience into ecstacies.

CHAPTER II.

A HAPPY FACULTY OF INTONATION—ITS ADVANTAGES.

As the effect and power of a speaker depends, in a very great degree, upon the intonations of the voice in the delivery of a speech, address, or argument of any description, it is an achievement of incalculable importance, in the field ot elocution, to acquire some specific tone of enunciation, which shall be peculiar to the person himself—that is, he should adopt it as an inflexible rule of action, to acquire some fixed mode of music in the matter of enunciation, into which he may easily and inevitably glide on every occasion, when he participates in speaking, just as a graceful dancer falls naturally into his own peculiar mode of dancing, whenever he passes through the evolutions of a dance, or as a charming vocalist, whenever he raises his voice in song, slides as easily into his own particular style of singing, as the hand falls to the side of the human frame, when it has been elevated for any particular object or purpose.

It may appear to an unpracticed ear in such matters, to be an unique expression, to apply the term music to the subject of elocution or oratory. But an axiom of any kind does not suggest the idea of greater intrinsic certainty, than the proposition that every successful or engaging speaker has a style or intonation in speaking, which may be denominated his own peculiar music. For unless he grafts this special property upon his oratory, it will present no definite quality or characteristic, and whenever he commences the performance of speaking, he will have a tendency to fall into the ever-shifting varieties of indifferent and imperfect enunciation.

A large proportion of those who speak from the pulpit, from the hustings, amid the pursuits of the bar, and in the deliberative assemblies of the country, may be truly said to possess no generic style of music or of intonation in speaking. They invest their hearers with the possession of their intellectual wares, just as a Saturday-night fiddler at a rustic dance puts his patrons in possession of his resources of music, by a profuse expenditure of physical exertion. The legitimate fruit of this want of style and tune in speaking, is that the speech made by a speaker on any particular occasion, is only recollected by the hearers as such, some pure particles of intellectual gold, which are drawn forth from the mind of the speaker by the exigencies of the occasion are treasured up in the memory of the audience as incidents distinct from the speech; but the effort itself, as an integral thing, leaves no fragrant or pleasing reminiscences in its train.

Whilst sitting in the gallery of the House of Representatives, some years since, our attention was engaged, amidst a wilderness of uninteresting debaters, by one whose delivery was peculiarly fine in its mould, and on fixing our observation steadily upon the speaker, we noticed that the same agreeable sensation which was imparted to our own breast by the speaker, had also been communicated to others, for the members of Congress were collecting in a dense group around him. This attraction exerted by the speaker, was purely the result of intonation, and it earned for him the highest honors of the house, unaided by any peculiar powers of ratiocination. For though imbued with the elegancies of classic lore, he was fortified by no giant energies of mind.

We once saw that great master of the music of the human voice, Henry Clay, followed in an address by one of the most celebrated speakers in the southwest, and notwithstanding the speech of the last-mentioned speaker was embellished with the varied gems which sparkle in the treasury of science, history and poetry, his enunciation fell upon the ear like the croaking of the raven after the dulcet strains which preceded it. The two addresses appeared side by side in one of the city journals a day or two afterwards, and though the speech of Mr. Clay was not deficient in beauty of phrase, yet we thought its literary features presented a quiet aspect in juxtaposition to the gorgeous decorations which marked the production of his associate.

And it may be here affirmed, that the peculiar charm of Mr. Clay's intonations of voice, was neither a casual nor a natural accomplishment, it was perfected and secured by the enduring application of all the aids derived from retired and public practice in the art of declamation, and from a studious and vigilant observation of the best living models in the accomplishment of speaking. This representation is not based simply upon some popular tradition, which is incapable of being traced to any definite source, but is fortified by the declarations of the possessor of these rare graces himself, on some literary occasion, though the occasion itself is not distinctly remembered. Yet when admired in the perfection and maturity of his unrivalled perfections as a speaker, he was regarded as a partial recipient of the beneficent endowments of nature. His elevated reach of intellect, it is certain that nature gave, but the aggrandizing medium through which his intellect was surveyed, was the fruit of persevering personal labor.

CHAPTER III.

AN EFFECTIVE STYLE OF DELIVERY A SPECIFIC QUALITY LIKE THAT OF TUNE.—THE PUPIL IN ELOCUTION SHOULD CAREFULLY FIX IN HIS MIND SOME MODEL OF EXCELLENCE IN THAT DEPARTMENT.

THERE is rarely a person who has bestowed any attention on the mode and manner of speaking in others, but who has found his admiration on some particular occasions, fired with raptures by the inimitable beauties exhibited by some speaker in the matter of delivery. Many speakers also, who are not distinguished for a habitual or uniform excellence in the performance of delivering a speech, will at times, under the influence of some casual combination of circumstances, display a music and power of intonation in speaking, which will excite both the astonishment of the speaker himself, and that of his acquaintances.

Now, whether the beauty of intonation in the matter of delivering a speech, to which we have just referred, has been recognized in another speaker, or whether a person, contrary to his current experience, has been favored in finding this beauty of intonation unexpectedly connected with his own speaking on some isolated occasion, it is a definite, fixed, and subsisting quality or property, like that of music or language, which may be acquired—which may be matured into a fixed habit—which is transferable, if the beauty of delivery has been noticed and admired in another—and which may be identified, seized, and rendered available to a speaker himself, if it has unexpectedly communicated a charm to his own speaking, on some particular occasion.

The person who has been smitten by peculiar beauties of intonation on any occasion, whether that beauty characterized his own effort, or that of another speaker, will frequently find it difficult afterwards to identify and to reduce to a specific personification, the precise qualities or beauties of sound in the particular speech or speaker which forcibly engaged his admiration. The effort to personify and bring a matter of this kind practically and visibly to the memory, so that the person desiring it, may give a taste or sample of the peculiar intonation to another, is similar to the effort to personify and bring up to the memory some favorite tune or air, which a performer would play off immediately, if it were only made known to him by the process of whistling or singing.

But however difficult it may be to revive the recollection of special beauties of intonation or delivery, so that the pupil may imitate or repeat the precise intonation when he wishes it, yet it may be accomplished, and that unfailingly, where the requisite attention is yielded to the subject. The best mode of commanding the specific mode of intonation when required, is to revolve the matter over and over in the mind, just as one exerts his memory to recollect a name, or some particular tune; and the personification of the specific beauty of intonation demanded, will (after persevering efforts to catch it) arise to the memory vividly. The object then should be to paint the impression of the particular intonation which the speaker admires, enduringly on the tablets of his memory, by keeping the invisible entity continually before his memory by reflection, by declaiming it extempore, and by connecting the precise intonation with the reading of some particular speech.

The student in elocution may apprehend in some degree, the certainty with which an excellent mode of speaking may be grafted upon his voice, by referring to the instances in which he has seen persons of a curious or grotesque enunciation in ordinary conversation, successfully imitated by observers of a mirthful and comic turn of mind. Imitations of this description are frequently accomplished with such a punctilious degree of accuracy, that persons in an adjoining room to that in which the mimic is stationed, will suppose with surprise, that acquaintances are present, who may be then at some distant locality. On other occasions, an assembly will be sustained in shouts of merriment for a considerable space of time, by well conducted imitations of persons who are characterized by vocal peculiarities. Another illustration of the perfect competency of the student to acquire the excellencies of intonation, is the facility with which he sometimes involuntarily imbibes the defective traits in the enunciation of a preacher, or a public speaker of any profession whatever, whom he often hears. He will sometimes detect a nasal or a drawling tone in his colloquial exercises, or some defective pronunciation of a word, which, on reflection, he will be enabled immediately to trace to some speaker that he has been in the habit of listening to.

It is true that valuable and agreeable peculiarities in speech, like those in music, are more difficult of acquisition than imperfections and defects. But still the certainty with which defects may be imitated by exertion, demonstrates infallibly the certainty of acquiring excellencies by the application of persevering exertion.

CHAPTER IV.

BY WHAT MEANS AN EFFECTIVE STYLE OF DELIVERY MAY BE ACQUIRED.

The first duty of a pupil in elocution, who may be desirous of acquiring a faculty of perfect intonation, is to cast about his recollection amongst the public speakers of the country, and to select amongst them that which has proved itself the best and most engaging intonation. Or if there be any peculiar tone or music of enunciation which has occurred to his own taste, as possessing high beauties and advantages, let him select that as his model of style, in what may be termed the music of speaking, and make it his own.

To reduce a particular style of intonation into possession, and to command the use of it when he chooses, there is one method of discipline which will as certainly achieve this object for a pupil as it is for the sparks to ascend upwards, when an explosion of any sort occurs. Let him select some speech or address remarkable for the brevity of its sentences and for the smoothness of its style, and let him adopt it as his daily habit to read the particular speech or address until he can read or declaim it just as he chooses to speak it. He should peruse, reperuse the particular speech or address, until he can give his voice any degree of elevation or depression he pleases in speaking the different sentences in it, so that he may accentuate each word in a sentence distinctly, and assign to each word in the sentence its proper emphasis. He should then read over the particular speech or address, until the whole production becomes set or tuned to the music of his voice. After this important preliminary has been achieved, he should then, when he takes up this speech or address, early in the morning, or at midday, or at whatever time he selects for commencing the speaking of it, fix in his mind the style of enunciation or intonation which he has chosen as his habitual music of speech, just as a leader in the music of a band or choir brings up to his mind the particular or favorite tune in sacred music, which he intends to raise for the congregation to follow in or unite with him in singing. He should run over the first sentence of the speech mentally, and blend the particular mode of intonation or style of music, with the sentence, before he utters a word audibly. He should then gently repeat the first sentence or two so as to perceive whether or not he can communicate to them the particular intonation, sound or style in speaking, which he desires. When he discovers that he has succeeded in this point by repeating the first sentence or two, let him add a third and other additional sentences in the speech, taking great care to preserve the style of intonation he began with, through the whole speech, or such portion of it as he may choose to read, declaim, or speak at the time. If a pupil will adopt this mode of acquiring a desirable intonation or style of music in speaking, and practice it several times in each day, or even once every day, he may, without doubt, command any mode of intonation or style of enunciation in speaking he chooses.

The simplicity and practicability of this formula of practice, may be explained by reference to performances in vocal music. Every person who is at all familiar with the practice of singing, knows that a vocalist will be able to blend a tune with much greater facility with a hymn which he has sung often in connection with that particular musical composition, than he can any other tune. The intonations of the voice, by being frequently combined in a particular arrangement or organization of sound with the particular hymn, song, or composition, by habit is so disciplined or broke as to correspond, after the necessary amount of practice, with the language, measure, pauses, breaks and time contained in the selected piece of music.

Thus it is in regard to any particular speech or address which a speaker daily reads or declaims, his voice by habit gradually becomes attuned to the words and to the particular measure of the sentences in it, so as to attain a great degree of flexibility and ease in repeating it over. So much is this the case, that the pupil or speaker will, after a term of practice, be enabled to speak it with any intonation or style he chooses.

CHAPTER V.

DEEP AND MUSICAL TONES OF VOICE—THE MODE BY WHICH THEY ARE PRODUCED.

In presenting the view which is designed to be unfolded in this chapter, it may be premised that the startling impediment to a production of deep and musical tones which meets almost every beginner in speaking at the early stages of his career, is what appears at one time to be too level a surface about the root of the tongue, and on other occasions a surface of too much convexity, to admit of the production of deep, full, and melodious tones in speaking. And this is a sensation in speaking which will be experienced in some degree through life, unless it shall be corrected and removed by the creation of what will appear to the speaker himself to be a hollow or concave surface about the root of the tongue, by a persevering exercise of the voice on the highest key in declamation or in music, or in both, if he chooses to adopt them.

When the pupil, in the morning of life, is discouraged in all his first attempts to speak, by that perpetual obstacle to the creation of musical sounds which exists in what appears to be too level, too convex, or too unyielding a surface about the root of the tongue to admit of the formation of agreeable and melodious sounds, the young aspirant pants for a hollow space or concave surface at the root of the tongue, almost with the same intensity of desire with which a subject of the nightmare covets a channel for free respiration. The pupil wants more room or depth of space about the root of the tongue, in which to create and forge melodious, full, and musical sounds.

The room, hollow space, or concave surface about the root of the tongue, which may be regarded by the pupil or beginner in speaking as essential to the creation of deep, musical, and full tones of voice, is produced by that tension or stretching of the muscles about the throat which is imposed upon that portion of the machinery of speech by exerting the voice habitually with its utmost strength on the highest key in declamation and in music.

Immediately after the voice shall have been exerted on a very high key, either in music or in declamation, the pupil will feel as if the whole pressure of the exercise had been brought to bear upon the root of the tongue, or on that portion of the organs of sound near the root of that member. The portion of the throat about the root of the tongue, after the pressure exerted by the act of singing or declamation shall have been removed, appears as if it had yielded considerably to the exercise, and that it had sunk lower down under the stress which had been imposed upon it. In a few moments, too, after the pressure exerted upon the organs of speech shall have been removed from what appears to the performer to be the root of the tongue, he will find the voice to be in much better tune or condition to utter deep sounds and to accentuate and emphasize correctly. The pupil will also find, when the voice shall have enjoyed a brief interval of rest, after the pressure first spoken of has been removed from what his physical senses indicate to be the root of the tongue, that it will be more full, clear, and deep than usual, and that he can both read and speak with more than his habitual clearness of note. The root of the tongue will seem either to have receded or sunk lower down in the throat, under the influence of the exercises which have been referred to in the early part of this chapter.

But whether it be the root of the tongue that is acted upon in the exercise of declaiming or singing on a high key, which produces that expansion or deepening of the organs of speech that renders them more competent to produce with ease deep, full, and swelling sounds, and which invests them in a more perfect degree with the faculties of modulation, articulation, and accentuation; one thing is certain, that the person performing in music or declamation on a key of great elevation, will feel, when the exercise has ceased, that greater room than before has been afforded about the root of the tongue for the exercise of speaking; and it is also certain, that it is the very expansion which is thus felt about the root of the tongue immediately after severe exercises in singing or declamation, which gives depth and compass to the voice, when the expansion shall have become habitual, by repeated and persevering exercise. And wherever the voice may be formed, whether it be in the glottis, or still lower in the throat, if the pupil himself should feel that the voice is beneficially affected by a pressure which shall be apparently brought to bear upon the root of the tongue, although it may in fact be brought to bear elsewhere, and yet lower down in the throat, it is enough if the student feels that the benefit is produced by pressure exerted upon the root of the member in question; for he will know that he is laboring for the improvement of his voice with some returns of benefit to himself, although he may not be able to designate with technical accuracy what particular portions of the organs of speech are particularly affected by his disciplinary exercises. If a patient who is afflicted with a chronic disease of the liver, shall find that a pain in his left side is greatly alleviated by the daily application of a brush to that side, a physician would be regarded as very unfaithful to his trust, if he should prohibit to the diseased person the use of his brush, because ne might not be able to specify, with professional and technical accuracy, that part of the vitals which had been beneficially influenced by the application of the brush.

Every system of instruction touching the formation of the human voice, concedes the point that all deep sounds of the voice are formed far down in the throat, and that they are accompanied by a much greater tension of the muscles about the throat than common or conversational tones which appear to come from the lips. And the pupil or performer certainly feels immediately after having exercised his voice on a high key, that the organs about the root of the tongue have given way, to some extent, under the pressure exerted upon them, and that the voice immediately afterwards is formed much lower down the throat than it previously was.

An accomplished writer on the subject of elocution in referring to the exertion of the organs of speech in producing deep tones or sounds of the voice, expresses the following views:—"This peculiar voice (referring to the deeper tones) when it is adapted to the expression of what is solemn, grand, and exciting, is formed in those parts of the mouth posterior to the palate, bounded below by the root of the tongue, above by the commencement of the palate, behind by the most posterior part of the throat, and on the sides by the angles of the jaw. The tongue, in the meantime, is hollowed and drawn back; and the mouth is opened in such a manner as to favor as much as possible the enlargement of the cavity described." The same lecturer observes in the same connection, "that the deeper formation of the voice is the secret of that peculiar tone which is found in orators and actors of celebrity."

CHAPTER VI

THE DEEP AND MUSICAL TONES—BOTH ACQUIRED AND PERPETUATED BY THE PERSEVERING CULTURE OF THE VOICE.

In the view of the human voice which was presented in the chapter immediately preceding this, (the proposition was included,) that the deeper tones of the voice are formed at a point of some depth in the throat. It sometimes happens that the faculty of sounding such tones is a natural endowment. But this is an event of rare occurrence. The original inclination of the human voice is, almost universally, to the production of superficial tones—those which appear to proceed from the lips, and in the formation of which the throat of the speaker appears to have no agency whatever.

It is by the adoption and daily application of disciplinary exercises to the organs of speech, that the capacity for uttering the deep and musical notes is acquired, and it is by a tenacious adherence to these exercises that they are preserved in perfection.

Much the greatest number of those who have charmed the world on the dramatic boards, and on the yet more sacred theatres for the employment of the faculty of speech, were originally endowed with a very slender share of vocal attractions. It was by a martyr-like submission to the most taxing, laborious, and continued disciplinary measures, that they grafted upon their voices the eloquence of sound. And these remarks apply as truly to those who have delighted eager assemblies by their accomplishments in music, as to those who have borne away captive multitudes by the seductive influence of eloquence in speech. They have almost universally commenced life with the conviction vividly painted on their minds, that they had to draw on the treasury of art for the great faculty of interesting and pleasing the world.

And, after all which has been said or written on the subject of the secret power of charming an audience which may be possessed by accomplished tragedians, the whole of this exuberant spring of attraction may be clearly recognized in the superior depth of their voices. It is in this quality, simlar to a wand of magic, that the creative principle of power may be found, which draws tears from the eyes of the heartless, shouts from the lips of the dumb, action from the limbs of the halt, and laughter from the stoical amongst the multitude.

It may not be denied that when depth of tone may be once acquired for the human voice by the application of the exercises which have been prescribed by the intelligent experience of the world, that other excellencies may be added to this prolific source of power. Its softness may be increased, its capacity for receiving the necessary inflexions is extended, its power of modulation will be improved, and its competency for the important duties of accentuation and emphasizing will be greatly heightened.

But all these faculties are the precious progeny of that prolific parent, depth of sound in the voice. They depend on that precious property in the voice, as truly as the leaves and the fruit depend upon the parent tree. Blend that quality with the voice, and all other graces will be spontaneously added, obliterate that estimable feature, and they will decay and disappear.

The very term, superficial sound, is at variance with the idea of music, flexibility, and softness. That quality, where it predominates, is an insuperable bar to grateful notes in instrumental music, and it is an impediment equally as formidable to engaging performances in the sphere of the voice.

The first duty of every person then, who desires to convert

the voice into a spring of power and celebrity, is to displace its superficial tones, by grafting upon it those of greater depth. And this will not prove the work of an hour or a day. Like every creation of art and labor which is highly appreciated by mankind, or which wields a commanding share of influence over the progress of human affairs, it is the fruit of persevering labor.

The pupil will be apt to suppose, after he has taken his earliest lessons in that system of training for the human voice which is recommended in this work, that the depth of tone which may be so eagerly sought, will never assert its presence. The voice will appear deeper and clearer, immediately after it shall have been exercised on a high key, either in declamation or in vocal music. But that apparent depth will give way in a short time to what may appear to be sounds of the voice, hopelessly and incurably superficial.

But let not the pupil despond or despair. That transient depth of tone and clearness of note which is almost certain to succeed every exercise of the voice on an elevated key, by the persevering use of intelligent training, will be ultimately ripened into a permanent faculty.

And an ample stream of encouragement flows from the fact, that the most prolific sources of vocal melody which have ever charmed the world, were opened and supplied by the culture of art. Similar to those beneficent and prodigal soils, which have been raised by labor and art upon the surface of rocky and sterile deserts, the notes which are grafted by art upon harsh and discordant voices, are those which yield the most bountiful and grateful returns of music to the world.

And the pupil should not be affected by surprise or pained by discouragement at the tardiness of the process by which deep and musical tones are acquired. If it be a natural tendency of the voice (which it is in a majority of cases) to emit superficial and unmusical tones, this, like other constitutional properties or conformations, requires time and labor to remove it, and to substitute a faculty for different and more desirable tones. For all natural properties of the human system are difficult to deface.

But the very sensation which is experienced about the roof of the mouth, about the root of the tongue, and about the muscles of the throat, when a pupil in elocution is passing through the process of exercising his voice on a key of great elevation, satisfactorily discloses to his own judgment that an operation is then in progress, which will eventually qualify his organs of speech for the production of deep and full tones. This exercise will reveal to him the fact that the vocal machinery is subjected to the principle of tension or stretching, which will not only afford more room in the posterior portion of the mouth and throat, for the utterance of deep and musical tones, but which also renders the muscles about the tongue and throat more nimble and flexible in the creation of sounds of any description.

The influence exerted upon the muscles and membranes about the tongue and throat, by the intense pressure of sound upon them often repeated, seems to him who experiences this pressure, like that which is imparted to the covering of a drum by the stress of the fingers upon it. The covering of a drum will yield but little to the pressure when applied the first time; and when the finger is removed, the covering will resume its level surface—no trace of the finger being visible upon it. But when the finger, or any other solid substance, shall be repeatedly and perseveringly applied to the covering of the drum, it will become more and more yielding, until at last it will become flexible to a very slight application of the finger. Thus it is with the organs of speech: the impression made upon them by the earliest exercises in declamation and in song, no matter how stretching and straining these exercises may be, will seem exceedingly transient in their duration.

But when the organs of speech shall be subjected to sharp and straining exercises, often repeated for a considerable length of time, they at length begin to yield to this continually-repeated pressure of the voice upon them, they become divested of their stiffness and rigidity, and receive that flexible and elastic nature which places them completely under the control of their possessor.

And is it at all strange that the organic machinery by which the voice is formed should yield to the pressure of sound continually and repeatedly brought to bear upon it? Even the hardest rocks are worn and hollowed out, after years shall have passed away, by the continued but gentle attrition of water upon their surface. Is it a proposition more formidable to the belief, to suggest that the functions of speech may be rounded, incurvated, or rendered more hollow by the continued attrition of sound upon them?

Sound is as much an agent as water, although it may not be as visible, tangible, and operative to the senses as that element. It is the force of the breath continually brought to bear upon a spongy surface of mere flesh, blood, and muscles, which is a much more pliant and manageable sur face than that of stone.

But the plain and substantive fact, that at the commencement of a system of disciplinary training, the voice of a pupil or beginner is found to emanate from the lips outwards, and that the same voice is found issuing from a posterior point to the root of the tongue or in the depths of the throat, at the termination of six months afterwards, is a fact which supplies a much more nourishing aliment to the human faith on this subject, than any reasoning which may be afforded by speculations merely theoretic in their character.

The great object of the pupil, then, in commencing any systematic efforts to train the organs of speech, should be to deepen the voice; that is, he should so stretch the muscles about the throat or root of the tongue, by daily exercise, as to form the voice deeper in the throat than it was natural for him to do. This is the simple but punctual performance through which he is summoned to pass. And the simple fact, that no person has patiently worshipped at the shrine of labor, in search of vocal improvement, without reaping the reward of success, whilst it stifles the voice of cavil, is qualified to waken into life the stoutest exertions of the ambitious.

Another symptom of difficulty in forming deep and musical notes which is experienced both by speakers and vocalists, is what appears to be a stricture or tightness about that portion of the throat which is adjacent to the root of the tongue.

This tightness in the integuments or muscles about that region of the throat, will not admit of full, deep, and swelling sounds of the voice. It is this stricture or tightness which a speaker or vocalist has to remove, by imparting an habitual relaxation or flexibility to those particular muscles. And after he shall have kept the organs of speech under a daily recurring discipline for some months in succession, the pupil will feel at the end of that term as if he was actually emitting sounds from a different organ from that which ushered them forth at the commencement of his exertions.

And there is another feature blended with the results of these exercises, and it is, that the improvement of the voice resulting from them will be revealed to the observation of others long before the pupil will be perfectly assured of their presence himself. The fulness and melody of his voice in common conversation will be a subject of remark among his acquaintances, before the student is conscious of the improvement himself.

CHAPTER VII.

THE DEEP AND MUSICAL TONES WHICH ARE OCCASIONALLY BLENDED WITH THE VOICE OF A PUPIL IN THE EXERCISES OF MUSIC AND DECLAMATION —IS IT POSSIBLE TO TRANSFER THEM TO THE PRACTICAL BUSINESS OF SPEAKING?

If, in the course of exercising the organs of speech, in declamation or in song, the voice shall be frequently or occasionally sounded in deep and musical tones, these desirable tones will be produced by the application of a degree of exertion which a speaker or pupil can recognize, estimate, and identify. If he can call back to the mind, can recognize and identify the specific measure of exertion which produced the rich and musical tones, he may be able to indulge himself in exerting the same degree of force again. And he can acquire the faculty of repeating the application of the same degree of exertion to the organs of speech, which in the first instance produced the musical tones, until he shall eventually glide into the habit of applying the specific degree of force with mechanical and unfailing accuracy.

The conclusion which may be legitimately derived from the premises assumed in the preceding paragraph, is this; that if the pupil can, by practice, bring to bear, with mechanical and unfailing accuracy, that measure of force upon the organs of speech, which in the first instance produced the musical tones of voice, he will, as the necessary result of this attainment, become qualified for the mechanical and unfailing production of the musical and sweet tones of the voice whenever he shall choose to do so.

Upon the two preceding propositions a third is suspended from which will be drawn the conclusion which is sought in this chapter. The third proposition is,—that if the organs of speech shall be mechanically and intelligently trained to the production of certain sweet and musical tones, by the unvarying application of a specific measure of force to them, then we are justified in adopting the conviction from the science of the human voice, from the anatomical developments of the human system, and from the general analogies of the case, that the organs of speech themselves will receive from the habitual application of the specified measure of force in question to them, an inflection, curvation, or determination, which will fit them for the mechanical production of the musical tones which have been spoken of.

The conclusion from the preceding propositions combined, is this; that if the organs of speech, by the habitual use of them in producing musical tones, shall receive a formation or curvation which will qualify them for producing the tones in question, at the pleasure of the pupil or speaker, then this formation or determination of the organs of speech, is an acquired or permanent physical property, which may be transferred to other duties performed by the voice, more important and momentous than the preliminary exercises. It may be transferred to the practical business of speaking, it may be habitually blended with the grave discussions of life, and may become an integral element in the composition of the speaker's voice.

The conclusion which has just been expressed, is sustained by the example of all masters of the science of the human voice, who have yet delighted the world. With few exceptions, the most accomplished and bewitching vocalists, who have shared the admiration of the world in a measure of redundant fulness, were originally destitute of any peculiar charm in the entertainment of song. It was by a persevering resort to the most approved modes of discipline, that they grafted their powers of fascination upon the voice. And when they once succeeded in producing an isolated note or sound of unusual sweetness, they never suspended their exertions on the subject until they succeeded in the precious enterprize of incorporating the attractive note as an integral portion with some entire and complete musical performance.

CHAPTER VIII.

EXERCISES IN VOCAL MUSIC BENEFICIAL TO THE VOICE.

The voice, like the mind, is improved, expanded, and conducted to its highest reach of perfection, by an almost indefinite range of appliances; and amongst the exercises which conduce to its improvement, the exercise of singing deservedly takes a high rank. The daily practice of singing communicates to the voice volume and expansion, invests it with energy where it is feeble, corrects its hoarseness, deepens its tones, and grafts upon it in the exercise of speaking a portion of that melody and sweetness which attaches to some of its notes in singing. And the introduction of vocal music in the exercises of many primary schools, as a branch of discipline essential to the perfect development of the pupil, can not be too highly commended. For, independent of the aid which it yields to the voice in subsequent life, it is a powerful auxiliary to health, in augmenting the vigor of the lungs, in promoting freedom of respiration, and yielding a healthful tone to the whole system of the physical functions.

The object here is to consider vocal music in connection with the benefit which its daily practice yields to the human voice in the exercise of conversation and public speaking. And there is one principle blended both with the mental and physical constitution of the human race, which clearly demonstrates, before we advance farther, the soundness of the principle here contended for, and that is the immense amount of improvement which is yielded to every faculty of the mind and every function of the body, by continued perseverance in any well-selected exercise. Is there any substantial reason which forbids an application of appropriate correctives to the voice. Without indulging in a retrospect so comprehensive as to include Demosthenes within its limits, we may scan the roll on which the names of the most successful speakers of modern times are inscribed, and we will discover that the most finished models in the art of enunciation, acquired their chief graces and skill from a constant attention to the interests of the voice.

In relation to the persevering practice in vocal music, we have never known an instance in which a beginner in the accomplishment of singing, who might have been indifferent or even insufferable at the commencement of his career in singing, failed to take rank in one of two classes of performers—that of being an agreeable or very excellent vocalist. And we have never known an instance in which a pupil in the art of elocution, habitually indulged in vocal music with the view of improving his voice in speaking, who did not reap perceptible improvement from the practice; an improvement too, which continued to be progressive, as long as the pupil persevered in paying his devotions at the shrine of the same auxiliary. We know one very conspicuous instance, in which the voice of an acquaintance, though possessed of incalculable strength, was yet harsh, monotonous, hoarse, without any depth of tone, without flexibility, without any power of modulation, and as one may naturally suppose, without the slightest pretension to melody, and who, yet by singing in every variety of way when opportunity presented itself, attained a height of improvement, which eventually astonished himself and his acquaintances. When the person in question, took occasion to participate in debate, every person was impressed with the fulness, clearness, and flexibility of his voice; and when he conversed in private, both strangers and his former acquaintances were in the habit of remarking upon the mellow and rich tones of his voice, and even on the sweetness of its music.

Almost every person is in the habit of observing the superiority of the voice of the slave population of the country, over that of the whites, in vocal music. In regard to the superior melody and sweetness of the African voice, we do not accede to the proposition; for there is something wild, vulgar, and indicative of a want of intellectual culture in the intonations of the African population in singing, which is characteristic of the race. But the superior compass and energy of the African voice, is so palpable as to defy all efforts at contradiction or refutation. The superiority of the African voice at the point which we have just admitted, is manifested in the surprising facility with which a band of sable choristers in the gallery of a church, will drown the more feeble efforts in sacred music, of the white race in the seats on the lower floor. We also observe the vast sweep of their voices, when engaged in sacred music in their cabins on the Sabbath, or in their nocturnal meetings. The same distinguishing property will present itself in their miscellaneous musical exercises, when passing from one part of their master's farm to another, or from the residence of their owner to that of a neighbor. The voice of a juvenile vocalist of this race, even without any extreme effort, will be heard from one boundary of a large plantation to its opposite. In addition to this, it may be safely affirmed that the voices of the slave population exhibit greater energy in ordinary conversation, or in communicating with persons at a great distance, than those of the white race. Their superiority in these respects, may be safely attributed to their constant indulgence in the practice of singing and hallooing about their masters' farms from infancy to maturity. A practice to which they are equally lured by an inherent fondness for music, and by a temperament naturally mirthful.

Another illustration of the vast addition to the strength of the human voice, which may be acquired by a habitual indulgence in singing, may be recognized in the extended reach which is usually acquired by the voices of ferrymen, simply from the daily and sometimes hourly practice of hallooing in answer to those on the opposite shores of a river, who may be applicants for their assistance at ferries, where no better or more artificial signal may have been adopted. Every person may also refer to the great additional clearness and fulness which will be communicated to his own voice immediately after having finished a hymn or song of any description, provided they may not have sung with so much vehemence as to superinduce a temporary hoarseness.

CHAPTER IX.

THE MODE BY WHICH VOCAL MUSIC IS RENDERED BENEFICIAL TO THE VOICE.

It may be adopted as an axiom, that the voice of every human being may be rendered more available for the purposes of public speaking, by a constant resort to the discipline afforded by vocal music. Voices of unusual strength and compass may be improved in sweetness, in softness, in depth of tone, and in the power of modulation, by the persevering application of this exercise; dull and monotonous voices may receive from it animation and melody; whilst feeble voices, in addition to the benefits already enumerated, may reap from it a vast augmentation of strength.

But the mode of applying this discipline has not been specified. And it may here be observed, that whilst every candidate for the honors of superior excellence in speaking may instinctively adopt some exercise for the improvement of the voice peculiar to himself, and which he will also instinctively correct as its defects may be disclosed to him by daily practice and observation—yet, in relation to the practice of singing, it may be observed that there are certain rules to be observed, by the faithful application of which the pupil may greatly abbreviate both his labors and the length of the route to the goal of excellence.

One of the primary exercises of the pupil, in the application of the discipline of music to his voice, is, whenever opportunity may present itself, to select a verse of some hymn or a portion of some song with which he may be familiar, and having first pitched his voice on a key of as much elevation as may be consistent with his vocal powers, and with a due regard to the safety of the lungs, then to sing the verse throughout at the utmost reach of his voice. The object to be attained in pitching the voice on an alto or high key, is for the purpose of imparting to it elevation of reach and depth, as well as sweetness of tone, by the process of tension, or stretching the organs of speech.

This exercise will prove in some degree irksome to a pupil who has not been much habituated to singing, but the fatigue resulting from the operation will certainly be vanquished by daily repetition. And by way of diminishing the amount of labor connected with this discipline, a pupil who has not been previously trained to any great extent, by the exercise of vocal music in church services or elsewhere, may adopt as his daily exercise for the first few days after he has commenced this mode of improvement, one verse of some familiar hymn or song, and sing it with the utmost reach of his voice, and then abandon the labor until the next day. And when he repairs to his selected place for practice on a succeeding day, let him sing his favorite verse again, and then pause, and after having paused for the space of five minutes, if his voice has not been too severely taxed by singing the verse over one time to admit a repetition of it, let him sing it over again, on the same elevated key which has been already recommended. Let him continue the method of exercise here suggested, until he may be able to sing the one verse on a high key with perfect ease, and he will find that his ease in singing it will be increased at each instance in which it is repeated, provided he may not repeat it so often in rapid succession as to produce hoarseness.

After he has ascertained that he can sing the selected verse with perfect ease, let him then from time to time daily add another verse to his lesson, as his improvement may require, and the strength of his lungs may permit, until he can sing the whole hymn or song.

And although, in his future and more advanced exercises, he may retain the hymn which was adopted as his first lesson, as a daily or occasional exercise, yet for the purpose of yielding to his voice a varied kind of discipline, he should bring into his service other hymns, songs, and tunes, which he may find by practical experience to be conducive to the improvement of his voice in elevation of reach, and in sweetness and profundity of tone.

The use of a single verse to beginners, has been recommended only in those instances where the voice will not bear the exercise comprehended in singing a greater number of verses, without inducing fatigue or injury to the lungs. Where a pupil, even at the commencement of the exercise, can sing a considerable number of verses without incurring fatigue, and without taxing the lungs and the vocal functions too greatly, he may sing any quantity he pleases, having a view at the same time to the prevention of hoarseness, which, though not a permanent injury to the voice, will render the subject of this exercise, in some degree, incompetent on the succeeding day, and perhaps for several days, to engage in the desired exercise with ease and advantage to himself.

But it may be here suggested to the pupil, as an indispensable rule, even at the commencement of the mode of discipline pointed out in the previous portions of this article, after having finished the daily exercise of singing one or more verses, on the highest key which the voice can bear to advantage, then to sing the same verse, or the verses of another hymn or song, on that key which will afford perfect ease, without descending to a pitch which will prove so low as to be both destitute of melody and of the benefit of discipline to the voice. The exercise last pointed out should be an unfailing supplement of the alto key in singing; and whilst the first will give to the voice elevation, compass, and depth, the latter exercise will preserve for it flexibility, ease, the power of modulation, and the natural key.

CHAPTER X.

THE MODE BY WHICH VOCAL MUSIC IS RENDERED TRIBUTARY TO THE ACCOMPLISHMENT OF SPEAKING.

It may, perhaps, be shaping the proposition too broadly to instruct a pupil in the art of enunciation to sing a verse or verses on the natural key of his voice, immediately after having engaged in the exercise of singing with his voice raised to its highest pitch, for almost any degree lower than the highest, appears so easy when sung just after the vocal functions have been released from the straining effect of an alto key, as to seem at the time to be the natural one. But it will be a beneficial exercise for the pupil to exercise his voice on some of the intermediate keys below the highest, immediately subsequent to singing on that, for the purpose of tuning the voice or of bringing it down to its natural level again. He may probably strike the natural pitch or level of his voice, immediately after having raised his voice to its highest pitch in singing a hymn or song, but the probabilities are against the happening of any such event, and if it should happen to be the case, it will be merely an accidental circumstance, unless the pupil has, by long practice and study, acquired great skill and expertness in the management of the voice. For the voice, immediately after having been subjected to intense exertion, is not in a tuneable state, and cannot be naturally brought to its usual level in conversation or in singing. It may appear to be the natural level at the time, but the pupil will find, after he has repeated a verse or two in singing, that there is still a key a little above or a little below the one which he has selected, which is the natural one.

The best method by which to strike the natural key, is to postpone the effort to obtain the natural key, or level of the voice, until some hours afterwards, when the voice has gotten over the straining effects of an alto key, and descended to its wonted and natural key or level. When the pupil does succeed in obtaining the natural pitch of the voice for singing, he should sing some favorite hymn or song, or any number of them he chooses, on this particular key, for the purpose of habituating his voice to it, which is the only one upon which he will be enabled to speak with a remarkable degree of fluency or grace through life.

When singing on this key, he will discover the benefit which he has reaped previously by exercising on a high key, only in one way, and that is in the great comparative ease with which he sings on the natural key—just as a historical work, or any work in general literature, appears almost as easy as a primer or a spelling-book, just after the mind has been released from the taxing process of solving some severe problem in mathematical science.

But notwithstanding the benefit of having previously exercised the voice on a high key in singing, may not be palpable to the practitioner, when he afterwards sings on the natural key of his voice, yet the benefit does exist, and he will discover it in the exercise of speaking or reading on the natural key of his voice, immediately after he has finished the exercise of singing a hymn or a song on the natural key.

He will find that the voice, after having been previously taxed up to its highest capabilities, by the alto key, performs its offices with a surprising increase of facility on the lower and natural key, just as a racer runs with a vast increase of ease and celerity when he puts on light shoes at the commencement of the race, after having had his feet encumbered for some weeks previously with heavy brogans or thick-soled shoes.

CHAPTER XI.

THE QUANTITY OF TIME WHICH SHOULD BE DEVOTED TO VOCAL MUSIC BY A PUPIL IN ELOCUTION.

There can be no definitive length of time prescribed for exercising the voice daily in singing on an elevated key, at the terminus of which the pupil must stop, and beyond which improvement to palpable observation cannot extend. Nor is there any specific number of tunes in each day for the exercise of the voice in this way, which is clearly preferable to any other number. On this point the pupil often having applied the exercise to his vocal improvement for a considerable space of time, whether that space of time shall be measured by weeks, months, or years, will be enabled to determine with a nearer approach to certainty from his own progress in improvement, than by any other standard or rule.

But it may be regarded as a tenable proposition, that though the exercise of singing on the specified keys is not to be persisted in daily, until the close of life, to the end that the desired improvement may be reached; yet the pupil should submit to this exercise daily, or as often as opportunity may permit him, for a sufficient length of time, whether it be six months, a year, or even more, to satisfy him that he has achieved the objects for which the exercise was originally commenced. This he will be enabled to ascertain with almost infallible certainty, from the improved facility with which he can read a speech or address, or any passage in a book. He may discover the improvement which has been effected by this exercise, after he has persisted in it for a considerable length of time, by the enlarged compass of his voice, and by the improved melody of the intonations of his voice, both in declamation and in singing. And his friends, perhaps to his surprise and gratification, will begin occasionally to remark on the tuneful fineness of his voice.

When he has progressed sufficiently far in the daily adoption of this exercise to discover that the excellence imparted to his voice has become in some degree habitual, he may then suspend it as a daily exercise, and resume it occasionally again when opportunity presents itself, for the purpose of preserving the benefit acquired, and of rendering it a permanent possession.

After the voice has been once augmented in its vigor, deepened in its tones, and sweetened in its notes, a resort to this exercise may be made once in a week, once in a month, or at such returning periods as may be afforded to the pupil by solitude or by his general convenience, reference always being had to the preservation of the improvement which has been acquired by previous discipline.

As to the number of times a pupil should engage in this exercise each day, it may be suggested that once is sufficient, but he may indulge in it more frequently if opportunities present themselves, and it should be dictated by his own convenience and pleasure.

CHAPTER XII.

THE EXERCISE OF VOCAL MUSIC CONDUCTED ON THE NATURAL KEY OF THE VOICE—ITS EFFECT.

SOME remarks have been made in a preceding chapter in commendation of the practice of singing a hymn or song, with the voice pitched to its natural key. The object in adopting this practice as a daily exercise, is to train or habituate the voice, by daily discipline in this particular mode, to that pitch or elevation in speaking, which is natural and easy to the speaker. Every human being has some grade or key in his voice, on which he converses, speaks and sings with greater facility and effect than on any other key. Persons may converse and speak intelligibly on a lower key than the natural one, and they may speak and converse intelligibly on a key of greater elevation than the natural key. They may also sing agreeably on a key of greater or less elevation than the natural one. But they cannot engage in either of these exercises with such perfect ease and grace, and with so much satisfaction to others, on any key except that which is natural or constitutional to the person.

It should be an object of constant solicitude then, with every pupil who is seeking either improvement or perfection in the art of enunciation, to ascertain by constant attention and effort, which is the natural pitch of his voice for singing and speaking. And when he has once ascertained this fact, then he should by daily singing and speaking less or more on that key, aim to make himself so perfect a possessor and master of it, as to be able to summon it to his aid whenever he commences speaking.

As to the time when the exercise of singing on the natural key should be put in requisition by the pupil, there is no period which is decidedly wrong or incontestibly right. The pupil may be governed in the selection of the time by his own opportunities and pleasure, and may indulge in the exercise when he chooses, and as often as he chooses. But it is not the most favorable occasion for striking with certainty on the right key of the voice, immediately after the pupil has been practicing the voice in music, on an alto or very high key. The voice at that time having been just released from an intense exertion, which has given it an unusual expansion, will not be in a condition to yield notes on the natural key with unerring certainty. And although the pupil may beneficially practice on lower keys than the highest, immediately after having practiced on an alto or high key, yet he cannot rest perfectly assured then, that he has selected the right key of the voice, for the reason already assigned, that any key at that time will appear so easy in comparison with the straining effect of the highest, as to seem to be the natural one.

The preferable and most certain mode by which to ascertain the natural key, is to practice the voice some hours after it has been exercised on the alto key in singing, on the lower keys, until the one which is perfectly easy and natural shall be discovered.

CHAPTER XIII.

VOCAL MUSIC ON THE NATURAL KEY OF THE VOICE—CONTINUED.

To guard against error and misconception in this particular, it is proper to suggest to the pupil, that in making his efforts to obtain the natural key of the voice, he may select a key sufficiently low to be perfectly easy, but which yields no music, and the exercise afforded by which, will yield no melody or improvement of any kind to the voice. In making the selection then, a great degree of attention is requisite at times, to enable him to discriminate between various pitches of the voice, which are very similar in regard to the measure of ease with which he may sing on them, and also in regard to the portion of sound which they respectively yield.

It is known to every person who has participated even to a limited extent in vocal music, that in almost every hymn or song, sharp or alto notes occur in every verse or stanza, either at the middle of a line or at its close. These notes tax the voice at times, to carry them out full and perfect, to the utmost limit of its powers. At other times the voice, from the fact of these notes being at a point of sharpness beyond its reach, will drop them, skip them over, or sound them with a broken or imperfect intonation. When the voice fails, in the exercise of singing, to give to the alto or sharp notes which have been mentioned, a full and swelling sound, this fact furnishes positive proof that the pupil is not on a key natural to his voice. And the habitual practice of singing without giving a full and perfect sound to the sharp or alto notes, is injurious to the voice in the same way that the habit of dropping any portion of an evolution in dancing injures the pupil in that species of performance. It grafts upon his person habitual irregularity, and is a bar to the acquisition of the graces of motion. This habit in singing, most assuredly as an exercise in connection with improvement in speaking, should be sedulously avoided.

The certain way of enabling the pupil to appropriate the proper and natural key to himself, is to sound the different pitches or keys of the voice, previous to commencing the exercise of singing, and he will thus, after repeated efforts, be able to perceive the natural key or pitch, from its adaptation to his voice.

When he has discovered the right or natural key, let him then sing a verse or an entire hymn or song on that key, as circumstances may dictate. And let him repeat the exercise regularly every day for such a length of time as to acquire the perfect mastery of it, and establish it as a habit. And he may also practice it occasionally when opportunity may permit, until the close of life.

When the pupil has sounded the different keys of his voice, for the purpose of finding the one which is natural, and commences a hymn or song, supposing he has struck the right one, if he should find after exercising for a short time, that it is the wrong key, he should suspend the exercise for awhile, and renew his efforts to obtain the right one, for the object which he is seeking is not obtained until he finds the right key. That object is to acquire a habitual practice of singing and speaking on the natural key.

CHAPTER XIV.

THE ALTO OR HIGHEST KEY TO BE ADOPTED IN MUSICAL EXERCISES ONLY WHEN THE PUPIL IN ELOCUTION GIVES FULL SOUND TO THE SHARPEST AND HIGHEST NOTES.

It must not be apprehended, from the remarks in the preceding chapter, which cautioned the pupil against the adoption of a high pitch for the voice when practicing on the natural key, with a view of making the latter key habitual, that it is considered advisable that the alto pitch should be discarded altogether as an exercise. The whole tenor of the early numbers on this subject clearly prohibit any such conclusion. The alto key, which may be the treble to some voices, the tenor to others, and the counter to another class, is regarded as an invaluable exercise. But it is principally to be regarded in the nature of a preliminary discipline. It is intended to augment the energies of the voice, to give it elevation of reach and depth of tone, to clarify it, and to increase the music of its intonations.

The exercise of singing on this key should never be succeeded by an exercise in declamation or reading, without the intervening exercise of singing on the natural key of the voice. For the pupil, without the adoption of the last-mentioned exercise, will not be able, without a mere accident, to strike the natural key of the voice in speaking, where he has been previously engaged in speaking or singing on the highest key of his voice.

And here it is necessary to remark, that when the alto key is advised as a profitable exercise for the human voice, no such elevated key is advocated as will not permit the pupil, in the exercise of singing, to give full and perfect sound to every note in a hymn or song—the highest and sharpest, as well as the flattest and lowest. By habitually or even occasionally pitching the voice on such a high key in singing as to compel the pupil to drop the sharper notes or to give them an imperfect sound, the voice is injured both for the exercise of singing and speaking.

For whenever the voice may be pitched on a key of such great elevation, the disposition to omit the sharper notes becomes habitual in the exercise of vocal music, and it will be transferred in some degree from the exercise of singing to that of speaking. Not that the pupil in speaking will omit words in a speech or address, because he has previously omitted to give a full and swelling sound to a note in singing, but because his voice, when raised in speaking, will give an imperfect sound to words, from the fact of having been previously habituated to giving an imperfect sound or no sound at all to certain sharp notes in vocal music.

The great object to be attained in exercising the voice on an alto or high key in singing, is to raise it to the very loftiest pitch which will permit the pupil to give a perfect, full, and swelling sound to every note in a hymn or song. Every time he accomplishes this object, on an alto or high key, he adds to the powers and resources of his voice. This extreme exercise is to the human vóice what the highest branches of mathematical science are to the human mind.

CHAPTER XV.

VOCAL MUSIC, CONDUCTED ON THE NATURAL KEY OF THE VOICE, TO BE SUCCEEDED IMMEDIATELY BY AN EXERCISE IN READING OR IN DECLAMATION ON THE SAME KEY.

WHAT has been designated, in the previous numbers, as the natural key for the human voice in vocal music, corresponds with the same key in the voice when employed in speaking or in reading. And every person who chooses to make the experiment, will find that when he has finished a piece of music of any description, which he may be competent to sing, on the natural key, giving to each note its full sound, that the exercise of reading or speaking adopted after an interval of five or ten minutes shall have elapsed from the close of such musical exercise, will be conducted with an ease and freedom which can be rarely attained under any other circumstances.

It may be also clearly ascertained, by a due share of attention to the subject, that when any performance in vocal music has been sung on a high or sharp key, and is followed in quick succession by an exercise in declamation or in reading, the exercise of speaking will be executed very imperfectly and with great difficulty.

The cause of this imperfection and difficulty may be traced to the fact that the voice in speaking falls immediately on that key which has preceded it in the labor of singing. It has contracted its character temporarily from the key on which it was exercised in music, and it takes its direction so strongly towards that key, whilst the influence of the previous exercise in singing remains, that it will adhere to the voice throughout the declamation or reading of an entire speech or article of any kind which is commenced immediately after the hymn or song is closed. To illustrate the justness of the preceding remarks, we uniformly see how vehement, irregular, and destitute of flexibility the voice of a minister will be in preaching a sermon immediately after having raised the hymns in the church service for his congregation, provided he has sung with sharpness and vehemence.

A pupil in the art of singing, if he intends to engage in the exercise of reading or declamation on the natural key of his voice in the evening, may sing a piece of music on the highest key which his voice will permit on the morning immediately preceding the intended exercise. And so may a public speaker, in the maturity of his experience, participate in the exercise of singing on an alto or high key, in the morning, where he designs to make a public speech on the evening of the same day, or on the day immediately succeeding, for the voice, in this instance, will have time to contract and descend to its natural key before the exercise of speaking commences either with the pupil or the speaker in full practice. Or if the pupil or speaker should be distrustful of the voice resuming its natural key at the required or appointed time, it will be very easy for him to sing a hymn or song on the natural key of the voice, and it will certainly perform its functions on the proper key, when the exercise of reading or speaking has to be commenced.

And the pupil, when he wishes to read with ease or declaim with ease, should daily precede this exercise, when practicing, by having previously trained his voice, by singing a hymn or song on its natural key, and the lawyer or member of any deliberative assembly, should adopt the same preliminary exercises, when he intends to make a speech in court, or in a deliberative assembly.

CHAPTER XVI.

THE PARTICULAR TUNES BY WHICH THE VOICE OF A SPEAKER SHOULD BE EXERCISED IN VOCAL MUSIC.

The safest and most infallible criterion by which to be governed in the selection of music for the exercise and improvement of the voice, is to consider the tunes with which the pupil is acquainted, with reference to their adaptation to the easy elevation and cadence of the voice. And he will inevitably derive the largest share of improvement from the habitual repetition in song of those tunes, whether they be connected with hymns or songs, which admit of the loftiest elevations and lowest depressions of the voice in singing the different verses which enter into their formation, or in singing any portion of a verse. When a portion of a verse is referred to, it will occur to every one who may be at all familiar with vocal music, that some pieces of music may be sung throughout with the voice upon an uninterrupted level, there being no point in them at which the voice of the vocalist is raised to an exalted pitch of elevation, or subjected to a very considerable descent or depression.

There are other pieces of music again, in which the elevations of the voice, and its depressions or descents, occur once or more in every successive verse. And there are other musical compositions, in which the elevations and descents of the voice occur only in every alternate verse, the intermediate verse being always sung with the voice on a perfect level, without imposing any effort or exertion on the vocal organs whatever.

In each of the foregoing descriptions of music, to which reference has been made, it is the exercise of the voice in singing the particular verses in a composition, in which the elevations and descents of the voice are easily combined in one line, or where the elevation occurs at the commencement of one line, and the descent takes place at the termination of a line which immediately succeeds it, that yields a special degree of benefit to the voice of a pupil in elocution.

The source of this improvement may be found in this fact, that when the voice is frequently subjected in the exercise of vocal music to a sudden and easy transition from lofty elevations to sudden descents or depressions, then it is improved by this very exercise in the qualities of flexibility and softness, and in its powers of modulation.

As the limbs, by a frequent indulgence in the exercise of running and dancing, may acquire a peculiar degree of nimbleness and elasticity for that particular exercise, which may be beneficially felt in walking and other exercises of the person, which require less exertion than those of dancing and running, and which may be transferred to the more moderate exercises of the person; so in a similar manner the human voice, when frequently subjected to elevations and depressions, combined with very short intervals between them in the same verse of a piece of music, will not only be visibly improved for musical exercises by this particular discipline, but the benefit will be transferred to the voice in conversation and in public speaking, by rendering it softer, more flexible, and sweet in its tones.

In speaking of elevations and descents of the human voice in this chapter, the two extremes of the voice, the high and the low, are referred to in this exercise as a combination of two different notes in one measured stretch or sound of the voice forming an unit—just as the hand is deliberately raised by an exertion of the will to the forehead, and brought down again quietly to the side, or just as a person may be smoothly elevated to the highest story of an edifice by the application of a tackle, and is deliberately lowered again to the basement or ground-floor, by letting the tackle down again. In this exercise the human voice is deliberately elevated in one strain to its highest pitch, and without any suspension of the sound let down again or lowered by almost imperceptible gradations to the lowest key.

The preceding exercise for the voice is broadly different from that discipline which consists in great elevations and depressions of the voice in declamation and in vocal music, which, instead of being prosecuted or conducted in a blended form, are executed and perfected distinct and separate from each other, as pure elevations or pure depressions or cadences. The voice in the exercise of vocal music, is sometimes raised to a very great pitch of elevation, without lowering it again at all. This exercise is merely intended to give the voice reach, expansion and depth of tone, by the application of the principle called tension, which is the operation or act of keeping it on a continuous stretch for several moments.

The voice may also in declamation and in vocal music be placed on a very low or moderate key, and kept there during the entire exercise, for the purpose of inuring and disciplining the voice for the easy articulation of soft and low tones in public speaking, which may be greatly essential at times to the perfection of its beauty in speaking, as well as to invest it with peculiar effect. This last, instead of forming a combination or blending of two sounds, the high and the low, in one stretch of the voice, like that referred to in the early stage of this chapter, may be regarded as a pure depression of the voice throughout.

CHAPTER XVII.

EXERCISING THE VOICE IMMEDIATELY PREVIOUS TO RETIRING TO REST—ITS EFFECT CONSIDERED.

There is a beneficial influence exerted on the voice of a speaker by exercises in reading, in declamation, or in vocal music, immediately previous to retiring to rest at night, which will be clearly realized and felt in delivering a speech or argument on the next succeeding day. This improvement communicated to the organs of speech by an exercise, which is succeeded by some hours of repose previous to their employment in executing any of the duties of life, is similar to the increased vigor and elasticity which is plainly experienced in the limbs in jumping, or in running on a day immediately succeeding that in which they have been moderately but vigorously trained by exercises of a similar character. A practitioner in jumping may have failed in repeated efforts to jump a certain number of feet on one day, which he may have prescribed as a maximum, whilst on the next day he may bound over the given number with the nimbleness of the antelope. The secret of this fresh accession of activity to the limbs and muscles by exercises applied in this particular manner, may be recognized in the fact, that the fatigue of previous exercise will be entirely removed, if it has not been too severe, by a few hours of succeeding rest, whilst the benefit given to the muscles by the force of tension, has been fully preserved.

Thus it is with the organs of speech. They will have been rendered flexible and expansive, for the exercise of speaking on a succeeding day, by the exercises of an immediately preceding night, which are followed by an interval of rest. When the voice shall have been severely trained in declaiming aloud, or in vocal music conducted on a very high key, only a few moments before the exercise of speaking commences, it is highly probable that the speaker may not possess that control over his vocal functions which may be essential to agreeable and effective speaking. For the organs of speech having been subjected to a high degree of expansion by severe exertion, will not in all cases yield an agreeable enunciation immediately after the force or pressure of this exertion shall be removed. An interval of an hour or two between the preliminary exercises of declamation or singing, and an argument, will in most instances afford the organs of speech time to resume their equable and natural state, under the influence exerted by rest, whilst the benefit of the exercise will be recognized in the increased expansion and flexibility of the voice. If the whole or the greatest part of a night shall intervene between such exercises and the speaking of a succeeding day, as has been remarked in the commencement of this chapter, the benefit will be yet greater.

If a speaker should indulge himself in an effort to improve his voice for speaking, immediately before the duty is commenced, he should either sing a few verses or read a few pages in some well-selected speech, on the natural or middle key of his voice, unless the voice should be so contracted at the trial, or should betray such an obstinate degree of hoarseness as to require an exercise in declamation or in vocal music on its highest key, in order to give it expansion or to remove its hoarseness. When this exercise shall have been closed, too, after about fifteen minutes shall have elapsed, the speaker or pupil should sing a few verses of a hymn or song, on the natural or middle key of his voice, or should read a few pages from a speech, with remarkably brief sentences, on the same key. This exercise will secure the natural key in speaking.

CHAPTER XVIII.

MISCELLANEOUS REFLECTIONS ON THE TONES OF THE VOICE.

The softer sounds of the human voice are acquired by practicing it in speaking or reading low on the middle or conversational key; for habitually reading or speaking loudly disqualifies the organs of speech for executing soft tones with facility—just as the constant practice of walking rapidly renders one less at ease in walking at a very slow pace, and as the constant practice, also, of stamping heavily in the act of walking, renders one less able to walk or creep with a feline lightness of tread when he wishes to do so.

But notwithstanding the habitual practice of loud reading and speaking renders it difficult for a speaker to execute the softer tones in speaking when he wishes to do so; and, although for the purpose of acquiring that ease, it is necessary to practice the voice in reading and speaking lowly on the middle or natural key, yet the voice is greatly assisted in its efforts to acquire the softer tones, by being frequently subjected to exercises on the more elevated keys of the voice. This latter exercise, when it is not carried to an extreme, as has been frequently affirmed in the course of these commentaries, expands and deepens the voice and renders it more flexible, and as a matter of course fits it in a much higher degree for the process of modulation—just as the leather which enters into the composition of a shoe, though stiff at first, becomes flexible and soft by constantly subjecting the leather to the pressure of the foot.

If the voice is contracted and superficial in its character, it will be utterly incompetent to execute in perfection the softer tones; and it is the expansion and depth, as well as the additional flexibility which is imparted to it by exercises on a high key, which increases its capacity for uttering the deeper tones. But it is not immediately subsequent to exercising the voice on a key of great elevation that the benefit of this exercise will be experienced in producing the softer tones. It will be after an interval of rest, comprehending some ten or fifteen minutes, and then special care must be taken to pitch the voice on the natural or middle key.

If the voice of a speaker should be feeble and effeminate, and will yield none other than treble notes, and those of an insufferable and screeching nature, he may succeed in rectifying its tones, and in imparting to it a more masculine character, by declaiming, singing, and hallooing with the utmost strength of his voice, whenever an opportunity shall be presented for indulging in those disciplinary exercises.

CHAPTER XIX.

THE ESSENTIAL IMPORTANCE OF CONFINING THE VOICE, IN THE ACT OF SPEAKING, TO THE NATURAL KEY—AND IN WHAT THE ADVANTAGE OF THIS COURSE CONSISTS.

The high importance and precious advantage which results from confining the voice, through life, in the practice of speaking or reading, to the natural key, consists in this—that whilst the voice confined to this pitch or key reaps the full benefit, as it regards volume of sound, depth of tone, and sweetness of intonation, which may be conferred on it by the various other modes of discipline to which it may be subjected; it may, at the same time, be truthfully affirmed that there is no other pitch of the voice on which each individual speaker can reach the highest and fullest measure of success which his capacity and resources may fit him for attaining.

There is no other pitch of the human voice on which a speaker may be able to command and maintain that happy level in speaking which may be termed the conversational style—which is the most acceptable and engaging of all others to those whom it may be his duty to address. There is no other key of the voice in speaking, on which the speaker, during the progress of an argument, speech, or address of any kind, will be perfectly competent to let his voice rise or descend at pleasure, as the exigencies of the case may require. It is the only key in speaking on which the speaker may pause when he pleases, and resume the thread of his argument again with an appropriate share of facility and grace. It is the only key of the voice on which the speaker may conduct an argument with due deliberation. And it may also be alleged with perfect fidelity to truth, that it is the only pitch of the voice in speaking on which the speaker may descend with perfect ease into the most minute particulars of an argument, narrative, or subject of any description, and press into the service of his cause or proposition the smallest particles of reasoning which may be qualified to assist in accomplishing the object which he may have in view. And the reason why a speaker may descend into minute particulars with greater ease on this key of the voice than on any other, is, that whilst he is engaged in speaking on this key he is at perfect ease, and he will be at perfect ease during the continuance of a very protracted argument, if he may be perfect master of the subject discussed. And it may be safely stated that when speaking on a key above the natural level of his voice, the voice being under the pressure of a straining exertion during the whole course of an argument, the speaker will be actuated by an impatient spirit from the irksome character of the process of speaking on a key of too great elevation; and from a feeling of repugnance to the labor involved in the undertaking, he will omit the minute particulars, facts, and data pertaining to his cause or proposition; and will confine himself almost exclusively to the boldest and most prominent points, which will not be presented with any peculiar degree of felicity.

In connection with this branch of the subject, it may be very appropriately suggested to the pupil, that the natural key of the human voice is the only point of elevation in speaking at which the speaker may be able to acquire and command the graces of action, and reduce them to practice whenever he participates in the labors of a discussion, delivers an address, or indulges in the exercise of reading. For the purpose of testing the justness of this proposition, the pupil may declaim a speech which has been committed to memory, read an address, or a chapter in any book, and practise gesticulation in conjunction with either of these exercises, and he may perceive with perfect clearness the imperfect nature of his gestures, on every pitch of the voice he may strike or select, except the natural one. And this key of the voice proves itself to be the proper one, because gesticulation is conducted with perfect ease whenever the pupil may be able to command that particular key, in the exercise of reading or speaking; and because in addition to this, the gestures are certain to become difficult, irregular, and broken, whenever he deserts this pitch of the voice, for any other on which it may be exerted, in the article of speaking.

This inability of a speaker to move his hands with perfect freedom and facility, results from the fact that those functions of the body, the exertion of which produces the voice, do not at the moment of speaking act and move with perfect ease and freedom themselves. Speech or sound is produced by the motion or action of certain organs or parts of the body, as much as gesticulation is produced by the action of certain members of the body called the hands. The organs of speech have not extension, like the hands, and their action is not perceptible, like that of the hands, to the organ of vision. But yet they are moved at the will of the possessor, by putting them in motion, just as the hands are moved at the will of their possessor by a certain amount of exertion. But if the organs of speech, when speech is intended to be produced, are not in a condition to act with perfect flexibility, the hands will act in sympathy with these organs, and will fail to move with flexibility of sweep when they are put in motion by the will, to produce gesticulation. Or if the speaker, when he commences the business of speaking, should bring to bear upon the organs of speech, too large an amount of pressure to admit of their executing their functions with ease, then the hands will also refuse to execute their functions in motion with a graceful measure of ease. Just as the voice, no matter how tuneful and flexible it might be at the time, would certainly yield a broken current or measure of sound, if the speaker, in delivering a speech, or a sentence in a speech, should, when attempting to raise his hand to make a gesture at any giving point, find it bound to his side, or encumbered by an amount of weight which would prevent him from moving it at all, or which would prevent him from moving it backward and forward, or upward and downward, without the application of considerable exertion.

The operation of the foregoing principle will be clearly detected in machinery of any description, in which, if an undue amount of pressure is brought to bear upon any one spring in a machine, or an undue amount of weight is suddenly attached to any one of its balances, the regularity of motion in every other part of the machine will be disturbed and deranged, until the pressure is diminished, or the undue weight removed.

The foregoing sympathy which has been affirmed to exist between the voice and the hands, in the matter of speaking, may be illustrated by a reference to various other examples

Let us assume, for instance, the case of persons who have been instructed in the accomplishment of dancing. Many persons familiar with this agreeable and sprightly exercise, sometimes choose to indulge in the recreation of dancing after their own music. Now, if a person acquainted with the art of dancing should commence singing some lively tune on that pitch of the voice which would render the exercise perfectly easy to the performer, and he should simultaneously commence the dancing of some step, the motions in dancing will be conducted with the most perfect nimbleness and ease, as long as the voice shall be preserved on that key in singing, which will continue the functions of song at perfect ease. But let the dancer suddenly pitch his voice, in singing the same tune he commenced with, on a more elevated key of the voice than the natural one, and the motions of the feet in dancing will simultaneously become rugged, irregular, and laborious.

As further illustrations of the operation of the principle of sympathy, which exists between the action of the voice and the hands in the exercise of speaking, we may refer to the grace and flexibility of motion with which almost every person engaged in a cotilion, or dance of any description, at the same time almost involuntarily moves, whilst the spirits and limbs of the dancers are propelled by a tune pitched on the right key, and played to the proper measure and time. Let the same or another tune be suddenly pitched on a wrong key, and played to a defective time and measure, and the movements of the same party of dancers suddenly becomes spiritless, cumbrous, and laborious.

Let an accurate performer on the violin or flute, consult his past experience in matters of music, and he will vividly recollect how nimbly his fingers have at times covered the holes in the flute, and with what incalculable facility they have touched the strings of a violin, when these instruments have been tuned to the proper key for playing those tunes, which he chose to play at the given time. He will also remember at other trials, how heavily and irregularly his fingers fell on the holes of the flute or the strings of the violin, when either of these instruments were pitched on a wrong key for playing any required tune.

Those who have observed the exercise of speaking amidst the discussions of the bar, of deliberative assemblies and popular meetings, will not fail to remember speakers whose gestures were exceedingly irregular and broken, and who frequently in gesticulation extended beyond the person only that portion of the arm which is comprehended between the elbow and the extremities of the fingers, the elbow itself appearing at the same time to be pinioned to the side. They will recollect at other times speakers who seemed to labor so much in speaking, that there seemed to be a threatening prospect of their falling on their faces. All these labors and all these imperfections were the product of the voice being pitched on a wrong key at the commencement of the exercise of speaking.

It is very true that the voice may be in a condition at times, owing to the effect of hoarseness produced by a cold or extreme exertion, or relaxation produced by excessive labor in speaking, or contraction produced by various causes, to bid defiance to any previous precautions of the speaker to pitch the voice on a proper key. This chapter has not been written for the purpose of providing for defects which are positively invincible, but for the removal and alleviation of imperfections which are clearly within the reach of human skill. But it is certain that if a speaker should have previously paid a sufficient share of attention to the voice to ascertain its properties and wants, that he can almost assure himself of the certainty of previously providing for the embarrassments to speaking just pointed out, by reading, by declamation, or by vocal music indulged in to some extent on the natural key of the voice in some retired place, an hour or two before he may be summoned by his duties. In cases of hoarseness, unaccompanied by cold, the same remedy will be serviceable.

CHAPTER XX.

DOES IT EVER HAPPEN IN THE EXERCISE OF SPEAKING AND SINGING, THAT THE HUMAN VOICE IS PITCHED ON A KEY TOO LOW TO ADMIT OF EASY AND EFFECTIVE SPEAKING?

MUCH has been said in the previous numbers on the subject of pitching the voice on a high key in the exercise of music, both in the nature of a preliminary training, to give compass and depth of tone to the voice, and to correct its various defects. And many suggestions have also been made heretofore in regard to numerous difficulties and disadvantages which result in the exercise of speaking, from the fact of placing the voice whilst thus engaged on a key of too much elevation. Now the question recurs, does the human voice ever fall in speaking or in singing upon a key too low to admit of easy and melodious sound in speech and in song?

There is nothing more certain than that the voice does frequently fall upon a key in both these exercises, which the speaker or singer will discover as he progresses in either (as the case may be) to be entirely too low to be consistent with his own ease, or to be productive of full and melodious sounds. The speaker or pupil can easily determine on the certainty of this occurrence himself, by adopting an experiment which is very simple in its nature. Let him take up a speech or chapter in a book, and purposely select a low or bass key for his voice in the exercise which he chooses at the time, and he will find after he advances a little way, that the sound of his voice will be deficient in melody and fulness, that gesticulation will be difficult and imperfect, and that he cannot yield the proper emphasis to the words and sentences which are embraced in the speech or chapter he may be reading or declaiming at the time. The same remarks are strictly true in relation to vocal music. If the voice should be pitched on too low a key, by a leader in church-music, the music will be drawling and monotonous, and entirely destitute of animation, and the leader will frequently be compelled to pause and commence the music on a key of greater elevation.

This difficulty of pitching the voice on a lower key than the natural one in speaking and in music, is entirely different from the voluntary determination of the speaker or singer to exercise himself in speaking or singing low on the natural and easy key of the voice. For there is no exercise which in its proper place is more beneficial to the voice in producing softness, flexibility, and facility of modulation, than the one last mentioned, and it is advisable to indulge in this practice daily, as a powerful auxiliary to the other exercises which are recommended in this treatise as correctives to the voice. But no matter how the speaker or singer may read, speak, or sing on that key which, for the sake of simplicity, may be denominated the natural pitch of the voice, he will uniformly find that the restricted volume of the sound does not prevent the voice from yielding a quiet melody, or from giving each note and sentence in either exercise an easy, full, and perfect sound or intonation.

In regard to the corrective which ought to be applied to this embarrassment, when it occurs, a brief chapter will be hereafter especially devoted to that subject. But it may be suggested in this connection, that if the speaker should find in the course of delivering a speech at the bar or elsewhere, that his voice is pitched on a key too low for easy and tuneful speaking, the most eligible mode by which to remove the difficulty, is to pause until he shall have time to breathe and collect himself, without taking his seat, and to fix in his mind a higher key when he resumes. We have known this difficulty frequently corrected in the discussions of the bar, by reading at length when the pause is made, some author applicable to the subject, and by then resuming it.

CHAPTER XXI.

THE PRELIMINARY EXERCISES WHICH MAY PREVENT THE EMBARRASSMENTS WHICH RESULT FROM PITCHING THE VOICE ON AN INCORRECT KEY IN SPEAKING.

The most effective discipline to which a public speaker or a pupil in the art of speaking can possibly resort, to place the voice in tune for easy, flexible, and acceptable enunciation, is to select some favorite hymn or song with which he may be perfectly familiar, and sing it on such a pitch as will allow the pupil to yield a full, swelling, and musical sound from the beginning to the end of the selected piece of music, without extraordinary labor or difficulty to the person practising. And let him repeat the same hymn or song, or sing another which he may execute with equal facility, until the voice shall have received from the exercise a proper degree of expansion. And this the person practising in this manner will be enabled easily to perceive by his own feelings, and by the degree of flexibility and ease with which the voice executes, its functions in singing.

After the speaker has continued the exercise of vocal music to a sufficient extent as just prescribed, then let him pause for the space of five or ten minutes, or for a sufficient space of time to afford the vocal organs a little respite from the previous exercise of singing, or to enable the ear to determine with accuracy the measure of sound to be used in speaking or reading. Then let him declaim from memory a committed speech, if he should be prepared to do so, on that key of the voice which will admit of his speaking the speech throughout in a natural and easy manner, and which will also admit of his giving the proper emphasis to each sentence and word in the speech. And let him continue this exercise of declaiming the speech in question until he shall have assured for his voice that set or proper level on which he wishes to speak in whatever exercise may await him.

After having finished the exercise of vocal music as heretofore prescribed, if the pupil or speaker has no committed speech, or he should not choose for any reason to exercise himself in that particular mode, let him read four, five, or ten pages of some easy and agreeable speech, in which the sentences may not be remarkable for their length. If he should not have a speech at command, let him read as many pages in some author which may be convenient as the exigencies of his voice may require at the time. And he can ascertain with some degree of certainty when he has declaimed or read enough, by the fact of finding his voice in a condition which will permit him to let it rise or fall at his pleasure, to sound the words with clearness and with some degree of melody and flexibility, and to allow him to give the proper emphasis to the words which occur in the speech or author.

The exercise specified in the preceding portions of this chapter will generally assure for the voice a proper degree of fulness, and also the necessary power of modulation in any exercise of speaking which is to follow in the course of the same day.

But if when the speaker or pupil in commencing the exercises heretofore pointed out, should find his voice in a condition of too much rigidity and contraction to be corrected by the mild exertion of singing on the natural key of the voice, then having first pitched his voice on the highest key which will admit of his yielding a full and swelling sound to each note in a song or hymn, let him indulge himself in singing a sufficient number of verses to satisfy him that he has sufficiently expanded his voice, or succeeded in correcting for the time the impediment to flexible sounds under which it temporarily labors. Then after having paused for some five or ten minutes, let him adopt the exercises in singing and in reading before described in this chapter.

CHAPTER XXII.

THE MODE BY WHICH A PUPIL IS TO CORRECT THE IMPERFECTIONS OF HIS VOICE WHO POSSESSES NO EAR FOR MUSIC OR SENSE OF TUNE.

It frequently happens that persons with the highest capacity and most refined and correct taste on general subjects, and who are also adorned by the richest and most varied mental culture, are yet entirely destitute of the perception of tune, or what is more usually designated an ear for music. The question here presented is, how are persons of this description to improve the voice for public speaking and to correct its imperfections?

This question may be answered by the affirmation that such persons have at their command the whole volume of sound, and the broad field of reading and declamation, in which to give full and profitable exercise to their vocal functions. And let it be remarked, in this connection, in the first place, that there is no exercise known to man, the daily adoption of which yields a larger amount of expansion to the voice, than the practice of declamation on the most elevated key which will admit of a full and perfect sound being given to each word in the speech which may be read or spoken in this way. Nor is there any other exercise, the daily use of which more greatly improves the voice in depth of tone and in increase of melody.

In order to avail himself of the foregoing exercise to the greatest advantage, a student, if he resides in a town or city, should resort to some retired place without the limits of a city, with his speech in his memory, or his book of speeches in his pocket, and at the appointed spot, after having first secured for his voice a pitch on which it will sound melodiously, let him declaim a committed speech, or such portion of it as he may be competent to declaim without injury to his lungs or throat, at the very loftiest pitch of his voice. In the early stages of this exercise, a single page of a committed speech will constitute a sufficient daily exercise for his voice, and he should, at the commencement of this exercise, content himself with the performance of it once in each day. When the voice has become in some degree inured to the exercise, he may increase the number of times at which it is repeated, should he choose to do so.

And it may be proper to remark, that inasmuch as the frequent speaking of one speech accustoms the voice to that particular production, and renders it much easier to speak than one which the pupil has not repeated over a number of times in speaking, it will be well for him to retain one speech for an exercise so straining as that of declamation upon an elevated key of the voice, for some time after he may have commenced this exercise. A portion of any one speech will answer for this exercise, until the end of the pupil's life, as well as any number of speeches; for the object sought in this exercise is not improvement in accentuating and emphasizing the language contained in the speech, but to improve the compass and musical qualities of the voice. And as any one speech is rendered easier to speak again every time it is enunciated on a high key or on any other, it is suggested, for the comfort of the pupil himself, to select and retain a portion of some one speech, as a daily formula for the practice of this exercise.

After the pupil shall have subjected his voice to the process of training which is comprehended in the exercises of declamation, as has been just advised, let him return to his chamber and read some speech, or a portion of some chapter in a book which he may select for the purpose, on the natural or easy key of his voice. And if he should strike this key in reading, which he certainly may if he makes persevering efforts, he will discover with what a large increase of facility he can read, after having placed the voice under the severe discipline of declaiming on a key of unusual elevation.

But if the pupil should for any reason prefer not to indulge in this exercise, by daily declaiming a speech which has been already committed to memory, he may perhaps, without the loss of any very important advantage, adopt as his daily exercise the reading of some page or two in any speech which he may select for the purpose; for a person may read on the most elevated key of the voice, as well as declaim and sing on that, though not perhaps with an equal degree of ease. He should select for this purpose, too, some speech which contains very short sentences, for the longer the sentences in a speech or production of any kind may be, the more difficult it will prove to read or to declaim that speech. This exercise of reading on an elevated key of the voice should be succeeded, when the pupil or speaker returns to his chamber, by the exercise of reading at length, and that on the natural and easy pitch of his voice, some speech or chapter, in order to accustom and discipline his voice habitually to that particular key.

CHAPTER XXIII.

THE MODE BY WHICH A PUPIL WHO POSSESSES NO RECOGNITION OF TUNE IS TO ASCERTAIN WHEN HIS VOICE IS PITCHED ON A WRONG KEY IN THE PROCESS OF SPEAKING.

It is not in accordance with nature, or with the deductions of daily observation, to expect that a person entirely destitute of the perception of tune, will frequently indulge in the practice of song. But the want of a proper ear for music or tune is not by any means inconsistent with a just taste for music. For it is an event of almost daily occurrence to observe persons who are not able to distinguish one tune from another, who are just as accessible to the delightful influences flowing from agreeable tunes, as the most accomplished proficients in the science of music; and who appear also to be equally as sensitive and as much revolted by indifferent music and discordant sounds, as those who have the organs of tune developed in the highest degree of perfection.

In addition to these observations, it may perhaps be very justly and truthfully remarked, that it is highly probable that many of the most finished masters of the accomplishment of eloquence, who have engaged the admiration of the world, were defective in the perception of tune.

If persons in this condition have a clear perception of sweet sounds, and a just appreciation of such sounds, though destitute of a discriminating ear in relation to different tunes, they may be perfectly competent to the task of discerning when agreeable or disagreeable sounds are produced by their own voices in speaking, as well as by the voices of others. And if they possess the faculty of perceiving and annexing a proper appreciation to pleasant and unpleasant sounds, it must follow as a necessary deduction from this proposition, that they possess the power of correcting and of changing the different notes of the voice, as they from time to time arise to the observation of the speaker.

If a person of this description perceives and admires an agreeable intonation in his own voice while engaged in the exercise of declaiming or reading, he will be also able to identify such sound, and repeat it again, and continue to repeat it until he perpetuates it and renders it a permanent possession. The same person too, will be conscious of sweet or engaging intonations in the voices of other speakers, and by a proper degree of attention, may identify such agreeable sounds or intonations, after the sound has passed from his ear, and by repeated efforts, may graft the power of producing similar sounds or intonations on his voice in the exercise of speaking.

It is equally certain that the person who is destitute of the faculty of discriminating between different tunes, is equally competent with any other speaker to know when he is speaking with a distressing amount of labor and fatigue to himself. He is also equally capable with other persons, of knowing when he is reading or practicing himself in the exercise of declamation on a pitch of the voice which renders the voice easy and flexible in performing its functions, or on one which entails upon him an irksome amount of labor and exertion.

If, then, a pupil or speaker without a just perception of musical relations may be competent, as he certainly is, to know when he is speaking or reading with ease to himself, it is not a strained inference to affirm that he can exercise his voice in declamation and in reading until he discovers that key on which he can speak or read with perfect ease to himself. And having once ascertained such key of the voice, he can daily engage in the exercise of declaiming and reading on that particular pitch of the voice, until it ripens into a permanent and settled habit.

Speakers who are destitute of the organ of tune, are usually endowed with a sense of hearing as acute as that of the most skilful votaries of musical science; and they can ascertain with just as much precision as persons of that description, what measure of sound is essential to the development and improvement of the voice at the various stages of the exercise which they may choose to adopt for their discipline.

When persons in this condition are desirous of enlarging the compass of the voice, they may retire equally as well as other persons, to some solitary or unfrequented spot, where they may indulge at pleasure in the loftiest flights of the human voice, in hallooing, or in declaiming a speech of any description, or in giving a sound of peculiar loudness to any particular words, which may be qualified, as they may believe, to improve the voice.

If, also, the same class of persons should be desirous of improving the voice in softness, in flexibility, and in the power of modulation, they may indulge themselves in the quiet repose of the chamber or office, in reading a speech or author from the point of being distinctly audible to those who may be moving around them, down to reading in a whisper, which may be so low as to be scarcely heard by the performer himself.

From the foregoing observations, it must be evident to a pupil of this description, that with the exception of exercises in vocal music, he has at perfect command the whole catalogue of appliances, which may be qualified to improve the human voice.

CHAPTER XXIV.

WHEN A SPEAKER DISCOVERS IN THE PROGRESS OF SPEAKING THAT HIS VOICE IS PITCHED ON AN ERRONEOUS OR DIFFICULT KEY—THE REMEDY.

It not unfrequently happens in the practice of speaking, even after the preparatory precaution has been adopted of commencing the exercise on a very low pitch of the voice, that the speaker having extended the compass of his voice as he becomes warmed by the subject, will discover that his voice has been pitched on an improper key to admit of the requisite ease in speaking. It has been placed upon a key too low or one of too great elevation. This may sometimes occur even if the speech read or declaimed shall have been at first commenced on a pitch of the voice so low as that of a whisper scarcely audible. And the difficulty of adjustment in regard to the pitch of the voice, results either from the want of previous discipline and culture to this faculty to accustom it to the natural pitch, or from the fact of its not being in a tuneable condition from the influence of some supervening cause or impediment of temporary duration.

The discipline essential to the prevention of difficulties of this description, has been pointed out in a previous chapter. The present object is to secure relief from the pressure of this impediment when it may attest its presence in the course of delivering a speech or in reading an author. And though it is not a very easy matter to effect this object at all times after the voice has taken a particular set or direction in speaking, yet it is nevertheless frequently accomplished.

The most successful mode by which to correct the voice when its improper pitch shall be detected by the labor and difficulty of speaking after the exercise has commenced, is to pause a few moments to afford the organs of speech a very brief interval of rest, and in resuming the subject again to strike or aim for a different pitch of the voice, a higher key if the previous pitch of the voice was too low, and a lower key if it was previously too elevated. And this is an interval of rest which the speaker must snatch from the exercise in progress, without resuming his seat, and that in such a way as will not create the impression with his audience that he is abont to relinquish his subject. These pauses are frequently indulged in by many speakers without reference to the state of the voice itself, for the purpose of enabling the speaker to survey with due deliberation the ground of discussion over which he may be passing at the time.

In the impatience of the moment some speakers make an effort to overcome this difficulty by suddenly raising the voice to an unusual point of vehemence, and getting apparently into a terrible fervor of passion. But the most efficient and certain of all modes by which to relieve the difficulties connected with speaking on a wrong key, when the impediment shall be discovered in the process of delivering a speech, if the subject under discussion is one to the elucidation of which authorities may be applicable, is to take up a book and read from it at as great length as its appropriateness to the subject may permit, and then to resume the business of speaking again. We have frequently known the temporary impediments of the voice in speaking to be corrected in this way both in the discussions of the bar and of deliberative assemblies.

One thing is certain that both the prevention and the correction of this embarrassing impediment justifies the expenditure of immense care and attention, for it produces monotonous speaking when the pitch of the voice is too low; graceless and irregular declamation when its pitch may be too high; and broken and imperfect gesticulation on either key.

CHAPTER XXV.

ARE ALL THE DISCIPLINARY EXERCISES USELESSLY EXPENDED ON THE VOICE OF A PUPIL IN ELOCUTION, WHO SPEAKS ON ONE KEY ONLY?

THE proposition has been frequently affirmed, that there are persons who speak exclusively on one key of the voice, and there are many conspicuous examples which go very far to establish the justness of the proposition. For no matter how much the voices of some persons may be raised in compass and in animation by the fervor excited by debate, yet the voice uniformly retains its flexibility, power of modulation, and beauty of intonation, and when at its ordinary level, the voice of this class of speakers presents an uniformity of sound which identifies the key on which they uniformly speak as a single one. In other speakers who appear to speak on one key of the voice exclusively, the intonation produced by the exertion of the voice in speaking, may be very indifferent in its quality—it may be a very hoarse or very sharp and screeching sound, but the sound is sufficiently uniform to produce the impression that persons of this description are confined in the exercise of speaking to one key.

But the important question to settle in this number, is whether persons who speak on one key alone, if there be such persons, may be benefited by the exercises prescribed in this treatise. The voice is similar in this respect to the mind or the body, where any particular function is capable of being almost indefinitely improved by the application of appropriate exercises. The intonations or sound of the church-bell, are clarified and improved in point of melody by the process of ringing it, and a very lame performer on the violin will be competent to the discovery that the tones of a very common instrument are perceptibly improved by the use of it.

It matters not then whether the voice of an individual is susceptible to one or many keys in speaking, as far as the point of improvement may be involved. Persons with one key, equally with others, may enlarge the compass of the voice, deepen its tones, and sweeten them by indulging in vocal music on the most elevated key of the voice, and by participating in declamation or reading on the same key. They are presented too with the same privilege with others of softening the voice and of imparting to it the power of modulation and emphasis, by indulging in the milder exercises for the improvement of the voice, which have been prescribed in the preceding numbers of this treatise, such as singing on a pitch of the voice which may yield a full and swelling sound with perfect ease to the pupil, declaiming on the same key and reading on it. And it may be suggested in addition to these remarks, that if a person should learn from previous observation, that his voice habitually strikes a key in the exercise of speaking which produces harsh or indifferent sounds, he may by repeated efforts procure a pitch for it which will habitually produce more melodious and agreeable sounds in the exercises of music and declamation.

It may also be observed, that should a speaker habitually speak on a bass key, which of course will produce very hoarse intonations of the voice, he may by persevering exercise increase its sweetness and melody. If, on the contrary, he should habitually produce treble notes by the exertion of his voice, he may by proper exercise soften it, augment its energies, and impart to it a more masculine character.

CHAPTER XXVI.

THE PRACTICE OF DECLAIMING, WHEN ALONE, ON QUESTIONS WHICH MAY BE SELECTED BY THE PUPIL HIMSELF.

It is a proposition which is firmly fortified by the best and most enlightened experience of the world, that there is no theatre of exercise which yields a more powerful and productive impulse to the faculties of the young aspirant for the glories of finished oratory, than a juvenile debating society, properly organized and conducted. And there is no species of discipline, yielded by any school of oratory that the wisdom of the world can furnish, which is more conducive to the development of the beauties and powers of the voice, or which is better fitted to train the faculties of the mind for the sharp contentions which arise in the discussions of the bar, the legislature, and the hustings, than trials of strength which spring up in a hall devoted to youthful polemics. It is a fact of incontestable certainty, that many of the finest and most engaging ornaments which have ever reflected lustre and celebrity upon the political and professional discussions of this country, imbibed the divine art of touching with effect the keys of human will, human passion, and human energy, within the precincts of the juvenile hall of debate. Amongst the ornaments to which we have just referred, William Pinckney, Patrick Henry, and Henry Clay hold a prominent and commanding position.

But notwithstanding the almost incalculable advantages which may accrue to the young disputant from the theatres of juvenile strife, yet the advantages which institutions of this kind afford, are not at all times within the reach of those who may covet them. And even if they were, the exercise which we are now about to suggest, is one which may be adopted with vast returns of benefit to the pupil, either in the character of an auxiliary to the debating society, or as a source of discipline and improvement, entirely distinct and independent of such an institution.

The discipline to which we refer, is the habit of selecting, for solitary discussion, either legal questions or queries in general politics, literature, history, and moral ethics, and allowing the pupil to advocate that side, *pro* or *con*, which he may prefer at the time. This involves what may be denominated a *solo* in the exercise of discussion, and if properly conducted and managed by the pupil, may be rendered productive of an amount of improvement to the voice and mental faculties, second only to those acquired in the more serious discussions of life.

This is a discipline for the mind and voice, in the benefits of which a pupil may be able to participate when he is travelling alone along the highways of the country—when he is perambulating the parental fields—when he is drinking in the sweets of retirement in the forest, or when he is immersed in the quietude of his own chamber. It may be a timely caution, however, to observe, that the practitioner or pupil will not be expected to conduct a solo or solitary discussion with as much animation or vehemence in his own chamber (unless he be a bachelor, and live alone in the country) as he would when exercising himself in a place of greater retirement.

To furnish a very simple elucidation of this mode of conducting a discussion, in which the pupil himself is to be the only disputant, we may here suggest to him that there is nothing easier than to choose some proposition with which he may be in some degree familiar, and after having selected either the affirmative or negative side of the question, and having revolved in his mind the prominent points involved in the side he has chosen, together with the array of facts which may be collected at the time to fortify that particular side, to begin the discussion with the proper degree of method, earnestness, and zeal. And for the sake of prosecuting the exercise in question to a still greater extent, he may immediately turn around and advocate the affirmative side of the question, if he previously sustained the negative, or *vice versâ*, and engage in the work of overturning without mercy the propositions which he had previously sustained.

But if the pupil should be too greatly fatigued, either intellectually or physically, to engage in the labor of answering a previous argument of his own, made on an opposite side of the question, he may with great advantage postpone the exercise until a subsequent day or occasion, when he may be enabled to meet the labor with that freshness of mind and voice, and with that accumulation of views, which may result from the intervening interval devoted to meditation and reflection.

There is another mode by which this exercise may be prosecuted with immense advantage to the pupil. In the branch of discipline now under consideration, a practicing member of the bar will enjoy a very important advantage over persons not similarly situated with himself, for he will be apt to retain a tolerably vivid recollection, not only of all the important cases tried in the courts, in the labors of which he may have personally participated, but also of the prominent facts and points connected with those cases which have been tried in his hearing. But whether a person desirous of advancing his improvement in the art of speaking be a member of the legal profession or not, if he be intelligent, and has been in the habit of observing the trials which occur in the courts, he will probably retain in his memory a sufficient recollection of the facts disclosed in every important trial conducted under his observation, to know with a tolerable approach to accuracy the points on which they were ultimately decided. If thus situated, he has only to establish a moot court of his own, to make up cases from the facts contained in the causes which have been formerly tried in his hearing, to argue the side of the prosecution to-day, and to answer himself by making an argument in behalf of the defence to-morrow. Or if he chooses a civil cause for discussion, he may prosecute in behalf of the claim of the plaintiff in an action in the morning, and answer his morning speech by an argument in defence of the interests of the defendant in the evening.

This exercise may be conducted, by one who adopts it in good earnest, with as much system and method as the trial of a case in court. But a person practicing himself simply for improvement, can scarcely be expected to assume upon himself a greater amount of labor than to note down upon a small slip of paper the prominent facts disclosed in favor of that side of a cause which he intends to advocate, and to refer to this *quasi* brief, when he begins the discussion or is progressing in it, for the purpose of refreshing his memory. And after he has disposed of that side of the question first chosen for discussion, he may then write a brief note of the points and facts discussed by himself, and answer them at such time as he may choose in behalf of the opposite side of the case.

The field of Congressional and of Legislative debate, too, opens to those who are ambitious of improving themselves in speaking an almost, inexhaustible mine of wealth; for the pupil has only to peruse the leading speeches delivered on the important questions discussed in these bodies, to make a compendious synopsis of the best arguments used on each side of a question, and to make a speech in his moments of retirement on one side of a question, and to answer it when opportunity or inclination may dictate.

In the exercises which have been pointed out to the student in the preceding reflections, a treasury of materials is presented to every person whose bosom may glow with a thirst for excellence, the assiduous use of which would enable them to ascend to any height of excellence to which ordinary ambition may legitimately aspire. But the materials prescribed are too simple in their nature, and may be commanded with too small an expenditure of labor, to be justly appreciated. In the course of our past experience, we knew an individual of moderate powers, of meagre education, and of still more limited pecuniary resources, who commenced the labors of the bar with a most imperfect and ungainly elocution, who, by invincible perseverance in using the exercises prescribed in this chapter, became a very powerful speaker.

It is somewhere affirmed of the celebrated William Pitt, that he adopted it as the constant practice of his life to listen with the most devout attention to every speech which might be delivered in the Parliament of Britain by the enlightened speakers who figured in his day, that he carefully noted down the prominent grounds assumed by them, and silently taxed his reasoning powers to discover the best arguments which might be made in reply to the points taken by them. This is a labor to which he subjected his mind merely to sharpen its faculties and to increase its promptness in debate, independent of any design, in most instances, on his part, to answer the particular speaker whom he might be observing at the time.

In a public address delivered by the late Henry Clay, on some occasion of a literary character, he took occasion to remark, in reference to the superior excellence which had been ascribed to him in the department of speaking, that the excellence in question, if it really existed, was attributable to no ordinary cost in the way of labor and pains-taking; that from an early period of his life he had been accustomed to the exercise of declaiming when alone on questions selected for the occasion, that he sometimes addressed the stock on his farm, at other times a tree in the forest; and he might have added no doubt, consistently with a punctilious reverence for truth, that in the more advanced stages of his progress towards the goal of perfection in the accomplishment of speaking, that he indulged himself in the habitual practice of replying to some hypothetical argument which had been made by some able debater of real existence. And it is a proposition within the grasp of even a very feeble measure of faith, to believe that if the secret history of a great majority of those distinguished masters in eloquence who have impressed their character and views indelibly upon their race and country were revealed to the world, that it would be found that they had reached an enduring eminence by the use and application of every resource conducive to improvement which came within their reach. And if the youthful candidates for glory in eloquence, who are now rising up in this country, shall faithfully use all the simple appliances adapted to their improvement which may come fairly within their reach, they will never have just cause for regretting the absence of the pebbles of Demosthenes, or the want of his sea-beach to practice on, or the seclusion of his cave.

CHAPTER XXVII.

THE POWER OF GIVING MARKED EFFECT TO PARTICULAR WORDS IN A SPEECH.

THE power of giving peculiar effect to certain words in a speech or sentence, may be attributed in some instances to the fact of the speaker having previously set his voice to music on those particular words, by repeatedly conning them over; but may be more usually ascribed to that degree of flexibility and power of emphasizing, which has been imparted to the voice of the speaker by the application of previous discipline.

This faculty constitutes one of the most potent springs of power in speaking, for it is one of the most successful of all modes by which the attention of an audience may be fastened upon the orator whilst he is engaged in the act of speaking, and to impress upon the minds of his hearers a durable recollection of the speech. A very few words uttered or emphasized with marked beauty and force, will engage a special share of attention as they fall from the speaker's lips, and will be retained in vivid remembrance by many of those who heard them, perhaps during the remainder of their lives.

But if a speaker should possess the power of arming a large proportion of his words with an electric sort of energy, every speech he delivers will be impressed indelibly upon the memory of his hearers, their wills and judgments will be led captive by the force of his language, independent of the superior strength of his arguments and his own reputation will ascend to a lofty height in the public estimation.

This accomplishment was the secret spring of that unrivalled sway which Patrick Henry, during a large portion of his brilliant career, exerted over the juries, popular assemblies, and legislative bodies of his country. For entirely apart from that measure of influence which was infused into his speeches by the intrinsic vigor of his arguments, in which particular they were by no means deficient, yet the voice of tradition and the records of biography must have combined together to cheat the world of an accurate knowledge of the true properties of his eloquence, if he was not largely indebted for his pre-eminent success as an orator, to the astonishing degree of energy with which his words descended from his lips. The celebrated Lord Chatham, whose elocution was embellished with all the graces which could flow from intellectual culture of the highest perfection, a person of the most finished mould, action of the most graceful flexibility, a voice of the most tuneful intonations, and an eye as vivid as the lightning-flash itself, nevertheless drew a liberal share of the magic of his mighty sceptre, from the music of his words. And we learn from every intelligent observer of the elocution of William Pinkney, whose affluent fulness in the chief graces and powers of oratory, has left such an enduring impression upon the era in which he flourished; that one of the most prolific sources of his power was the accomplished skill with which he enunciated the words which he delivered.

In descending to orators who figured in more recent times, the name of George McDuffie will occur to every one in a state of almost inseparable association with the specific power now under consideration. A very intelligent gentleman who heard his celebrated speech on the removal of the deposits by General Jackson, observed at a period long after the speech in question had been delivered, that many of the identical words uttered by Mr. McDuffie in delivering that speech, continued then to linger upon his ear, and that the term "*Pandemonium*," which was used in some way as being applicable to General Jackson and his Cabinet, whilst it appeared to fall like a peal of thunder in the hall of Representatives when it was uttered, still seemed to ring in his ear at the time he alluded to the subject. When he addressed the Senate of the United States on the Oregon question, immediately after his election to that body in 1843, though then divested of his original fire and impetuosity by the enfeebled condition of his physical energies, yet this distinguishing property of his elocution presented itself with striking prominence, in answering the arguments of those gentlemen who had affirmed the perfect clearness of the American title to Oregon.

Mr. McDuffie remarked, in the course of his speech, "Mr. President, if our right to Oregon be as clear as some gentlemen assume it to be, why *slumber* upon it so long?" The whole sentence within which the preceding interrogatory is comprehended, was remarkable for the searching energy with which it was uttered, but the word "*slumber*" fell from his lips with a fulness, fire and vigor which produced a marked impression at the time, and which will probably be long remembered by many of those who heard it. Senator Preston, of South Carolina, also possessed the power in question in a remarkable degree of fulness, and it would assert its presence not only once or twice in the progress of a speech, but in every stage of its delivery. And this accomplished orator was unquestionably indebted for this controlling skill in sounding particular words, to the persevering use of the varied appliances which may yield an efficacious culture to the music of the voice and to its powers of articulation and emphasis. In addressing a multitude of human beings on the Canton course, near Baltimore, in the presidential canvass of 1840, he took occasion to refer to the notorious "hard cider" sneer which had been used during that excited period, in connection with the name of General Harrison, and whilst commenting in a strain of vehement eloquence on the sneer to which reference has been made, Mr. Preston remarked, "but, fellow-citizens, we took up this contemptible effusion of malice, and threw it *like a hand-grenade* into the ranks of the democracy, and they scattered like pigeons under the shot of the fowler." There was a musical cadence connected with the utterance of the words *hand-grenade*, which yet continues to ring upon the ear of the writer of these remarks, but the inimitable action which accompanied the utterance of these terms, appeared to suggest to the assembly at the time the reality of a hand-grenade being tossed amongst them, accompanied by an immediate explosion.

In what may be regarded as the more varied beauties of the human voice, no orator who has lived in modern times—perhaps there has been no orator who lived at any time—who surpassed the late Mr. Clay. In the expression of the feelings of deep and quiet pathos, and in the strains of elevated and impassioned eloquence, his voice was the perfection of music. But this great master of the human passions was gifted too with the power of lending magic to particular words. But the special effect given by Mr. Clay to any particular word, was derived more from the tremulous beauty of the inflexions and intonations of his voice, than from the electrifying energy with which he uttered them. Early in the year 1847, and immediately after the battle of Monterey had been fought, an immense meeting was held at the Exchange in New Orleans, to adopt measures for the relief of the suffering population of Ireland. Amongst the eminent speakers who addressed this meeting, Mr. Clay was one, and in the course of an address of about fifteen minutes in duration, which was marked as well by the beauty of its delivery as by the philanthropy of the sentiments it breathed, he remarked in a deep and tremulous strain of quiet pathos—"Refuse relief to the Irish, fellow-citizens! Refuse relief to suffering Ireland! when every battle-field in America, from *Quebec* to *Monterey*, has been crimsoned with Irish blood!" Taking the terminating points of the battle-grounds of America, both on our northern and southern frontiers, as far as they had been then fought, (for the battle of Buena Vista did not occur until some weeks afterwards,) he presented a practical illustration of his views in the most thrilling tones of sweet and measured beauty to which the human voice is susceptible. There were hundreds fresh from the heights of Monterey present at the time, and upon whose hearts this passage of the speech fell like electricity.

The late William Gaston, of North Carolina, possessed to a very remarkable extent, the faculty of infusing a stirring degree of energy into particular words, when wrought up to the pitch of unusual fervor in debate. When once addressing the legislature of North Carolina in opposition to some bill proposing relief for political grievances to a certain part of the State, and when his indignation was provoked by what he considered a measure of intimidation held out by the friends of the bill under consideration to coerce those opposed to it into a support of it, he remarked with an energy which seemed to penetrate the floor on which he was standing: "Mr. Speaker, if the friends of this bill desire the members from the East to vote for it, let them remove *their rod* sir." The word "rod" fell from the lips of the speaker with almost the startling energy of an exploding bombshell.

Whilst remarking on this subject, it is due to the present chief magistrate of the United States, General Pierce, to suggest, that a more conspicuous display of the capacity for investing particular words with a felicitous effect, is rarely presented than was afforded by him in speaking the following sentence, which is contained in his inaugural address: "You have summoned me here in my *weakness*, now you must support me with your *strength*." The people of the United States were supposed to compose the audience to which these remarks were addressed, and the relative position occupied by two words in the sentence, "*weakness*" and "*strength*," combined with the graceful animation and distinctness with which they were uttered, made an impression on the minds of those present at the time, which will not be speedily effaced.

Some care has been taken in this chapter, to present from the speeches of distinguished American orators, a few simple examples in illustration of the accomplishment in speaking, to the consideration of which this number has been principally devoted. In the number next succeeding, an effort will be made to point out and simplify, as much as possible, the means by which this faculty may be acquired and perpetuated.

CHAPTER XXVIII.

HOW THE FACULTY OF YIELDING PECULIAR EFFECT TO CERTAIN WORDS MAY BE ACQUIRED.

It is a proposition which requires no profuse expenditure of reason to demonstrate it, that the capacity for giving an effective or impressive sound to particular words, in a speech or sentence, arises more from that improvement of the voice in melody and flexibility which is produced by long perseverance in using the proper modes of discipline, than from any particular attention which may be yielded to the particular words themselves. For every intelligent observer who possesses any skill in musical performances, must be conscious of the great expertness which he acquires by practice in producing certain sounds, in the application of the bow and the fingers to a violin. It is thus with the voice itself, when it is improved by the application of discipline, in the general character of its intonations it is also improved in its capability for pronouncing particular words as the speaker or reader chooses to pronounce them. Just as the limbs of the body, when improved in their general elasticity, by exercises of any description, not only receive from this discipline an adaptation to running, jumping and wrestling, but are also qualified by the same exercises to acquire, with greater facility the graceful faculty of dancing.

It is a proposition which requires no profuse expenditure of reasoning to demonstrate it, that the capacity for giving an effective or impressive sound to particular words, in a speech or address which the pupil may read or speak, those which may be justly denominated the leading words in a sentence, whether they are located at its commencement or at its close.

And when the leading words are discovered, it should be the object of the pupil to give to them a very conspicuous utterance in speaking or reading the sentence. And by the faith ful observation of these prominent words in a sentence, aided by the energetic pronounciation of them when they are reached in the exercise of reading or speaking, the speaker or pupil will not only sharpen his faculties of discrimination in such a way as to be enabled to detect the locality of such words in other sentences entirely distinct from the one in which he is exercised, but he will fall habitually also into the practice of yielding to all prominent words in sentences a full and stirring measure of sound; but more particularly will he give an engaging sound to words of a similar form with those on which his voice has been previously practiced.

CHAPTER XXIX.

THE EFFECT OF GIVING A ROUND, FULL, AND DEEP SOUND TO THE VOICE BY THE REPEATED VOCIFERATION OF CERTAIN WORDS.

There are certain words, sentences, and expressions contained in the treasury of human language, which, by the daily exercise of repeating them, a pupil will find exceedingly beneficial in the effect of giving to the voice a full, deep, and melodious sound. This exercise may be conducted on the various pitches of the human voice, from an alto to the bass key.

The words to which reference will be particularly made in this connection, are those either commencing with the letter O, or having their characteristic sound determined by the appearance in them of that particular letter. As an illustration of the proposition under consideration, we may take the words, "bold," "cold," "hold," "gold," "roll'd," "mould," "poll'd," "scold," "toll'd," and repeat them on the various keys of the voice with very improving results.

When these words, or words similar to them in which the letter O gives the determining sound or accentuation to the word, are frequently repeated in succession, with a pause occurring of a few seconds between them, on the loftiest pitch of the voice, they tend to give to it reach and tension, whilst the particular sound of the words improves the voice in rotundity, in fulness, and in depth.

But the idea is not intended to be conveyed to the mind of the pupil, that the exercise of the voice on words of this description is to be confined to its highest key alone. It may be exercised in this way on its various other keys with very great advantage. The highest pitch of the voice is selected in the first instance, in order that the voice, in sounding words of this description on that particular key, may be stretched to its utmost point of tension and reach.

Let us take another example of words in which the letter O gives the determining sound—words which commence a sentence with the letter O in them, and which contain a command or request, as the case may be. A speaker may be referring, in a speech or address of any kind, to the indiscriminate havoc produced by death amidst the different ages of the human race, and may present as a request to his audience, the sentence—"*Go* to the grave-yard, and you may there find graves of every length. *Go* to the death-bed scene, and you there see stretched beneath the icy sceptre of the grim monster victims of every age. *Go* to the house of mourning, and you may see the tear of grief streaming for charming infancy and blooming youth, as well as for mature manhood and hoary age." The frequent repetition of the word "go" in sentences of this description, yields an improving influence to the voice on any of its keys, but particularly on the highest key, when sentences of this kind may be adopted as exercises.

A speaker, for the purpose of illustrating the baneful fruits of intemperance, may say to his audience—Go to the prisons of your country, and behold them literally crammed with the victims of intemperance. Go to the halls of justice, and cast your eye on the criminal dock. Go to the chamber where squalid wretchedness reigns with absolute sway, &c. Go to the dramshops of your country, &c., and finally, Go to the fatal tree, and there behold the victim of intemperance closing his days in anguish and in infamy.

In referring to examples of countries which may serve to illustrate the baneful effects of tyranny, ignorance, or any other destructive moral or political agency, we may refer in the speech to a great number of countries in the following manner: Go to Russia, and see there the blighting effects of tyranny. Go to Turkey, &c. Go to Persia, &c. Go to Poland, &c. Go to Spain, &c.

But whilst the foregoing sentences occur occasionally in a speech or address of any description, and serve merely for the purpose of exemplification in an exercise for the voice, they may be pushed to any length which the pupil may choose. He may take every State in the American Union, beginning with Maine, without adding any expletives or other words, simply repeating the brief sentences, Go to Maine, Go to New Hampshire, &c., until he runs through the whole catalogue. And in a similar manner run over any number of the States of Europe, Asia, or Africa.

CHAPTER XXX.

LOUD SPEAKING CONSIDERED.

A PUBLIC speaker should never acquire the habitual practice of speaking in a loud and vociferous strain. There may be exceptions to this proposition, but they are exceedingly rare, and are of such a partial character as not to disturb its general accuracy and force. It may be perfectly legitimate that a speaker should expand his voice to the farthest limit of its strength to the end that he may be distinctly heard by a very multitudinous assembly which is spread over a very ample surface; or it may answer a very useful purpose that the fullest range should be given to the voice when a speaker arises to address a popular assembly which is already raised to a very high pitch of excitement, touching any very important topic which may be in the progress of discussion before it. But the speaker should take a special degree of care to assure himself that his audience is in an excited state of feeling before he undertakes to address it at the topmost key of his voice. For whilst he may be fully appreciated in addressing with unusual energy and vehemence an assembly, which has contracted from previous speaking, a very fervid state of feeling—yet a speaker will appear to be entirely ahead of his audience, and will indicate a childish excitableness of disposition in addressing in a very animated and boisterous manner an assembly which is perfectly calm and self-possessed. And when a speaker does address even an excited assembly with the utmost strength of his voice, he should take the precaution to be exceedingly brief in his remarks; for neither his own voice nor the sympathies of his audience will sustain him in speaking with peculiar advantage in a strain of unusual fervor more than ten or fifteen minutes. His voice will in all probability begin to relax in some degree; to contract a partial hoarseness, and to exhaust a portion of its melody from speaking in a strain of unusual vehemence more than fifteen minutes; and it will be difficult to preserve the feelings of an audience at the acme of their interest for a longer space of time than that which has just been suggested, except in the instance which has been mentioned in the outset of this chapter, where the speaker, in order to be understood, is compelled to speak loud; the feelings of an audience will also become fatigued by a lengthened strain of vehement declamation. To assure to an orator the patient and well-sustained attention of an audience through the delivery of an extended speech or argument, there must be elevations and depressions or descents in the voice of the speaker.

But as an additional and very persuasive reason why a speaker should not habitually indulge himself in very loud speaking, it may be very truthfully affirmed that speaking, in proportion as its volume of sound is extended, sinks in the same ratio in the scale of intellectuality. So much is deliberation, calmness and placidity associated in the human mind with intellectual operations, that the best and most cogent reasoning which ever falls from human lips, loses to some extent its appearance of intelligence by being conveyed to the ear of an audience in a boisterous manner. The stunning roar of the voice will attract the attention of hearers so much to the impetuous energies of the physical man, that they will not have the power of estimating properly the intellectual man.

To illustrate in a still more lucid manner the reality of the principle asserted in the commencement of this chapter, it may be suggested to the pupil that the divinest and most touching melodies in music are conveyed to the senses through a soft and flexible medium of sound. And it may be received as a proposition of infallible certainty, that all music which is characterized by unusual loudness of sound, is not calculated to touch any congenial chord or key of sympathy in the human breast, unless it be an invocation to arms, a song of exultation at some public jubilee or festival, or an anthem at some religious celebration.

Another reason why a peculiar loudness of sound is apt to depreciate the effort of a speaker in the estimation of his audience, is the almost inseparable connection which exists in the human mind between unusual compass of voice and the subordinate intelligences in the scale of creation. For instance, sounds of this description, as a characteristic property, are usually attributed, as far as they are used amongst men, to uncultivated and savage life—and amongst brutes, to the ox, the ass, the lion, and the alligator.

CHAPTER XXXI.

THE FREQUENT REPETITION OF INTERROGATORIES IN SPEAKING A BENEFICIAL EXERCISE FOR THE VOICE.

In connection with the subject of declamation, it may be appropriately observed, that there is one very important exercise for the voice which a speaker should certainly include in his disciplinary code. This is not declamation in its perfect character, but approaches the nature of that exercise to some extent, and may be denominated a fragmentary declamation. This discipline for the voice consists in the repetition of the various interrogatories which are used in conversation and in speaking, in regular succession, and for a considerable interval of time, on each occasion when the exercise shall be resorted to.

Most persons have observed the animation which is communicated to a speech, when an energetic speaker pours out a number of interrogatories in quick succession. And it is a circumstance which is perceptible to every person who has yielded even a superficial degree of attention to proceedings of this description, how much additional vigor is exerted by the voice of a spirited speaker in the act of propounding questions to an audience.

The terms, the use of which is here enjoined on the student in elocution, are the following: *How? Who? What? Where? When? Why?* and various other words which usually constitute the leading terms in any interrogatory which may be used in the delivery of a speech or address, but which do not at all times, when standing alone, form a full and perfect interrogatory, without the accompaniment of other terms or language applicable to the information apparently or really sought by the interrogatory.

To avail himself of the benefits of this exercise, whenever an opportunity of doing so may present itself, the pupil may frame if he chooses a declamation formula, containing an extended list of interrogatories, preceded in each instance by the different terms which have been heretofore presented in this number, and by any other terms which usually assume a leading position in questions of any kind.

A pupil in declamation may frame a formula for his own private exercise in the following manner, assuming to himself the position, as is usually the case where questions of the kind are propounded, that some proposition has been affirmed by a previous speaker in which he does not concur. He may begin his formula thus: If the proposition which Mr. B—— has just affirmed be true, how is it that no person besides the honorable member himself has been competent to discern the justness of his position? *How* is it that the proposition in question is contradicted by the past history of the world? *How* is it that the proposition affirmed by him to be just, has been tacitly and impliedly condemned by the practice of every free government of the world, both in ancient and modern times? *How* happens it that the proposition of the honorable member has been condemned in all ages and in all countries by the principles of sound morality? *How* happens it that the dictates of public and private interest condemn the proposition? *How* happens it that the principle of decency condemns it? And, beyond all other considerations, *how* is it that the solemn warnings of the Holy Bible condemn it?

The preceding skeleton is of course intended only to serve

as a specimen or sample of the artificial formula which every pupil may adopt for his personal improvement in the private exercises which are designed for the amelioration and correction of the voice. The formula in question may be ex tended to any length the pupil may choose. And the formulas should be prepared in such a manner that all the questions propounded in each of them separately, should be preceded by only one of the terms heretofore suggested in this chapter; that is to say, each formula should be devoted exclusively to one of the leading terms of a full interrogatory heretofore mentioned, viz.: How? Who? What? Where? &c., accompanied with the necessary amount of language to render each interrogatory full and complete.

In reference to interrogatories commencing with the term "*Why*," we are presented with a very beautiful example in one of Doctor Channing's sermons, devoted to the elucidation of the principles of Christianity; and this is a sermon which may be very justly commended to every one, not merely as a beautiful exemplification of the exercise here recommended, but because it is also a spring of profound thought and elegant diction; and from the easy, smooth, and flowing style of its sentences, will serve as a selection of unsurpassed excellence in which the pupil may daily exercise himself to very great advantage, both in reading and in declamation. This sermon begins as follows: Why was Christianity given? *Why did Christ seal it with his blood? Why is it to be preached?* &c. The preceding example has been given to the pupil to show him clearly, by a practical instance of the kind, in what way interrogatories may be properly commenced with the word *Why?* But the pupil may adopt for himself a formula, in which interrogatories commencing with the same word, may be extended in immediate succession, to any reasonable length.

As an example of interrogatories commencing with the word "Where," a very brief extract is here presented, from a speech delivered by the late Daniel Webster, at a dinner given in honor of his public services, by the people of Boston, June 3d, 1828. Having previously referred, in the course of his remarks, to an attempt which had been made in some parts of the confederacy, to draw a line of discrimination between New England and other States of the Union, by a classification of the States in which the States of New England were designated as the "New England States," and the other States of the Union, termed "the Patriot States," Mr. Webster, in a stream of indignant eloquence, propounds the following questions to his audience:—"Where but in New England did the great drama of the revolution open? Where but on the soil of Massachusetts was the first blood poured out in the cause of liberty and independence? Where sooner than here, where earlier than within the walls which now surround us was patriotism found, when to be patriotic was to endanger houses and homes, and wives and children, and to be ready also, to pay for the reputation of patriotism by the sacrifice of blood and of life?" The pupil or person practicing himself in the exercise of declamation may adopt a formula for daily practice, of his own creation, in which questions similar to those immediately preceding may be extended at considerable length.

As an example of questions commencing with the word "Who," we present an extract from a discourse delivered December 22d, 1820, by Mr. Webster, in commemoration of the landing of the Pilgrims, at Plymouth. Referring to the peculiar circumstances which marked the early settlement of New England, Mr. Webster propounded in that particular connection the following questions: "*Who would wish that his country's existence had otherwise begun? Who would desire the power of going back to the ages of fable? Who would wish for an origin obscured in the darkness of antiquity? Who would wish for other emblazoning of his country's heraldry, or other ornaments of her genealogy, than to be able to say that her first existence was with intelligence; her first breath, the inspirations of liberty; her first principle, the truth of divine religion?"* In a formula framed and adopted for exercise, a pupil or practitioner may extend questions of a similar character with the preceding, to any length he chooses.

As an example of interrogatories commencing with the word "What," we submit the following. A speaker, in denouncing the improper application of the power of taxation by any legislative assembly, may be supposed, for the purpose of enforcing his views, to invoke the aid of the celebrated "tea tax," in the following questions:—What circumstance was it which caused the fires of the American revolution to blaze forth? What circumstance was it that stimulated the early apostles of liberty in this country, to pour out their blood like water? What measure of the British Parliament was it, which threw this country into a ferment from its Northern to its Southern extremity? What encroachment of the British Parliament was it which caused the friends of the revolution to brave every terror, to incur every danger, to share the fatigues of every toil, and the bitterness of every sacrifice?—it was the power of unjust taxation. A formula adopted simply for exercise, may contain questions similar to the foregoing, extended to much greater length.

As an example of interrogatories commencing with the word "When." A debater in speaking in praise of Mr. Jefferson's administration, may be supposed to propound, in the course of his remarks, the following questions:—When did our country enjoy a higher degree of prosperity at home and respectability abroad, than during Mr. Jefferson's administration? When were the duties of the government administered with a more single eye to the liberty and happiness of the citizen, than at that memorable period? When was the cause of science and of letters more munificently encouraged? When was the extension of free principles more ably advocated? A formula for practice, containing questions of this sort, may be extended as the practitioner may desire.

A sufficient number of examples have now been yielded to the student or practitioner on this subject, to explain to him, with some degree of clearness, in what manner interrogatories may be shaped and used, so as to serve as a daily practical exercise for the human voice. And it may be proper to observe, that in order to render them productive of all the benefits they are capable of yielding to the voice, the student should declaim these interrogatories whenever retirement may permit him, on the loudest key of his voice; and with a brief pause between each question, should repeat them for the space of ten or fifteen minutes on every occasion in which he engages in the exercise. He may exercise his voice on a formula containing the questions, beginning with the word "how" at one interval of practice; and he may select the formula which contains the interrogatories, beginning with the word "why" at another exercise. And he may repeat and re-repeat the questions contained in any one formula, and add to them new interrogatories as his pleasure may suggest and his invention may permit. Or he may take the formulas, one after another, embracing the interrogatories which commence with the various words that have been presented in the course of this chapter, and repeat them at one lesson or exercise of the voice. The particular exercise of the voice which is connected with the sounding of these interrogatories in an energetic and animated strain is the advantage which is sought, and it matters not how often they may be repeated over.

The adoption of these interrogatories in a speech or argument, imparts a very large accession to the animation of the exercise, if they should be repeated with a proper degree of energy. But the principal aim in this treatise is to inculcate the use of these questions as a very essential auxiliary in the important undertaking of improving the voice for speaking. And the philosophy of exercising the voice in this particular manner, may be traced to the fact that these interrogatories cannot be repeated with a peculiar loudness of sound without yielding a very improving discipline to the voice and great animation to the exercise in progress at the time. And in addition to this, it may be remarked that when the voice shall have been frequently exercised at stated times on these particular interrogatories, that from the influence of previous practice any of these questions, or interrogatories similar to them, will be invested with great effect and power whenever they may arise in any of the more important and serious discussions which pertain to the interests and the business of life.

From the particular structure of the word "how," interrogatories commencing with that term of speech, are qualified to yield to the voice in the simple act of pronouncing it on a loud key, great additional reach, depth, rotundity and fulness. And when questions commencing with this word are frequently repeated on a loud key, the pupil will find that the volume of his voice has been perceptibly extended after the suspension of the exercise. From this source arises the great advantage of exercising the voice at stated times by the frequent repetition of interrogatories commencing with this particular word.

The word "why" as a starting-point to a train of interrogatories set apart for the discipline of the voice, is also calculated to lend an important measure of assistance in the enterprise of improving it in energy, animation, melody and compass.

The word "who," when coupled with an interrogatory as an antecedent, is also available in a very eminent degree, when loudly and distinctly sounded, in giving tension to the vocal functions.

The words "what," "where," and "when," do not yield to the voice in the act of pronouncing them, the same measure of exercise in the way of tension as the preceding words, but they afford, when frequently repeated as heretofore suggested, a very profitable exercise for one who may be directing his attention to the improvement of the voice. And it may be very justly affirmed that these terms when legitimately introduced into a speech, argument, address, or public effort of any description, lend great additional grace, animation and attraction to the performance, whatever it may be.

CHAPTER XXXII.

KEEPING THE VOICE ON A CONTINUOUS STRAIN OF VEHEMENT DECLAMATION DURING THE DELIVERY OF AN ENTIRE SPEECH, CONSIDERED.

An address which may be delivered from its commencement to its close in a very vehement strain, will be rarely remembered by an audience with any very vivid sensations of pleasure. They may applaud in the most munificent manner, the ability of the speaker, for that will not be concealed from an intelligent assembly of men, even by the repulsive exterior of a graceless and ungainly delivery. But they will never single out fragments or parcels of a discourse of this kind, which they admire for its peculiar beauties, and hold it up to the admiration of their friends and associates. The reason of this failure on the part of hearers to seize on any special passages in such a discourse, and to honor them with encomiums, may be traced to the fact that a discourse delivered in the style to which we have referred, has nothing varied in its features to attract the spirit of admiration to any particular portion of it. We do not find in a discourse of this kind a patch of light here, and a passage of shade there, to make the picture interesting by the effect of transition; without anything of variation about it, without any undulations of surface from beginning to end, it presents the appearance of a monotonous unit.

An address to find a large degree of acceptancy with an assembly must present elevations and depressions on its sur face, the speaker must come down from the summit of the mount at times, and hold communion with his hearers as domestic and social beings. For if he keeps his voice on an alto or even on a continous strain of animation throughout the delivery of an entire production, they will cherish no sympathy with him in his labors; the divinest reasoning conducted with unbroken vehemence, will not wake a responding key in the bosoms of hearers, and they will feel as much relieved when such a discourse is brought to a final pause, as ever any mathematical class has been at the close of a tedious lecture of their professor before the black-board. The imagination of an audience is kept on a continuous stretch by speaking of this description. Human beings, to become deeply engaged by an argument, sermon, or address, must have rest during its delivery, and in order to secure this object, the speaker must come down occasionally from his lofty height, and converse with his hearers on the level plane below.

CHAPTER XXXIII.

READING WITH THE UTMOST STRENGTH OF THE VOICE, CONSIDERED.

In a succeeding chapter, the daily practice of reading at that elevation of the voice, which is usually reached in an animated and rational conversation, has been suggested to the student, because it is desirable that he should habituate his voice by constant discipline to that particular key which is calculated in the grave discussions of life to produce the most natural, persuasive, and effective oratory.

But the suggestion of that particular measure of sound in reading, has not been intended to exclude other modes of conducting this exercise. As a means of imparting expansion, clearness, and depth of tone to the voice, there is scarcely any exercise which merits a profounder share of attention than reading, when convenient, a page from some speech remarkable for the brevity and flowing smoothness of its sentences, on the topmost key of the voice.

This exercise demands in most persons a very severe exertion of the vocal organs whilst it may be in progress, and it should not be protracted beyond five or ten minutes. And notwithstanding the adoption of this mode of reading as a daily exercise in the retirement of the forest, will be attended with a return of very conspicuous benefits to the voice of the pupil, yet it will prove amply sufficient for the purposes of improvement to practice in this way about three times in each week.

And on each occasion when the pupil shall have practiced himself in this particular manner, he should invariably take the precaution, after the lapse of half an hour from the expiration of the exercise, to read some portion of an author at the conversational level of his voice.

The object to be attained in this procedure is, the beneficial influence exerted upon the voice by bringing it back to its natural elevation, immediately after having been practiced on a very high key. Unless the voice shall have been too severely strained by the previous exercise of reading on the alto key, it will be found much more flexible and easy to control in reading in the usual and natural mode, immediately after that discipline, than at any other time. And by making the exercise of moderate reading a supplement of the former, on every occasion in which it shall be practiced, the voice will not only be shielded by this precaution from the acquisition of any unusually harsh and vociferous sounds in speaking and in conversation, which might possibly be superinduced by practicing frequently on a key of great elevation, but the student will be ultimately conducted to an incredible degree of facility in modulating his voice, and in giving their proper measure and emphasis to words and sentences in reading. He will also be enabled, in this way, to acquire the faculty of giving the proper elevations and depressions to the voice which may be demanded in reading and speaking. The preceding theory has been derived from an experience so truthful and practical as to entitle it to the highest consideration.

CHAPTER XXXIV.

THE DAILY EXERCISE OF READING IN AN AUDIBLE TONE OF VOICE.

THERE is no branch of discipline, within the range of human attainment, which confers on the voice a more solid and enduring class of benefits, than the daily practice of reading, in a distinct and audible tone, a judiciously chosen speech, or a select chapter from a book which may be commended for the smoothness and facility of its style. Yet this important and effective auxiliary to advancement in public speaking, similar to light, air, water, and all other earthly advantages of easy acquisition, has been held in light estimation, from the simplicity of its character and the small expenditure of labor imposed by its performance.

The habit of reading daily from ten to twenty pages in an author, is to the human voice what the daily exercise of walking is to the human frame. The natural and easy operation of walking, put in requisition daily to a certain extent, pre serves the muscles and sinews of the body in that equable condition which qualifies a person for the perfect and vigorous execution of all the physical duties which may devolve upon him in the progress of life. Without professing to suggest how wonderfully the appetite and general health of the system of man are heightened and preserved by a movement of the body so gentle and free from excess as that of walking, it may be justly asserted, that all the physical exercises which are carried to the highest degree of perfection by the powers of a vigorous and elastic frame, such as heavy draughts from the ground, running, jumping and dancing, are chiefly dependent upon the very simple exercise of walking. If this natural discipline for the human frame should be totally suspended for a great length of time, the most active limbs would become in a high degree stiff and torpid, until a fresh stock of flexibility might be infused into them again by the full resumption of this exercise.

The daily exercise of reading occupies very much the same relation to the voice which that of walking does to the movements of the body; it preserves the voice in an equable condition. By subjecting the organs of speech to a moderate exercise daily, it preserves them in an open, expanded, and tuneful condition.

When the human voice receives its only discipline from that portion of speaking which is executed under the public observation, in the courts of justice and other assemblies of men which convene for the transaction of business, it misses an immense harvest of improvement, in the shape of intonation, emphasis, modulation, flexibleness and expansion, which may be most certainly derived from the daily practice of audible reading, in the closet, or in the silence of some sequestered grove.

When the business of speaking shall be resumed in the courts of justice, at the close of a vacation of some weeks, and the voice shall not have been exercised during that interval of time, except in the usual colloquial exchanges of life, it will inevitably experience that sensible decline in its general powers which will be realized by the human body when it is suddenly summoned to perform the highest exhibitions of celerity in motion, after a long period of total inactivity.

To secure for the exercise of reading a regularity and certainty which will be utterly beyond the reach of every ordinary contingency, a student in elocution should deposit his favorite author or book of speeches on a table or chair by his bed-side when he retires to rest, to be within reach of his hand when he awakes with the light of returning day. And when he shall have removed from his eyelids the leaden clogs imposed by the slumbers which have just passed away, he should read in a tone of voice a little louder than that of ordinary conversation about five pages. When this duty shall have been performed, he will have placed the measure of improvement derivable from that particular exercise beyond the inroads of business, the calls of pleasure, and the various accidents which may possibly consume his time during the day.

But it is not sufficient for the ends of improvement, that a speaker or student should barely pass through the formula of reading a certain number of pages. To satisfy the exalted aim he has in view, in adopting this mode of discipline, he should read methodically, intelligently, and cautiously. He should, before he commences this exercise on each returning morning or day, as the case may be, determine in his mind to blend with the exercise before him that which is his favorite mode or style of enunciation, and which he intends to adopt as his habitual mode of delivery in speaking, on the broad theatre of life. By thus daily practicing in privacy, what he may regard as the most accomplished and admirable of all modes of delivery, he may ultimately succeed in reducing that particular style of delivery so effectually and permamently into his possession, when speaking amidst the diversified business engagements of the world, that nothing will sever it from the aggregate of his accomplishments.

It has been heretofore affirmed, in the course of these commentaries, that a speaker can call up and fix in his mind his favorite mode of speaking a speech, when he is at the point of commencing an argument, just as a practical vocalist may be competent to bring up from the resources of his musical knowledge, when he is about to commence a hymn or song, that particular tune which he prefers singing in connection with the song or hymn before him. But that degree of accuracy and promptness, in regulating and in controlling sounds, which may enable a person to determine mentally the particular style in which he shall deliver a speech or sing a hymn which is before him; and which will not only qualify him to select this mode mentally, but will also empower him to transfer it to the exercise of speaking or singing, when he commences either, requires long and persevering practice either in a speaker or singer. And to render this faculty a personal appendage of a speaker, so as to hang constantly at his side, that he may use it with the same degree of facility that he uses his pocket knife, there is no species of discipline so simple, attainable, and effective, as that of daily reading.

When a student, on commencing his daily exercise in reading, shall have fixed in his mind the particular style of delivery in which he shall read the pages before him, he should then commence reading at an elevation of the voice scarcely above that level of sound which may be regarded as audible or intelligible to persons sitting in the same room. From this starting point he should gradually raise the voice until it shall attain that compass of sound which usually characterizes an animated conversation in the well-regulated circles of society. When the voice shall reach this pitch of elevation, the student should keep it there until the close of his lesson, with such occasional elevations or depressions as may be demanded by the character and nature of the particular production he may be engaged in reading.

The student should also yield the most devout share of attention in prosecuting this exercise to accentuation and emphasis. With an imperfect execution of this branch of a speaker or reader's duties, the most elegant and spirited production which ever dropped from a human pen, may descend in futile sounds upon the ear of a hearer. With a total absence of these grand essentials to agreeable and intelligent reading or speaking, the best and most intellectual productions on earth are converted into the most unmitigated nonsense. But from the practical and masterly blending of these sterling accompaniments with reading and speaking, there flows a degree of power at times which moves both assemblies and nations of men with the power of an earthquake.

In the preceding views presented in this chapter, the quantity of matter contained in five ordinary pages was prescribed for the morning exercise of the student in reading, not for the purpose of arbitrarily tying him down to that specific amount, but because of the great convenience connected with the operation conducted in that particular shape. Five pages is a lesson in reading sufficiently extended to afford a beneficial exercise to the voice, and not so long as to conflict with the performance of other duties. The morning has been suggested as the most eligible period for taking the opening lesson of the day, because the voice is in a condition in the morning, from the repose of the previous night, to be more easily moulded and tuned to the will of its possessor, than at any other portion of the day; because it will then be apt to retain through the day the particular intonation which it yields under the influence of exercise at that time, because a pupil will be more apt to enjoy the morning free from all external interruption and intrusion, than any other part of the day; and because when an exercise shall be taken early in the morning, a benefit is thus secured for the student on that particular day, which cannot be taken away from him by subsequent incidents which may happen in it. He is neither confined by the views presented in this chapter to a lesson of five pages, nor is he restricted exclusively to reading in the morning. He may read in addition to his morning exercise, in any portion of the day he pleases, and he may read as many pages as he pleases. But let him be sure not to permit the day to close, when he can avoid it, without taking a lesson of some length.

CHAPTER XXXV.

THE PRACTICE OF READING IN A TONE OF VOICE SCARCELY AUDIBLE.

A FREQUENT adoption of the practice of reading in a tone of voice so low as to be scarcely audible to those who may be sitting in the same room with the person engaged in reading, is strongly commended to the attention of a pupil in elocution, from the peculiar efficacy of this exercise in qualifying the human voice for the utterance of those sounds in public speaking which may be characterized by an unusual degree of softness and delicacy.

The adaptation of this particular exercise to the production of the effect just ascribed to it, may be realized in the superior expertness in picking up and handling very minute objects, which is acquired by persons whose daily business renders it necessary for them often to remove such objects of traffic from one place to another, in a store or workshop, by the application of the fingers. Persons whose sense of touch has been sharpened by constantly picking up small and minute particles of any substance, will pick up such particles from the surface of a counter or table, with the same degree of celerity with which a half-famished fowl will pick up a grain of corn from the floor, whilst unpracticed fingers may make several blundering efforts to accomplish the same object, and fail at last. A person whose vision has been constantly trained in the prosecution of any scientific or mechanical pursuit, to the discovery and inspection of grains of any chemical or metallic substance, which may be scarcely visible to the naked eye, will possess an incalculable advantage over eyes unpracticed in the same way in searching for small objects in the common routine of human pursuits.

The voice which has been patiently and perseveringly practiced in reading on a key which is but a few degrees raised above the level of an ordinary whisper, or at farthest, to a pitch of sound which may be regarded as being vocal in its character only so far as to be distinctly audible to the reader himself, will acquire, in uttering soft, gentle, and delicate sounds and tones in speaking, an indefinite advantage over a voice undisciplined in a similar manner. The voice in being regularly trained to the enunciation of scarcely audible sounds, will acquire the same promptness in articulating such sounds, when it becomes necessary for the voice to produce them again, which is attained in picking up minute objects by fingers habitually practiced in handling objects of the kind, or as may be reached in the search for almost impalpable objects, by a vision which has been long accustomed to the examination and observation of such objects.

It will be almost impracticable for a voice which has been accustomed exclusively to the enunciation of loud sounds, to descend to those of a soft and delicate character, when such intonations may be required in speaking. And the destitution of this faculty will frequently prove a serious impediment to the growth and perfection of a speaker's usefulness, influence and success. For it often becomes necessary, merely for the purpose of guarding against the blight of monotony in the delivery of a speech, to descend to a very low key. It is almost invariably requisite that a speaker should pitch his voice on a very moderate key in the commencement of a speech, to the end that he may by the gradual expansion of the voice, as the speech progresses, be enabled when he reaches the merits of his subject, to command just that specific measure of sound which is proper and no more. It is very frequently demanded of a speaker, to let his voice descend to a level of sound which is scarcely audible to his hearers, when he is giving vent to very peculiar emotions, or indulging in the expression of some particular sentiment. And it is apparent to the most inexperienced observers of the business of public speaking, that to give the required effect to many sentences which occur in arguments and speeches, it is imperative upon the speaker to let his voice descend at the close of such sentences.

CHAPTER XXXVI.

THE SUBJECT OF GESTICULATION.

It is very far from being a problem, the solution of which has been so clear as to place the matter beyond all cavil, that there is any precise class of gestures which a speaker should use in performing the duty of speaking, to the exclusion of all others. Any motion of the person or hand, which is free, full and flexible, and made in such a manner as to correspond with an idea or sentiment which has been expressed at the time, will serve in some degree to augment the attraction of the speaker.

The great impediment to completeness which one should

guard against in making a gesture, is that broken, cramped, and restricted way of gesticulating, which gives to the arm of the speaker the appearance of being regulated in its motions by a string or wire, that is pulled by some invisible agent. The elbow looks in these cases as if it might be pinioned to the side of the person speaking, for his arm, in the process of gesticulation, is never moved in advance of the person, with an easy and extended sweep; but in its action presents the appearance of being fettered or clogged, and each of its motions will appear to be by jerks and out of time, similar to the motions of a dancer who does not move in unison with the music, or like the stroke of a paddle aimed at a ball, in any game where such an article is used, after the ball has passed.

The gestures which we have just described may, in the case of an unpracticed speaker, result from inexperience or diffidence. For when the limbs and person of a speaker have not been trained and disciplined in the graces of motion, he will not, in every instance, spontaneously contract a facile and graceful mode of action at the commencement of his career as a speaker. And if a speaker, at the threshold of life, should be afflicted by a large stock of timidity, his action and movements, both in speaking and in social intercourse with strangers, where he may not be perfectly at ease, will be cramped and restricted by his feelings of self-distrust.

But the obvious source of imperfect and labored gesticulation in speaking, may be usually recognized in the want of flexibility and softness in the voice of the speaker himself at the time. Every one who speaks will be enabled to collect a sufficient fund of knowledge, from his past experience, to assure him that whenever he has spoken at any time with the voice in proper tune, that he has been able to gesticulate with perfect ease, and that when, on the contrary, the voice has been harsh, contracted, or unyielding in any of its organs, that the gestures have been labored, broken, and ungraceful. This perpetual sympathy which exists between the organs of speech and the organs of motion, if they may be so denominated, reveals the imperious necessity of subjecting the voice to such a constant discipline, if it should require it, as will tend to preserve complete harmony between the exertion of the organs of speech and the action of the hands.

In regard to the precise motions which a speaker must execute with his hand whilst he is speaking, it may be safely said that any full or extended motion of the arm or hand which he chooses to indulge, will be, in some degree, an auxiliary to the work in which he is engaged.

When a speaker is commencing a speech, he may fold his arms across his breast, and keep them in that condition until an increasing animation, inspired by the subject, may dictate the act of changing their position by moving them forward in gesticulation. The precaution of folding the arms across the breast, has been suggested at the beginning of a speech, because a speaker frequently feels ill at ease then from the fact of his arms dangling loose at his sides without any employment. Any other posture which may serve to place the hands and arms at ease, will answer as well as folding them together, such as holding a book or paper in the hand, or keeping the hands themselves folded together in front of the speaker.

One mode of using the hands in the article of speaking, by some persons, is to keep both arms extended beyond the person during the delivery of an entire address or speech, keeping both hands moving slightly upwards and downwards, or both inclining to the right or the left, as inclination or propriety may prompt. In this gesture the elbow may rest on the side, or it may project an inch or two beyond the side, witn each arm extending in a straight line beyond the person, except when moved upwards or downwards, or turned to the right or the left, as has just been suggested. This mode of using the hands, when executed with skill, is a mode of gesticulation which presents the blended advantages of grace and dignity both.

There is another mode of gesticulating which has presented itself with peculiar attraction in the persons of some speakers of very high distinction. It is one which is exceedingly simple in its character, and may be acquired with perfect ease. It is left to the speaking world to adopt or reject it, as their interest or pleasure may dictate. This gesture is comprehended in the act of keeping the left arm extended from the elbow beyond the person, with the palm of the left hand uppermost and exposed, and keeping the right hand moving gently upwards and downwards across the palm of the left hand, sometimes a little elevated above, and sometimes brought in contact with it, except when both hands are temporarily separated to make some more emphatic gesture.

A very effective gesture may also be produced by closing all the fingers on each hand except the front finger, and after the left arm shall be extended beyond the person from the elbow, then to bring the front finger of the right hand immediately across the same finger of the left hand. This gesture is adopted for the purpose of invoking a specific degree of attention in behalf of any particular fact or principle which the speaker may be submitting at the time. The speaker should bring it up quickly, too, and not resort to it in a drowsy manner, for it is intended to be an animating gesture, and it is one which is usually adopted when the speaker becomes somewhat fired by his subject.

There is another gesture which may be practiced with considerable effect, when the speaker wishes to draw an emphatic degree of attention to any special principle or fact, and that is the act of bringing the front finger of the right hand, with the rest folded up, in contact with the table before him, and to touch and retouch the table with this finger, in order to specify and single out, especially, the point he may be enforcing at the time.

There is another gesture which is adopted by distinguished reasoners, occasionally, for the purpose of calling a pointed share of attention to any pending proposition, and that is to bring the front finger to a perpendicular across the lips of the speaker, while he is discoursing. This is a favorite gesture of Bishop Timon of the Catholic Church.

It is not uncommon with some speakers to run the left hand under the right breast of the vest, and to keep it there during the greater portion of an argument, whilst they keep the right hand, at the same time, constantly engaged in gesticulation. This mode of disposing of the hands, may be well enough at any time, but the chief grace which commends it to the use of the student is derivable purely from the special share of beauty with which this passage of action may be conducted by any particular speaker.

Another way in which the hands may be disposed of, during the delivery of a speech or argument, is, after bringing the elbow of the left arm to an angle with the person, to rest the inner portion of the thumb of the left hand upon the left hip, and to gesticulate with the right hand. This mode of action may be at times resorted to, and so may that of putting both hands in that position which is called "akimbo;" but in usual acceptation these modes of action are strongly objectionable, if indulged habitually, for they present the impression of vanity, bravado, and a redundant stock of self-esteem on the part of the speaker.

Another gesture frequently resorted to, especially by nervous speakers, when they become considerably excited in a discussion, is to keep the right hand elevated all the time, with the palm downwards, and the hand constantly preserved in a tremulous motion, like the fluttering of a leaf agitated by a breeze. There is nothing to be particularly commended or condemned in this gesture, for though it may indicate animation and energy, it is destitute of grace and ease.

Another mode of conducting the process of gesticulation by some speakers, is to keep each hand alternately in motion during the business of speaking, and sometimes both at the same time. This method of action, when executed with entire ease, is about as perfect as any which may be acquired by a speaker, because neither hand seems to be paralyzed or bound to the side of the speaker, all the time he is speaking, from the fact of being idle. Both hands, from the fact of being alternately used in the work of gesticulating, become trained in such a way as to execute their work with an equal degree of expertness, and that in the proper place; and when they are both employed in the work of making gestures, the action of the speaker will be proportionally more animated and effective.

Another source from which a speaker occasionally derives a vast accession to the effect of his delivery, is, from holding a paper connected with his subject in his hand, or a book of authorities before him, and by gracefully pointing to and reading from the paper, or book, as the case may be. This exercise arms the speaker with the weight derived from a printed and solemn authority to support him, and gives him for the time what may be termed an air of erudition; but the chief attraction derived from it is the fact of interspersing the act of speaking with a legitimate sort of variety, every instance of which relieves to some extent the exercise in which he is engaged.

But the matter of gesticulation and of action at large must be regulated so much by the subject which is in the progress of discussion, by the occasion, and by the sentiment intended to be enforced by any given gesture, that it must always prove a difficult task to classify gestures so as to give them a personal identity which will enable a reader unerringly to recognize them, from the accuracy of delineation contained in any written description.

The student will acquire infinitely more knowledge in relation to the graces and the sterner properties of action from an intelligent observation of the most finished speakers of his time, than from any arbitrary rules compiled on the subject. He may take the mode of action which he has imperceptibly blended with the business of speaking himself, and add to his treasury of graces other attractive qualities and passages which he may have noticed in the best models within the sphere of his observation; or he may adopt for his model the style of some highly-approved master in action, and graft upon the style thus selected effective passages from the gesticulation of other patterns, as they occur to his observation.

It may be regarded as a safe proposition, in concluding this chapter, that a speaker should never hammer the benches before him with his fist, nor should he beat out the unoffending brains of the books against the tables, because he has been unable to beat into his own brains the contents of the books. George McDuffie used to indulge in this method of yielding peculiar force to his views of a subject; and it is also said that he used to stamp with his feet at a terrible rate. But there was a muscular power of thought and a volcanic fervor of imagination in McDuffie's composition which disarmed these deformities of action and of manner in him of their usual revolting tendency. This tempestous sort of manner appears very contemptible though in a speaker who possesses neither heat nor vigor.

CHAPTER XXXVII.

THE ART OF PRONOUNCING ACCURATELY, ITS GRACES AND ADVANTAGES.

The faculty of pronouncing with punctilious and graceful accuracy, is a resource to a public speaker which cannot be too highly appreciated. It lends a charm to public discourse which is just as conspicuous as that engaging quality in a musician, which enables him to yield each note in a musical composition in full melody, time, and measure. In point of influence, the blandishments which are thrown around language by the art of pronunciation, are infinitely more enduring than the most enchanting strains of music which ever descended upon the human ear.

The simple fact of pronouncing words with such a faint approximation to correctness, as to avoid animadversion, does not form a point for repose at which a speaker should suspend his exertions in search of improvement. A degree of accuracy of the kind just mentioned, ought rather to constitute a level from which he should ascend to loftier grades of excellence. And though it may not be the destiny of frail and feeble humanity to reach perfection, it should certainly be the unceasing aspiration of a speaker to approach and deserve that lofty elevation.

The person whose life may be devoted in a large degree to the business of public speaking, should cease to speculate concerning the advantages of a finished pronunciation, when he reflects that Lord Chatham, in whose memory Britain glories as the most radiant ornament of her past history, kept a dictionary constantly within his reach, for two important purposes; the one of which was to ensure to every word he uttered in debate, a pronunciation of incontestable accuracy, and the other of which was to enable him to select those words which would best express the idea which he wished to convey. It is scarcely necessary to observe that Lord Chatham stands on the extended path of centuries, almost without a rival, in both the music and the electric power of his language.

But the public speaker is not only enlightened in the art of pronunciation, by the faithful counsels which flow from the best dictionaries on that subject, he has within his reach the most gifted and accomplished scholars of the age, whose voices in the management of words, distil the classic music which charmed Athens in the perfection of her culture, and Rome in the palmy periods of her renown. He has before him the crowning graces in the department of pronunciation, which embellish the oratory of the most finished speakers that his country may boast. He is provided in rich profusion with decisive opinions on this subject, which are securely treasured up in the printed wisdom of the world. And in addition to these bright and faithful auxiliaries to the illumination of his judgment, and to the perfection of his taste, he has at command his own conceptions of music and measure to assist him in clearing his pronunciation of every asperity and defect.

It may be justly affirmed of a correct and graceful pro nunciation, that it is certain to ensure a grateful and flattering reception to solid reasoning, clothed in the garniture of elegant diction. But it wins its way to loftier achievements than this on the field of intellectual aspiration, it is almost certain to invest with the deceptive glare of artificial beauty, matter of an indifferent and ephemeral character. It is frequently affirmed of distinguished speakers, that they possess the faculty of making very poor matter sound handsomely.

It rarely happens that an orator of abounding attractions presents himself before an audience in the delivery of a speech, without engaging a marked share of attention on account of the inimitable beauty with which he pronounces some particular words. After the delivery of a speech has been closed by a speaker of extended celebrity, we frequently hear the exclamation,—Oh how delectably he pronounced some specified word. How did he manage to invest it with so much beauty? Because he yielded his patient devotions to the particular word, and to all the elements of the English language. O *how* delightfully a certain musician sounded the softer notes in his performance. By what means did he succeed in distilling such delicious melodies from his instrument? The question may be answered by affirming that the musician was enabled to draw the bewitching melodies from his lips or his instrument, by the same process by which the accomplished speaker is enabled to deliver his words in a dress of graceful music, to the ears of an audience, by having repeated the notes of enchantment over and over, without limitation, in the solitude of retirement.

A speaker of merited celebrity might deliver speeches wherever the English language is used as a medium of thought, and his pronunciation would be honored with the most grateful applause at every locality which would resound with his voice. For a marked superiority in the art of pronunciation, is one of the chief sinews of an orator's power. He speaks with effect, because he pronounces well, and it may be almost as appropriately said, that he pronounces well, because he speaks with effect.

There are certain words which are articulated in such tremulous and delicious tones of beauty, by some accomplished speakers, that the sound of these words, instead of fading from the memory of the hearer, continues to linger upon the ear, even to the gates of death. But those special words which descend upon the ear like strains of the richest music, may be appropriately compared to the brighter tints upon a cheek of unmingled beauty. These particular words engage the admiration of a listener, not because the great mass of language uttered by a finished speaker is imperfectly sounded, but because the striking words ascend some perceptible shades higher in the scale of excellence, than the other elements which compose the structure of language with which they are blended.

Each word which entered into the composition of a discourse delivered by a classic and polished speaker, might be taken singly, and scanned as units in connection with the most approved standards of pronunciation, and the fact would be explicitly revealed, that these words had been, without exception, pronounced with a share of skill and accuracy which would have reflected lustre on any ordinary speaker.

It often happens that persons in the very maturity of their experience, by listening to the more finished masters of the English language, are inducted into the art of pronouncing words so as to yield a musical enunciation, which they had loathed through life, from an inability to sound them in a smooth and grateful manner. Many of the proper names, both in biblical and profane history, produce an exceedingly uncouth and repulsive sound when they drop from the lips of a novice. But these words are as completely divested of every shade of asperity, when they emanate from classic lips, as the diamond when delivered from its native excrescences by the polish of the artist.

As an accurate pronunciation appears to constitute one of the most engaging ornaments of the business of speaking, the votary of that ostensible art will not be likely to devote too large an expenditure of time to its acquisition. He should not only consult the most authoritative dictionaries on this subject, but he should converse with men of classic taste and discrimination in the construction of language. He should yield a sincere and fervent measure of devotion to the most elegant and accomplished speakers who may come within the sphere of his observation. And he should exercise himself, in his more retired moments, in sounding words in a variety of modes, just as a person devoted to music sounds his notes in different ways, to ascertain by practice which method of sounding will yield the sweetest melody.

CHAPTER XXXVIII.

THE ADVANTAGES WHICH RESULT FROM A CLEAR ARTICULATION OF WORDS BY A SPEAKER.

A VERY classic and elegant writer has remarked that words in just articulation, "are delivered from the lips, as beautiful coins newly issued from the mint, deeply and accurately impressed, perfectly finished, neatly struck by the proper organs, distinct, sharp, in due proportion, and of proper weight."

An attempt to improve on a delineation possessing so much graphic beauty as that which has been quoted in the preceding lines, may possibly involve an useless consumption of time. It may be observed, however, that the contrast which is exhibited between a perfect and a defective articulation of language, is equally as glaring as that which is presented between the sound of two bells, the one of which gives out clear and glassy tones, and the other confused and lumbering notes. And for the purpose of presenting an illustration of the difference which exists between perfect and imperfect articulation, which will keep them perfectly distinct from each other in the contemplation of a speaker, it may be said that the line of distinction between the two modes of execution is as broadly marked as that which exists between two pictures, the one of which presents every person, object and plant, in a state of clear and beautiful definition, whilst the other yields its representations to the eye in a jumble of confusion.

Another chapter in these commentaries has been distinctly appropriated to the subject of pronunciation. And it may be justly remarked in this connection, that the faculties of pronunciation and articulation are so intimately blended in the offices which they perform in the business of speaking, that it requires a share of acute discrimination to preserve with perfect uniformity the boundaries between them with the requisite measure of distinctness.

The difference which exists between the pronunciation and the articulation of words, consists in this: a speaker may possess a very intelligent apprehension of the pronunciation of words, and he may very perspicuously show this to his hearers by marking in some degree the proper points for accentuation which occur in the words which he utters. But if there be any natural or acquired defect in the organs of speech, for instance, if the voice be exceedingly unmanageable, or if the palate should be gone, a person in this condition, although he may indicate by a very feeble and imperfect accentuation of words, that he possesses a due apprehension of the necessity of that quality in speaking, yet he cannot, owing to his poverty in the blessing of sound, give out the different syllables in the words which he utters with a distinct intonation, he cannot yield to each syllable and letter in the composition of a word that due degree of weight which will mark with distinctness and precision the divisions which exist in them, just as the transient pauses which occur between the notes delivered from a bell of a glassy intonation repeats the distinct existence of each sound which falls from it upon the ear. It may be said of a person whose voice does not come to the aid of his understanding in the pronunciation of words, that he is a correct pronouncer, but not a perfect or just articulator, just as it may be said of a performer on the violin, who is a perfect master of the science, but not of the sounds of music, that he is a correct but not a distinct musician.

To yield words in a discourse with every atom of sound which may be due to them in a measure of proper distribution amongst the letters and syllables, is the province of articulation. The speaker who understands pronunciation very perfectly, may execute that portion of his duties with a sufficient share of accuracy, to indicate that he is skilled in scholastic learning. And a musician may pass through an entire composition in music, in such a way as to convince every person in his presence, that he is a perfect master in the science of music. But from a defect of the ear, he may not produce the different notes in the composition, in such a full and distinct measure of sound, as to communicate a lively sense of entertainment to the audience.

It requires the acute and practiced ear, as well as the discerning mind, in the application of musical science to the entertainment of mankind, to deliver out the notes of music in the perfection of their distinctness and sweetness. And it requires the faculties of a disciplined and tuneful voice, as well as the mental acumen imparted by classic culture, to give out words in speaking with the proper distribution of sound which should be yielded to them. The intimate union which exists between pronunciation and articulation in the business of speaking, has been very distinctly affirmed in a previous portion of this chapter. Indeed it may be appropriately said that the one of these faculties merely presents a different phase of the other, carried to the most extended limit of its excellence. A person who very clearly apprehends the office of pronunciation, but who possesses a voice exceedingly deficient in volume and in modulation, may convince every person who hears him speak, that he knows how to pronounce, by recognizing the points of accentuation in the progress of speaking. But he may yield this accentuation with such a limited measure of sound, as to excite the attention of his audience in a very feeble manner. The fact of giving the accentuation even in a feeble and superficial manner, shows that the understanding of the speaker is right on the subject. The fact of giving the accentuation faintly and imperfectly, shows that the voice of the speaker is deficient either in strength or in culture.

The delivery of a speaker who articulates clearly and justly, is neither marred by an imperfect apprehension of the words he utters, nor by the inappropriate distribution of the measure of sound amongst these words. A speaker who articulates finely, not only discloses the fact that he understands the component elements in the language which he delivers, by giving these elements and divisions a faint recognition in the sounds of his voice, as he progresses in delivering a speech. He pays a full measure of homage to them. He speaks each word in a discourse as distinctly separate from every other word in it, as each shot which descends from a shot-tower is distinct from every other shot which falls from the same starting point. He marks the boundaries between the different syllables in a word, when he speaks it, just as explicitly as a smith marks the limits between each link in a chain, when he forges them in succession. And he assigns to every letter which determines the sound of a word, a locality in the utterance of that word, which is just as ostensible in its place, as the eye is in the human face.

For the sake of rendering the difference between pronunciation and articulation so broad as not to afford the pupil in elocution the slightest shade of hesitancy in discriminating between the two operations, it may be affirmed that pronunciation in relation to the quality of accuracy in sounding words, may be compared to an individual who shows clearly enough his recognition of an acquaintance by a nod scarcely perceptible, or by a formal and frigid shake of the hand. This shows that he has a just conception of the prevalent forms of social civility, whilst at the same time he reduces these forms to a practice which is warmed by a very faint spirit of cordiality. Articulation may be said to resemble a person who not only manifests his recollection of a friend when he meets him, but who also practically demonstrates that recollection by a countenance beaming with animation, by a salutation warmed by the glow of affection, and by a grasp of the hand strengthened by the joys of reunion.

It was said of President Jefferson, that he would dispense the compliments of a dinner party with so much elegance and address, that each of the guests he entertained at the time would retire from his hospitable mansion with the flattering conviction that he had borne away the prize compliment of the occasion. And if a speaker should articulate the words delivered by him with perfect distinctness and accuracy, his hearers may leave him with the belief upon their minds that each word he spoke was marked by a special beauty of sound.

But it has not been designed, in the preceding remarks, to depreciate the value of an accurate pronunciation of words. That quality in speaking is an essential which is so imperiously demanded, that without it a speaker must progress in his business with an execution as blundering and graceless as that which is yielded in the exercise of dancing by a person incurably crippled in his limbs. But whilst pronunciation marks the points of accentuation in words, articulation, similar to a faithful auxiliary, distinctly reveals these points to the ear by applying to them the property of sound in a proper measure of clearness and fulness. It may be justly remarked, that the inseparable union of these two accomplishments is essential to give elegance and effect to language which is spoken, the one to mark the points of division in words, and the other to give those boundaries the proper enunciation.

CHAPTER XXXIX.

THE PROPERTY OF CADENCE IN SPEAKING.

A RECURRENCE to the magical effect which has been frequently exerted on an audience by accomplished vocalists, in displaying a beautiful and tremulous cadence of the voice, will enable the pupil to appreciate properly the peculiar efficacy of this quality when blended with the delivery of an enlightened advocate. It is the fact, apparently, of permitting the voice to die away and retire into the depths of the throat, so as to be scarcely audible, which produces this species of intonation. It is usually possessed, in the highest degree of perfection, by celebrated singers and tragedians, because their voices are usually subjected to the most rigid, painful, and persevering culture, for the purpose of producing this sound equally with others which render the voice attractive.

But this accomplishment of the voice is not confined to professional vocalists or to dramatists. It asserts its presence, in a very attractive degree, in the delivery of skilful orators. And as it is chiefly the fruit of culture, it may be as extensively appropriated by speakers as by the dramatic corps. This proposition derives confirmation and support from the fact that almost every voice of music or of tragedy which has delighted the world on the theatrical boards, has been the product of incalculable toil and vigilance. And it is also sustained by the great advances to perfection, in this peculiar intonation, which has been exhibited by those public speakers in this country who have devoted a liberal share of attention to the matter.

The voices of some persons have been adapted by nature to the easy acquisition of this element in vocal beauty.

And it is highly probable that those who possess an original determination of the voice to the production of such sounds, are just as unconscious of the property as those who have had the faculty of ventriloquism slumbering in their constistutions until the meridian of life before they discovered it.

But even where nature has furnished the basis for this desirable acquisition, in blessing some of her children with a voice of rare flexibility and tunefulness, it cannot be rendered in a high degree attractive without the application of the most assiduous attention and labor. For it is not sufficient that persons should be endowed with a large fund of constitutional melody. It is also rendered incumbent upon them to regulate and discipline their natural stock of sweet sounds, in such a manner as will enable them to dispose of it correctly, and to distribute it in a proper measure to the world.

It is incontestably true, then, that the vocal faculty about which we are now discoursing, is, without an exception to the contrary, the result of acquired skill and art. It is even thus where nature has given the noblest elements for its creation. The proposition is pre-eminently true where the voice has presented obstacles to the attainment of this peculiar beauty.

But the invincible fact that a quality of the voice possessing such rare attractions for mankind, may be attained by persevering exertion, extends a measure of encouragement which should be highly exhilarating to a student in elocution. For it clearly reveals to him the proposition that his power of fascination as a public speaker, is a subject which is to a great extent under his own control, that it is a matter of volition.

The mode by which this accomplishment may be acquired, may prove somewhat difficult to define. But it may be assumed, as a starting point, in commencing a duty of such vast importance, that when the faculty of producing the deeper tones of the voice shall be once acquired by a speaker, that he is then provided with practical evidence that the principal barrier to the creation of those tremulous and beautiful cadences to which we have been referring, has been removed from his voice. For as it is impossible to yield this cadence without the power of producing the deeper tones of voice, the converse of the proposition may be assumed as true, that when assisted by the power of producing the deep tones, a speaker will find it an easy enterprise to command in speaking that cadence which is so agreeable.

From the preceding reflections, it will appear that, with the view of attaining the quality of sound which forms the subject of this chapter, the pupil should devote a patient degree of attention to the object of deepening the tones of the voice. After he has secured this essential preliminary, he should then observe with unwavering fidelity the delivery of the most celebrated speakers and tragedians within his reach, in order to become familiar with the varied tones of beauty which may be yielded by their voices. And he will not only be enabled, by the adoption of this course, to recognize and identify the beautiful and tremulous cadence of the voice to which we have referred, so as to know distinctly what it is, and in what it consists, but he will also ascertain by what agencies and exertions it is formed.

When a speaker has practically informed himself by an intelligent observation of the most distinguished masters of the voice, what the quality of cadence really is, how it is produced, and what sort of additional beauty he really wishes to engraft upon his voice, he should keep the desired passage of sound continually in contemplation, and practise it unfailingly whenever suitable opportunities shall be presented to him. If he shall resolutely determine to pursue the suggestions here submitted, he may summon to his aid in speaking the rare and beautiful quality of cadence with as infallible certainty as he can acquire the accurate knowledge of any branch of scholastic learning which may engage his fancy.

And the faculty of producing this note of the voice in perfection, merits the most fervent aspirations of a public speaker, as well on account of the inimitable passages of beauty which it enables him often to interweave with the process of delivery, as for the splendid conquests which it may enable him to achieve on the field of discussion. The act of causing the voice apparently to melt and sink away in the distance, whilst its sounds may be so distinctly articulated to the ear as to define and preserve their distinctive character, and to make them intelligibly known to the hearer, is an attainment which invests a vocalist or a tragedian with high powers of attraction; but to the delivery of a cultivated and gifted reasoner, it lends a charm of invincible power.

CHAPTER XL.

THE ABILITY TO YIELD A PROPER EMPHASIS TO WORDS.

One of the most copious springs from which a speaker derives his available supplies of influence and strength, is the art of giving the proper emphasis to the words which he utters in a discourse. And this accomplishment in a speaker is as distinctly felt by an audience in casting its appreciation of a discourse, as that creative faculty is felt in a painter which enables him to mingle together, in a felicitous proportion, the lights and shades which are blended in the formation of a magnificent picture. When destitute of the competency to give a proper emphasis to the words which he utters, a speaker will not only be subject to the passive injury of not being properly appreciated, but he encounters the painful penalty of being positively misapprehended in his remarks on a subject.

Those who may be familiar with dramatic exhibitions can

very justly apprehend how an actor that imperfectly comprehends his part, may, by adopting a wrong train of expressions and gestures, united with a blundering emphasis, succeed not only in veiling the nature of the character which it is his duty to personate from the conception of his audience, but how also he may positively transmute that character into an individuality utterly at variance with that which he has been appointed to represent.

The extremity of imperfection which has been alluded to, the public speaker seldom or never reaches. But it often happens that a cause of transcendent merit meets with incalculable injury from the total absence of that dramatic skill in an advocate which would enable him to marshal his words in such a manner, in delivering an argument, as to make each word produce its proper effect.

It has sometimes happened, that a word emphasised with masterly skill and address, has decided the fate of an empire. And it is a proposition utterly beyond the reach of controversy, that the dextrous disposition of a single word in a discourse has frequently taken captive the heart of beauty, and disposed of highly-important measures. These conclusions are not derived merely from the pages of history, nor from the voice of a floating tradition, but they are founded upon the solid basis of past observation.

When we hearken to the conversations of legislators and jurors, who explicitly confess to the impeachment of having been borne away by an argument transcendentally powerful in its character, what is the explanation that they usually afford concerning their tame surrender to the witcheries of eloquence? The declaration generally is, "O, the speaker drew such a hideous picture of the wrongs received by the prisoner, we were compelled to acquit him." "The statesman expatiated with such irresistible power on the frightful evils with which some particular measure was fraught, that we were compelled to vote against it." Another statesman drew

a field of such perfect enchantment, out of a different measure, by applying to it the creative wand of his imagination, that his audience really believed that they had the scene of magic practically revealed to them, and slided into the snare of the orator with as much docility and meekness as a be v
ridges would glide into the net of a fowler.

When the philosophy of the most miraculous conquests of oratory is critically analyzed, it will be found inclosed, in many instances, in the simple power of giving a superior emphasis to words in a discourse. This proposition is fortified in a very high degree by the tame appearance which is often presented in print by speeches which in their delivery inspired the populace with phrenzy. By pointing to the flag of the nation at times with dramatic skill, the orator touches a vein of enthusiasm in his audience which places them as emphatically under his control as would be a piece of melting wax in the hands of an artist. By pointing to an obnoxious individual, with a skilful command of the music of sound, an orator may consign that individual to hopeless immolation.

CHAPTER XLI.

THE CONVERSATIONAL STYLE IN PUBLIC SPEAKING.

It is the impression with many speakers that no decided effect can ever be produced on an audience, unless it should be addressed in a vehement and declamatory strain. But nothing can be farther from the reality. For whatever is most in accordance with nature in the pursuits of life, is alone qualified to produce any permanent good or solid satisfaction. And as walking is that exercise in the motions of the body which is most consistent with nature, because it is that application of the functions of man which is constantly and universally ministering to the wants and the pleasures of life, so the conversational mode of speaking is the style which corresponds in the highest degree with the tastes and feelings of a large majority of our race. It is that style of speaking in which an individual insinuates himself into the affections of both sexes in the private walks of life. It is that style of speaking by which the most important business transactions of life are usually conducted and perfected. It is that style of speaking in which the most momentous political negotiations are commenced and prosecuted to their close by the representatives of different nations. It is the style in which the members of every household, within the wide domain of rational nature, are endeared to each other; and it may be safely affirmed to be the grand circulating medium of our race throughout the world.

It is not a strained inference, then, to assume from the foregoing premises, that the hearts of an audience can be more successfully reached, and the strings of popular sympathy more powerfully touched, by the conversational style in public speaking, than by any other. If the attention of any individual in society cannot be arrested by an acquaintance who submits to him any matter of business or distress in a very earnest conversational appeal, it is not unnatural to suppose that the heart of the person addressed is widely estranged from the person addressing him, or that his feelings of sympathy are inclosed in a shield of impenetrable ice.

Even in the dramatic exhibitions of the world, it is very observable what an indefinite advantage the actor who conducts his part in a smooth and facile strain of animated conversation, possesses over the most cultivated performer who is constantly ranting on the topmost key of his voice. It is equally apparent with what celerity a celebrated actor engages the attention of his audience, when he descends from the heights of boisterous rant and declamation to the calm level of ordinary conversation.

When a speaker is declaiming to an audience of any description, the most finished and convincing argument in a strain of loud and vehement declamation, he is regarded by those whom he addresses as one who is playing a part, he is as distinct from the audience as the magician when exhibiting his mysteries in the field of ledgerdemain, and as the clown in the circus, who has temporarily foregone his original identity. A speaker of this description may command the admiration of an audience, by the splendor of his oratorical flights, by the vigor of his argumentation, and by the dramatic skill of his gestures. But he rarely sways their sympathies and affections. They view him whilst he is engaged in addressing them, as if he was a different being from themselves, as if he was making a speech instead of talking to them upon a matter in which they possessed a common interest with him. Let a speaker of this description be succeeded by one of respectable powers and attainments, who addresses them in the familiar strain of persuasive and animated conversation, and the change in favor of the conversational speaker will prove so glaring as almost to be incredible. Why is this so? Why it is a result which flows from the nature and constitution of man. The conversational speaker addresses them in that style which commands their attention at the festive board, at the fireside, in the fields of labor, on the public highways, and in all the simpler duties and pleasures of life. He talks to them as they have been accustomed to be talked to, and as they have been accustomed to talk to their fellow-beings, and they feel as if they would like to take a part in the conversation with him.

The conversational speaker simplifies the business of speaking to his hearers so as to bring a matter home to every-day sympathies, just as a writer remarkable for the simple beauties of his style, endears himself to those who read his productions, because the readers feel that the writer belongs to the same race with themselves. And as persons who read the works of a writer characterized by great simplicity of style, are apt to imagine that they could have written the works they may be engaged in reading themselves, so the hearers of an accomplished conversational debater will be apt to imagine that they could speak like him themselves.

The renowned Archbishop Tillotson, who has left imperishable memorials of his name and excellence behind him, in his sermons as well as in the traditional reports of his moral purity and loveliness, which have descended to posterity on more than a million of voices, regarded it as the highest compliment that had ever been paid to him as a pulpit orator, when, on descending from the pulpit at the close of his discourse on a Sabbath morning, he overheard some countrymen who came down to London to hear him, ask a city man with evident surprise, "is that your great Archbishop, why he talks just like one of us!"

The most successful speakers from the sacred desk, in legislative assemblies, on the hustings, and before courts and juries, will all be found in the colloquial department. And it is not intended to be affirmed in advancing this idea, that there are no speakers who are highly declamatory in their style of speaking, who succeed in engaging the admiration of the world. This proposition would be broadly and intelligibly overruled by the experience both of ancient and modern times. The page of history is adorned by the names of many speakers who have acquired imperishable fame both in the earlier ages of the world and in those which are more recent by the force of a vehement elocution. But the principle which is designed to be presented in this treatise, is that the highest degree of utility and effect is only to be attained in the conversational style.

The clergyman who Sabbath after Sabbath dispenses both the promises and the threats of the gospel through the meaum of a florid, theatrical, and declamatory elocution, may number in his train more noisy and enthusiastic admirers. But the quiet grace and simplicity of the conversational minister, will command more converts to the faith which he professes, and will also win for him a larger measure of silent and profound affection. The declamatory speaker before a jury, may have a larger number of those who are listening in the court-house to talk about his speech after it is finished, than the conversational speaker. But the lawyer or advocate who addresses a jury in the conversational style, will be most successful in fixing the attention of the jury, and will carry the most verdicts.

CHAPTER XLII.

THE CONVERSATIONAL STYLE IN PUBLIC SPEAKING CONTINUED.

THE conversational style in speaking recommends itself to the speaker, not only from its superior efficacy to all other modes in engaging the attention of those he is addressing, but also on account of the vast abridgement of the speaker's labors which it admits, and the power it affords him of explaining with perspicuity and minuteness every proposition which he may choose to support or oppose. When a public speaker is engaged in addressing an assembly of any description, in a strain of vehement declamation, the labor involved in this manner of speaking is so intense that it causes him to shuffle over his propositions very loosely and superficially, without taking time to indulge in any nice passages of reasoning on any point, or to yield attention to particulars.

The conversational reasoner, on the contrary, having the

perfect command of his voice, can proceed at a degree of celerity regulated by his own pleasure, and, whether he is speaking fast or slow, will be enabled to press into his service every fact and authority which he may remember, and may also reason minutely upon them, because he will be speaking perfectly at ease, and free from that intensity of exertion which will be an unfailing concomitant of any speaker whose habit it is to address an assembly at the topmost pitch of his voice.

When we speak of the colloquial style in public speaking, we do not enjoin that monotonous and drawling sort of enunciation in which the speaker can be hardly heard by his audience. A great deal of prosy nonsense, ignorance, and fustian are frequently delivered in that style, by a speaker who has not the enthusiasm to be excited to a pitch of animation, or from his inexperience in the business of speaking, cannot muster up the confidence to speak with much spirit, for fear of losing the path which he may have previously chalked out in the deliberations of the closet.

When the conversational mode of speaking is referred to, we mean that the speaker should commence his remarks in that simple and familiar manner, and with the same compass of voice which he would adopt in presenting his views to a friend or to a company of friends in the social circles of life. When he has advanced a short way in speaking, or shall become interested in the subject about which he may be discoursing, his feelings will gradually contract a glow from the exercise, and his voice will be also gradually expanded in its volume. And when the voice of the speaker is raised to the highest pitch which it commonly assumes in rational and well-regulated conversations, then he will be at that level of the voice at which he will do himself most justice and prove most agreeable to his audience.

There are many persons who will not find it very difficult to adopt the conversational mode in speaking, from the fact of their voices possessing that uniform and equable flow of sound which corresponds with the usual colloquial exercises of social life. But, in a great majority of cases, those whose business it is to address their fellow-beings, have voices which take so many shifting keys, in the act of commencing a speech, or they have trained their voices so long in the declamatory mode, that it will require a patient and persevering use of various exercises, to enable them to command at pleasure what is here termed the conversational mode.

One of the most successful modes by which to blend this mode of speaking with the style of a speaker, as a constant habit, is to resort daily to some retired locality either in the forests or fields, and having previously provided some book of speeches, which has been selected with reference to the shortness of its sentences and the smoothness of its language, to declaim a portion of some speech remarkable for the brevity of its sentences and the animation of its language, at the highest pitch of the speaker's voice. This exercise gives tension or expansion to the voice, frees it of its asperities, clears it of its hoarseness, increases its depth of tone, and improves its melody of sound.

After he has exercised his voice in declaiming upon a sharp or elevated key, let him pause some fifteen or twenty minutes, or at least for a sufficient space of time to afford the vocal functions rest. Then let him take up the speech or address which he has previously spoken on a high key, and read it over, deliberately and carefully, on a low key of the voice, and he will find with what remarkable facility he can go through a performance in the usual style of reading, immediately after the voice has been subjected to the previous severe training.

But declamation on an elevated key of the human voice is not the only preparatory training which will tune the voice for reading with facility. The student, by previously exercising his voice in singing some favorite hymn or song, will discover that, with an interval of rest between the two exercises, he can read a few pages in a book of any description, with an ease which he can rarely attain independent of such previous exercise in singing.

CHAPTER XLIII.

THE ACQUISITION OF DIFFERENT MODES OF DELIVERY—ITS ADVANTAGES.

The benefit of acquiring a fixed style or mode of intonation in speaking, and of rendering that style a personal accomplishment, has been heretofore presented to the attention of the pupil, in the course of these numbers.

And without aiming to trench or infringe in the remotest degree, on the force of previous suggestions, it may be proper to state to the student, in addition to that admonition, that it will prove an exceedingly valuable attainment to acquire various modes of delivery.

For instance, he may hear an accomplished orator who enunciates in the conversational style, and he may, by perpersevering exertion, transfer that particular style of delivery to his possession.

He may then be captivated by some admirable speaker, who delivers his views in the didactic style, and he may acquire that mode of speaking, without interfering in the slightest degree with the first style which has been mentioned.

He may then hear a finished orator in the declamatory style, and reduce that method of delivery into his possession.

And he may, with proper care and perseverance, intro duce into the cabinet of his personal accomplishments, all the captivating modes of delivery which shall be presented to his attention.

It would require more time to obtain the mastery over the whole circle of modes, than it would to acquire one of them. But it is just as much within the range of practicability to obtain them all as to obtain one.

Just as it is as practicable to solve fifty problems in mathematics as it is to solve one, if the student only has the time at command.

And as practicable to learn a hundred tunes in music as one, on the same principle.

The advantage of acquiring different modes of delivery may be recognized in the capacity with which this acquisition endows a speaker, of choosing at pleasure a mode of delivery on different occasions, to suit the audience he may be addressing, or to correspond with the spirit of the times or the circumstances in connection with which the address may be made, or with the character and quality of the matter he may be about to deliver. The acquisition of each new mode of speaking too, as it successfully arises, will tend to improve and perfect every mode that a speaker may have previously acquired ; just as a dancer is improved in every previous step he has learned by the exercise which he passed through in acquiring each successive new step or evolution.

These different styles or modes of enunciation are to the matter of which a speech is composed, in the hands of a speaker, just what tunes are to the verses of which a hymn or song is composed, in the hands of a vocalist.

And as the vocalist may fix in his mind the tune he is to sing in connection with a given hymn, when the hymn itself shall have been specified; so a speaker, when a speech has been arranged in his mind, or a subject may be presented to him at a meeting, which he shall debate, he may fix in his mind the style or intonation of voice he shall blend with the delivery of the coming speech.

A speaker having at command various modes of speaking, may blend in one speech every style of oratory, just as various temperatures of the atmosphere may, in a fickle climate, be experienced in one brief hour.

CHAPTER XLIV.

THE REGULATION OF THE VOICE IN REFERENCE TO THE VOLUME OF ITS SOUND FROM THE BEGINNING TO THE CLOSE OF AN ENTIRE ARGUMENT.

It is a matter of incalculable importance to a speaker, that his voice should be pitched on a proper key at the commencement of a speech. On the certainty of his attaining this preliminary object, his success and convenience in the effort then in progress, will be both suspended in a very high degree. If the key he chooses shall be too high, his voice and gestures will be conducted with painful exertion and graceless irregularity through the whole course of the performance; for there is a mysterious sympathy existing between the voice and the limbs in the process of speaking, which will not permit the latter to move with perfect ease and flexibility, when the former is acting or sounding out of tune. If the voice should be placed on a key too low, it will yield sounds distressingly monotonous and deficient in music, through the whole course of a speech. And this defect the speaker will not be adequate to correct, no matter how loudly he may sound his voice, until he shall have effected a transition to the right and natural key, which will attest its presence to the speaker, whenever he shall become competent to speak with perfect flexibility of voice and gesture.

In the selection of a pitch for the voice, when the speaker is commencing a speech, he should be regulated very much by the position he occupies in relation to the assembly he is engaged in addressing. If his position should be near the chair of the presiding officer when he commences addressing any assembly, he should speak loud enough at the beginning of his remarks to be heard by persons at the centre of the hall. If he should be standing at the centre of the hall, he should commence his remarks at that pitch of the voice which will cause him to be heard distinctly at the extremities of the hall. If he should occupy a position within four or five feet of a jury, at the opening of an address to a body of that kind, he should commence his remarks so as to be distinctly audible to them, and not louder, for his proximity to the persons he is addressing will render it ungraceful, unbecoming and injurious to his cause to speak louder at first than has been suggested, for he may enlarge the compass of his voice gradually as he advances in his address. If a speaker should be engaged in addressing a multitude in the open air, he should commence speaking precisely with that degree of loudness which would characterize his voice in opening a conversation with a person about the distance of ten paces from him. And he should permit his voice afterwards to swell in its compass, so gradually that it will have attained its acme, or what may be termed the ultimate limit of its volume, when he shall have spoken about fifteen minutes.

To ensure the possession of the proper and natural pitch of the voice at the commencement of a speech, and its continued or unbroken retention through the whole progress of an effort, requires not only the application of a habitual previous discipline to the voice, but a vigilant attention of the speaker to its progressive enlargement as he advances in his remarks. For there is in every human constitution, except those of the most frigid and impervious mould, a degree of fervor and excitableness which will be inevitably provoked into circulation and action by that peculiar sort of influence which is exerted on the temperament by the labor of speaking. This sort of caloric in the system of man, when it rises too rapidly and is expended too freely, communicates the same jarring impetus to the human machine which a redundant application of steam usually imparts to machinery in the mechanical world. When this impetuous fervency of feeling rises so high as to get the upper hand of a person, when he is speaking, it is certain to produce a painful vehemence and celerity in the matter of delivery, and a marked irregularity and precipitation in the work of gesticulation.

The discipline which has been prescribed in the course of these commentaries, will conduce much to correct the tendency of speakers to overleap the bounds of a discreet and well-regulated animation in delivering a speech. But previous discipline will not be sufficient in every instance to ward off the impediment to effective speaking which has been just deprecated. To repress this tendency to redundant excitation in speaking, and to keep it in tame subordination to the dictates of interest and convenience, the speaker will be frequently compelled to exert the same rigid control over his feelings, when speaking, that he would be called upon to exert in keeping down an enraged mastiff that might be chained in his presence.

The best models for imitation in the speaking world, almost without an exception, have sanctified by their example the practice of commencing a speech on the conversational key, and of permitting the voice to extend in its compass as they progressed in their remarks, in such a way that it generally attained the pitch of a highly-animated conversation about the time when they had occupied the floor about fifteen minutes.

To assure the command of the voice throughout the delivery of an entire speech, a speaker should not only commence his remarks in a very moderate tone of voice, but he should proceed very slowly at the beginning of a speech. He should permit brief pauses to intervene between the earliest sentences in the composition of his speech, and take his own time in the labor of expressing his views. He will thus blend in salutary and beautiful union two advantages which shine with a conspicuous and graceful measure of lustre, in the character of a speaker: he will exhibit a spectacle of dignified composure and serenity to the eye of the world, and he will be enabled to deliver a calm, well-considered and intelligent survey of the subject before him to those he may be addressing.

CHAPTER XLV.

IS IT POSSIBLE TO IMITATE THE DELIVERY OF AN ACCOMPLISHED SPEAKER WITH SUCH A DEGREE OF SUCCESS, AS TO ENSURE THE TRANSFER OF HIS PARTICULAR STYLE AND MANNER TO THE PERSON OF THE COPYIST?

The imitative faculties of the human race exist in a much stronger degree of perfection than the prevailing views of the world on this subject would induce us to believe. And it is by a specific measure of attention yielded to particular facts which frequently occur, that will demonstrate this proposition to every intelligent and unprejudiced mind in the most luminous and satisfactory manner.

The readiness with which children at a very early age will imitate anything grotesque or peculiar, either in the voices or manners of occasional visitors to the house of their parents, has been observable to almost every person. And the imitation is conducted with such a punctilious degree of fidelity and accuracy at times, on the part of the juvenile copyist, as to prove a prolific source of blended wonder and amusement to those who behold the exhibition.

Those who are familiar with the habits and characteristics

of the African race, will possess a vivid recollection of the surprising shrewdness they usually exhibit in detecting those passages in the manners and conversations of persons who visit their owners, which may be impressed in a high degree with an awkward, provincial, or outlandish tinge. And their incredible expertness in imitating peculiarities in voice, manner, and motion of the preceding description, has often yielded an abundant harvest of merriment to persons of whose observation the benighted copyists were utterly unconscious at the time.

There is nothing which excites the spirit of imitation in the breast of any person in connection with the prevailing manners, voices, and enunciations of the times. For these are so much in accordance with nature and daily experience, as to pass without observation. It is only what digresses from the usual path of human observation at either of these points, that provokes into action the spirit of mimicry. And it is singular to what heights of perfection the faculty of imitation is carried when any person presents himself to the world, either in high life or low life, who is distinguished by any marked peculiarities of manner, voice, or motion. Every person of this description is almost as certain to be honored with a mimic in his wake, as every solid body is sure to have its accompanying shadow, and the personation is executed with such perfect fidelity at times, that persons in an adjoining room have supposed the person thus burlesqued to be present, when perhaps he was more than a hundred miles distant from the scene.

The corrollary which may be safely deduced from the foregoing observations, is that inasmuch as the spirit of imitation is aroused into successful operation by the presentation of anything singular in the voice, manner, or motions of a person, simply because such singularity is a digression from the ordinary pale of human manners and observation; that the same spirit of imitation, if its possessor chose to apply it in that way, might be successfully exerted in copying the voice and manners of any person in society who might be prominent for no peculiarity

It may be safely affirmed too, that all mankind possess the faculty of imitation to some extent, and that every human being who may not be encumbered with an unusual share of dulness, may push this faculty, by the force of persevering exertion, to a degree of accuracy far beyond the limit of present estimation. This proposition is abundantly fortified by the facility with which the bulk of our race glide into the daily performance of the great catalogue of duties which are essential to the common business and intercourse of life. The only solid reason which can be assigned for the fact that some persons stand prominently revealed to the world as accomplished mimics, is that from a mirthful turn of feeling, or by some casual combination of circumstances, they have been determined to the work of commencing the imitation of some peculiar individual, and having commenced the work and received some compensatory recognition of their talents in the encouragement and plaudits of their companions and friends, they have been stimulated to cultivate and extend the faculty until it acquired for them some degree of celebrity. If they could infuse into the feelings of their acquaintances the same degree of amusement by the act of imitating men who possess no peculiarity, they would attain the same degree of success which marks their labors when taking off the manners of the odd and the curious. The evanescent distinction, or rather notoriety which is won by this exercise, is the grand incentive which conducts the accomplishment to a full growth and expansion.

In the further prosecution of this subject, it may be suggested that there is a great number of persons who find themselves involuntarily gliding into the imperfections of enunciation, which cling to ministers of the Gospel, whose preaching they are destined frequently to hear. They apparently catch by absorption at times, the nasal twang, the drawling monotony of voice, and sometimes the vociferous rant of the preacher under whose ministrations they usually or even occasionally sit. This assimilation to an imperfect speaker is not in all cases permanent; it prevails in patches, or to a partial extent, and is usually checked and repressed by a judicious speaker, whenever he observes its presence in the style of his own enunciation. But the fact serves to show the susceptibility of human nature to contract any prominent trait in the manners or habits of those with whom it may be frequently brought in contact.

It has often been the experience of persons who have participated in the duties of deliberative assemblies, to find, at the close of months after the expiration of their labors, that their own elocution at the bar or on the hustings, presented very legible traces of the style and intonation of some speaker, whose voice had frequently descended on their ears, in the business of legislation. And in this case they were not the defects of the particular speaker which were involuntarily imbibed; they were the valuable properties in the delivery of some distinguished debater, which silently, but perhaps too transiently, insinuated themselves into the enunciation of the persons, who recognized the similarity with some degree of surprise.

It may be thought by the reader that an exceedingly excursive range has been assumed in this chapter, but the proposition which it has been designed to establish, is one of incalculable importance to the student of elocution, and no expenditure of words can be considered too extravagant, which would serve to imbue the juvenile mind with a practical and available faith in the soundness and validity of the views here presented.

The object in introducing so many examples from human life, on the subject of the imitative faculties of mankind, has been to illustrate the capability which exists in every human being, endowed with a respectable quickness of apprehension, of transferring to his own person any prominent peculiarity which exists in the manners, motions, and voice of another, whether that peculiarity be stamped with the graces of excellence, or marred by the taint of deformity.

It may be alleged as an objection to the foregoing proposition, that the defective peculiarities of our race are much easier of acquisition, than the adorning excellences of their characters. This objection is fortified in some degree by a theory coëval with the origin of man, and which proclaims that every human possession which is commended to our love and admiration by great intrinsic value, appeals to labor and time to secure its perfection.

It is the assistance of this very theory which we invoke, in order to render effective and beneficent the proposition which has been feebly presented in this chapter. The young aspirant for the utility and glory of eloquence is earnestly and affectionately invited to encounter the most irksome and persevering toils in the precious enterprise of plucking from the example of others and rendering them his own, those shining graces and qualities which illuminate and guide the counsels of peaceful wisdom. But it is cheering to be assured that labor can win for a human being, these almost divine accomplishments.

It will occur to every intelligent reader, that those who have enrolled themselves amongst the wonders of the era in which they prospered, in the character of artists, sculptors, and painters, have perfected themselves in these much-admired accomplishments, not merely by the habit of observing the beautiful and perfect passages in celebrated paintings and statuary, in a blended form or taken as a whole, but it is also an incontestible proposition, that the most renowned painters and sculptors have habitually indulged themselves in the practice of singling out the most attractive traits in each work of art, and of transferring those particular passages or features to a work or production of their own creation, when occasion or opportunity would permit it.

The faithful pen of history has imparted to us the intelligence that many of the most finished models in oratory, who who have charmed admiring assemblies and countries with their eloquence, were eager in the desire to imbibe improvement from every living fountain; that they extracted some endowment of personal grace and motion from every finished speaker or actor who displayed his powers in their presence, and that they also caught some effective tone of music from every superior voice which was employed in executing any intellectual mission in their hearing.

It is said of William Pinkney, who occupied the topmost round on the ladder of forensic celebrity in this country, that when representing the United States at the courts of foreign governments, he worshipped, with the impassioned spirit of pilgrim devotion, at every shrine which presented to his colossal and ardent intellect the faintest assurance of improvement in oratory. He was a constant and vigilant observer of the most finished speakers, both in the Parliament and in the courts of justice in Britain, as has been revealed to us in his personal correspondence. And the voice of tradition informs us that when stationed at the court of Naples, that he observed the most finished specimens of statuary with the enthusiasm of an antiquary, for the purpose of snatching from these works of art any special grace of attitude or posture which engaged his admiration, for the purpose of engrafting them on his own manner in speaking.

And the votary of eloquence should not be palsied when success shall not attend his earliest attempts to command the brighter graces in speaking which captivate his heart. Unfaltering perseverance in reaching after any coveted beauty in the style or manner of a finished orator, will ultimately place it within his grasp, as surely as he may be able to aspire to its acquisition. And he recognizes the most cheering guarantees for the verity of this proposition, in the broad and incontrovertible fact that time and labor have never yet failed to achieve for an intelligent mind any earthly prize which the universal sentiment of mankind had not tacitly inscribed upon the record of impossibilities.

CHAPTER XLVI.

DELIBERATION AND SELF-POSSESSION NECESSARY BOTH IN THE OPENING AND IN THE PROGRESS OF AN ARGUMENT.

As a lady who has been endowed by nature with but a frugal share of personal beauty, will enhance her attractions for the evening by joining a dancing assembly with courtly elegance and grace, so a speaker of barely respectable endowments, may magnify his influence and fascination as a debater, by opening an argument with an appropriate measure of deliberation and self-possession.

And a speaker should never adopt a hurried manner in opening a speech, but in one instance, and that is when he takes some concluding remark of the speaker who has last preceded him, and commences his own argument with a reply to such concluding sentence. In this solitary instance, he may begin his argument by the time the opposite speaker has touched his seat, and whilst the replying speaker is scarcely erect in rising from his own. If an apt reply to the concluding remark, or indeed to any important remark of an adverse speaker, shall be made under the circumstances just specified, the opening remarks of the replying speaker will not only be appreciated for their own intrinsic value, but they will secure a favorable reception for the sequel of the speech.

Under all other circumstances, except those just pointed out, a debater should open an argument with a degree of deliberation and serene self-possession which indicate that he is perfectly at home on the intellectual ground over which he is about to tread. It is desirable that a speaker should not only appear to be at home, but that he should really feel himself to be so; but if he may not be adequate to the reality, he should certainly affect by his manner to be perfectly at ease, both in commencing and in prosecuting an argument. For self-possession in performing all the duties of life, especially those of a high and responsible character, is a draft upon the admiration of the world, which wil lnever be dishonored. And even if an affectation of ease and self-possession by a speaker should be skilfully executed, it will tell as loudly for him with his audience as the reality itself, for they will not be able to discriminate between the genuine coin and the counterfeit, if the latter should be adroitly assumed.

During the progress of an argument, a speaker should uniformly proceed at a deliberate and measured pace, and should never permit himself to slide into a hurried manner.

There have been occasionally eminent debaters who posted with lightning celerity through an argument, and there was one of that description whose colossal powers both illuminated and adorned the highest legislative counsels (of this country) for a series of years.* But debaters who are so largely endowed by nature and cultivation as the one to whom we have just referred, may secure an ascent to glory by a measure of giant strength which will tread under foot all defects of manner. But even debaters of the loftiest reach of intellect will receive a vastly higher estimate as speakers, if their delivery is commended to the public taste by a manner which is easy and deliberate, instead of being hurried. For the direct tendency of a rapid enunciation is to produce the impression with an audience that the speaker is diffident of

* The Lamented Calhoun.

his own powers, or wishes to hurry through a very onerous task, or that his mind has been imperfectly disciplined by education, or that he is compelled to proceed at a rapid rate because his mind is not provided with a proper amount of ballast to hold it to a dignified and steady pace in debate.

CHAPTER XLVII.

SPEAKING CONSIDERED WITH REGARD TO THE LENGTH OF A SPEECH.

In deciding a proposition of the character which is indicated by the head prefixed to this chapter, the business of speaking must be considered with reference to the present condition of the world. During more remote periods in the history of our race, and even within the limits of the present century, when the faculty of effective and polished speaking was confined to comparatively few persons, there was no conventional or prescribed limit annexed to the space of time which might be comprehended within the limits of a speech. Unless the speaker should be addressing some tribunal or body, the legal term of whose duration was exceedingly brief, or some meeting or assembly which would dissolve under the influence of rules drawn from considerations *ab inveniento*, the day it convened, he might continue to speak from day to day for an endless succession of days, making the verbal blast of one day serve only as a starting point for a prodigal expenditure of windy rhetoric on the next. It is true that a web of loquacity woven out to such an interminable length, would naturally impair the reputation of any particular speaker for brevity in his discourses, and would inspire his audience with some bodings of fatigue when he arose to address them; but still his liberty on the subject of speaking was as broad as the air. He was restricted by no rule in relation to the matter, except such as were necessarily provided in consonance with the brief span of time within which certain tribunals or bodies were confined, or which might flow from the immemorial usages connected with certain meetings of the people, which were dictated by mere convenience.

But the world within the last twenty years even, has passed through the process of a radical and entire revolution on this subject. From the more extended and minute circulation of the benefits of education, from an indefinite multiplication of the facilities for rapid and enlarged intercourse with mankind, and from the stimulating influence exerted by the spirit of the American Government upon the ambition and energies of man, the faculties of those within the sphere of its influence have been roused to an intensity of exertion on all subjects, unprecedented in the annals of our race. Whilst the transfusion of a new and electric element into the mental and moral constitution of the American people has prompted them to explore every track of science, and to labor in every field of enterprise, they have not proved insensible to the alluring rewards which cluster upon the path of oratorical renown.

Facility in speech being recognized as the potent and universal lever which elevates the ambitious to consideration in neighborhoods, counties, districts, States, and even on the broader and more imposing theatre of national contention, speakers have sprung up in a degree of profusion far beyond the demand of the popular wants in this Confederacy. Every neighborhood and county cross road, now presents its oratorical champions; every jolthead who has sipped even sparingly of Latin and Greek, at a mushroom university, thinks he incurs immortal infamy unless he enters the arena and becomes a speaker. Every coxcomb who has learned to write a joining hand so as to be legible, at a country school, or to calculate the cost of a load of pumpkins, on an ordinary slate, thinks he will gain a crown as unfading as the stars, by seeing his name registered in some village two-penny sheet, as the orator in chief of some piny woods' convention. Every member of a legislative assembly, no matter how freely his constituents would pardon him for the omission of such labors, believes he will go down to posterity with a mark upon his forehead as broad as the brand of Cain, if he does not publish three or four columns of unmeaning and vapid verbosity in the metropolitan organ of his party for home consumption. The truth is, that speaking may soon become almost a universal attribute—things are rapidly verging to that point, when every human being will become his own speaker, and when the number of those who speak will swarm like the locusts of Egypt.

When it is glaringly evident that the supply of public speakers, in this country at least, has greatly overpassed the demand for labor and talent of that description, it must occur to every rational mind that some precautions must be adopted to secure to every interest a full and intelligible hearing before the different tribunals which dispose of the most cherished interests of life.

In the popular branch of Congress, the time allowed to each speaker on the floor is one hour, and this amount will be abridged in the course of time, as the House of Representatives augments in point of numbers, until it will be reduced to half an hour. The Supreme Court of the United States allows two hours for the argument of a cause, except in cases where special application shall be made for an enlargement of the time allotted to the counsel. These restrictions have been imposed upon the original freedom of debate, from the entirely changed character of the United States on the subject of speaking. And though this innovation on the ancient latitude of debate was regarded with some degree of odium and distrust at its early introduction, it cannot be doubted that the necessities of the country will gradually cause this abridgment of the liberty of debate to insinuate itself into every deliberative assembly, and perhaps court of justice in the land.

It may be safely suggested to the judicious and intelligent student, that half an hour is the eligible and golden measure which should regulate the consumption of time in making a speech or argument, and this from a due consideration both of what is demanded by the daily increasing number of speakers, which in a few years will not admit of more than this amount of time being enjoyed by a single speaker, and also from a calm survey of what is enjoined by the interests of the speaker himself. An hour is usually a very unobjectionable length for a speech if it should be well employed, but in a short time this space will not be extended to speakers, from the supervening force of circumstances already mentioned. And in addition to this inducement to the habitual abbreviation of speeches, half-hour arguments, when pressed by luminous and vigorous minds, have proved the most effective in the annals of debate. They present plainly and forcibly the points disclosed and the arguments and facts by which these points are fortified—they are not diluted in point of strength by the admixture of a large share of useless and inappropriate verbiage, and the body addressed is sure not to be wearied by an address of this length in such a manner as to become disgusted with the speaker, and to depreciate his arguments. By selecting this particular space of time too, for the habitual delivery of an argument, a speaker will greatly narrow the field of his own labors, and improve the quality of his intellectual wares. When there is no definite length prescribed for a speech in the speaker's own mind, he is apt to be reaching after quantity rather than excellence, and he will cram every sort of lumber into an argument which presents the faintest approximation to reasoning. When, on the contrary, his time for discussing a question is short, a speaker will concentrate his attention on what is available in the matter of his defence, to the exclusion of everything in the shape of trash and tinsel.

It has been said of the celebrated Chancellor of England, Lord Somers, that he once delivered a speech in the House of Peers in the space of seven minutes, which was so replete with sense, wisdom, and intelligence, that the debate was closed on his resuming his seat, every one being satisfied that so wise a counsellor had embodied in his address all the information which was essential to the proper elucidation of the question then under consideration. The illustrious character of the speaker, it is highly probable, abridged the debate more effectually than the flood of light which was reflected by him within so brief a space on the field of discussion. For it would appear that a complex question, which was to be determined by the force of reasoning, and not by the application of any decisive fact or authority, could not be perspicuously presented in all its bearings, within the brief space which has been attributed to the venerable Lord Chancellor. For the very fact of rendering the points involved in an important question intelligible to an audience, requires that these points should receive that measure of extension, from the application of language and reasoning to them, that the precious metals require from the appliances of the mint when they are in the process of being impressed with those devices which may qualify them to act as a convenient circulating medium. The points embraced in a complex question sometimes require the same spreading out, under the influence of the reasoning faculties, which the scenes in a historical or sentimental picture require from the brush of the artist, to make them perfectly comprehensible to intelligent observation.

CHAPTER XLVIII.

HOW A SPEECH OR ADDRESS SHOULD BE COMMENCED.

To fix with absolute precision, by the application of a prescribed code of regulations, what a speaker's manner should be in the opening of an address, would be about as difficult an undertaking as an attempt to engraft on the person of a youth, through the medium of theoretic principles, the graceful and polished self-possession of the accomplished citizen of the world. So much depends in the acquisition of personal accomplishments, on the union of close and devout observation with instruction flowing from the experience of others, that it is impossible to accomplish, in a written treatise, much beyond the fact of pointing out to the student captivating graces to be won, and repulsive defects to be shunned, in the persons of prominent living actors upon the public stage.

It is a fact which is everywhere accessible to intelligent observation, however, that there are various passages in the delivery, movements, and manners of certain speakers, which paint upon the surface of the mind and memory vivid and enduring images of the most grateful character, whenever they are presented. In the very act of rising from his seat, one speaker will communicate a fascinating charm to an assembly by the grace of his manner. Another sends a thrill of delight through a multitude by the first sound which drops from his voice, so intelligent is the intonation it emits. A third will excite glowing expectations in the breast of an audience, by the classic sort of method with which he arranges his papers preparatory to participating in debate; and a fourth will invest the chair of the presiding officer in a deliberative body, which is usually a seat of barren formalities, with the most engaging elegancies of life.

One of the most powerful and accomplished debaters of modern times, Daniel Webster, has pronounced eloquence itself to be "action, god-like action." And in opening his celebrated speech in reply to that brilliant and graceful ornament of every attribute of his countrymen which may be considered glorious and ennobling, Robert Y. Hayne, in the debate which arose on Foote's resolutions, it is said that he yielded to his audience, in his own demeanor, a practical exemplification of the touching power of action. On the 21st of January, 1829, when the orders of the day were taken up by the senate, several speeches having been then made on the resolutions in question, by Messrs. Webster, Hayne, and Benton, Mr. Chambers of Maryland rose and expressed a hope "that the senate would postpone the discussion until Monday, as Mr. Webster, who had taken part in it, had unavoidable engagements out of the senate, and could not conveniently attend that day." Mr. Hayne rose and said, "*that something had fallen from the gentleman from Massachusetts which had created sensations from which he would desire at once to relieve himself—the gentleman had* (referring to an unanswered speech of Mr. Webster, made a few days previously) *discharged his weapon, and he* (Mr. H.) *wished for an opportunity to return the fire.*" Mr. Webster remarked "*that he was ready to receive it, and wished the discussion to proceed.*" Mr. Hayne then took the floor, and spoke at length. After which, Mr. Webster rose, and delivered that reply which has acquired such an unlimited celebrity in the reading world. And it has been said by gentlemen of great elevation of character and position, who were observers of the debate referred to, that Mr. Webster's acceptance of Mr. Hayne's implied challenge to continue the debate at once, exhibited an air of majestic authority which might have served as a rebuke even to royalty itself.

Elegant and graceful action may gild over some of the darkest and most repulsive duties of human life, as it cer

8

tainly veils from detection the hideous mien of some of the most fiendish actions. John Randolph, in speaking of the great suavity and courtesy of Sir John Bayley, one of the judges of the King's Bench in England, gave as an illustration of his graceful demeanor, that some gentleman observed "that Sir John was so supremely graceful in the discharge of his judicial duties, that it must be a luxury even to be sentenced to death by him." And a bailiff is somewhere commended for the charming politeness with which he could conduct a prisoner to jail; and a sheriff for the soothing assiduity and tenderness with which he would adjust the hangman's knot on the neck of a convict.

A speaker unquestionably possesses graces of manner and of delivery which may be in some degree innate or peculiar to himself; but that he may add to and enlarge the field of his attractions, by an intelligent and persevering observation of the action of his fellow beings, is a proposition so simple in its character as to dispense with the labors of a pains-taking demonstration.

A speaker in commencing an argument, should never take his position at a point too remote from his audience. If he is addressing a jury, he should never get at a distance greater than five feet from it, if he may command a choice of positions. In a deliberative or popular assembly, he should take his position about the centre of the audience he may be addressing, or by all means at that point in the space occupied by his audience which will afford its members the fairest opportunity of observing and hearing him, and which at the same time will yield to him the best means of speaking to the assembly as if he was addressing each individual in it.

The benefit which a speaker derives from being near the body to which his remarks may be addressed, and particularly a jury, is that sympathy which flows from their seeing him, hearing him distinctly, and in possessing the power of marking with precision the particular gesture and expression of countenance which accompanies each idea or proposition he presents for their consideration.

If a person should take his position at the door of the house in which he may be discoursing, having an audience in his rear, to whom he never turns his face in speaking, but keeps his face towards persons outside of the house, all the time occupied by the speaking, that portion of the assembly in the house without including the remotest suspicion of a slight being offered to them by the speaker, will not be as much influenced or affected by the remarks delivered by him, as that portion of his audience which were located in front of him. And why not? Because they were destitute of that measure of sympathy with the speaker; in conducting the business of speaking; which emanates from the great natural appliances which most successfully touch the strings of human sympathy, the expressions of the countenance and the action of the person and hands. But that portion of the audience in the house, which never saw the face of the speaker, would be much more actively influenced by his remarks than would be a number of hearers outside of the house, who could distinctly hear every remark uttered by the speaker, but who could not get a glimpse of his person at all.

As a general proposition, a speaker should not commence the business of speaking immediately on rising from his seat, but should take sufficient time to survey his audience, and to collect his ideas with every appearance of the calmest self-possession and of respectful but easy confidence. After a few preliminary moments thus occupied, he should commence his remarks in a moderate tone of voice, and in such a way as to introduce the subject before him directly to the attention of his audience. He should also take due care to begin his remarks with the briefest sentences within the reach of his powers. For no circumstance is better calculated to throw a speaker out of an easy style of enunciation than a long sentence at the very opening of an argument. It requires a great expenditure of breath to speak one of these sentences through, where it is so long before a pause is reached. And independent of the irksomeness of the operation connected with the delivery of such sentences, it is difficult in speaking, as it is in singing, to blend any particular measure of music or intonation with the speaking of them. And if the measure or music of the speaker should be wrong at the commencement of the speech, as it will be difficult to rectify it when he has once gotten under way, his style of speaking will be apt to continue erroneous through the whole speech.

An exceedingly graceful and convenient way of commencing an argument to a jury or to an assembly of any description, where the speaker follows immediately after a debater on the opposite side of the question, is to take some proposition of the speaker who has just concluded, and to make some remarks on that in the very act of rising. This forms one of the most simple and agreeable methods of opening an argument which is known to the speaking world, for it at once introduces the speaker and the subject to the jury or audience in a very practical and easy manner, without the vapid circumlocution which is usually embraced in an exordium. And in taking up at the start, and in the very act of rising, some proposition of the preceding speaker, the one who is engaged in answering the other may remark by way of commencing, "that he entirely concurs with the gentleman on the opposite side in the opinion that the case is a plain one, but not plain for the benefit of the gentleman and his client." Or he may express a concurrence with the preceding counsel or speaker, in any proposition or affirmation he may choose, but deny the application of the proposition for the benefit of the opposing speaker and his side.

Another convenient way of opening an argument, is to commence it just at the very point where the preceding speaker leaves it, by selecting some fact which conflicts with the principles and propositions urged by the opposing coun sel, and that in the very act of rising. Or the speaker who follows immediately after another, may with infinite benefit to his own side of a question, observe (if the anecdote or incident be a good one) that the gentleman on the opposite side, or his client, reminded one very forcibly of some very apposite and ludicrous incident or anecdote, which may be then stated by the replying speaker. All these modes of commencing an argument, a speech, or address, have been dictated by an observation of the great benefit which has frequently resulted from a resort to them by debaters. They are easy and familiar in their nature, and are calculated to arouse a jury from a state of torpor, lethargy, or indifference, and to place them at once in the kindest and most friendly relations towards the speaker.

CHAPTER XLIX.

WHAT PARTICULAR SPEECHES A PUPIL SHOULD SELECT FOR THE EXERCISE OF DECLAMATION.

There is no duty which devolves on a speaker who may be ambitious of acquiring a felicitous and graceful enunciation, which requires a more accurate fulfilment, than the choice of the speeches which he is to read or declaim in his daily exercises. Whilst a comprehensive system of discipline might prescribe on this subject a recourse to the productions of all, or at least a large number of finished performers in oratory, for the purpose of attaining facility in delivering speeches marked by every variety of style, yet a regard to the structure of our nature, which is dictated by the faithful counsels of experience, loudly warn the student against the adoption of any such course.

Every human being, when he is engaged in reading purely for the acquisition of knowledge, should certainly read the books within his reach, which contain the most precious lessons of wisdom, the most just and vigorous thoughts, and the profoundest and most rational views of human nature, without a predominating regard to the peculiar style or phraseology of the works.

But when the student is exploring a work in quest of an entirely different object—when he is paying his devotions to an author for the purpose of contracting a particular mode of expression, or of grafting upon his person a particular style of enunciation, he should choose with the most punctilious accuracy, that work which extends to him the brightest assurance of accomplishing the desired object.

If a book of speeches, addresses, or essays, containing sentences of great length, should be placed in the hands of a beginner in the art of elocution, for the purpose of being daily read aloud or declaimed by him, they would inevitably exert a discouraging or damping influence over his ardor in the pursuit of improvement, from the intrinsic and inherent difficulty of delivering them.

The same pernicious influence will be exerted over the energies and industry of a pupil in elocution by placing in his hands speeches for declamation, which are stamped with invincible obstacles to a facile and smooth enunciation, which paralyzes the strength and revolts the taste of the early votary of science or of classic literature, when at the very threshold of his researches, a work exceedingly difficult of acquisition is given him to study. His heart falters and his industry flags from the vivid apprehension with which he becomes inspired of never being competent to accomplish the enterprise in which he has just embarked.

For the purpose, then, of averting a difficulty which would

be so startling to the young mind when entering on a fresh path of labor, a book of speeches should be placed in the hands of a student at the commencement of his labors, distinguished for the brevity of its sentences, and for the smooth flow of the language it contains. Speeches, addresses, or essays of this kind can be read with the expenditure of much less labor, by the most practised reader or declaimer, than productions characterized by the lumbering length of their sentences; and as a necessary result of this fact, they can be spoken or declaimed with vastly greater facility by inexperienced speakers.

The juvenile performer will find it greatly to his interest to read and declaim speeches of the preceding description, because it should be his chief aim when laboring to improve himself in elocution, to master and to reduce into his permanent possession some very desirable and accomplished mode of delivery, which may have been previously commended to his attention by a judicious counsellor, or which had been adopted by himself under the influence of a high admiration for it. The accomplishment of this object will be attended with incalculable difficulties, if the works of a writer or speaker should be assigned him for daily declamation, in which the sentences should be marked by unusual length, and in which the language might be deficient in smoothness and flexibility.

Every citizen of this country who may have enjoyed the benefits of a collegiate or academic career, in which the exercise of declamation was included as a branch of youthful discipline, will recur with pleasing emotions to the easy and flowing sentences which were contained in the speeches delivered by Lord Chatham, Lord Mansfield, Lord Erskine, and William Pitt, whilst the speeches of Burke and Sheridan, though adorned by the most precious properties of thought and language, are rendered too stiff for easy declamation from the length of their sentences.

The speeches of George Canning, Lord Lyndhurst, and of T. B. Macaulay, are commended to the consideration of a pupil in elocution for the smoothness of their language and the neatness of their sentences, whilst those of Lord Brougham, though impressed with an herculean energy of thought, and enriched by the wealth of universal acquisition, are difficult to declaim or read, owing to the inordinate length of their sentences and the prevailing stiffness and hardness of their language.

When the student explores the American field of debate, in search of speeches suited to disciplinary declamation, he will realize a rich vein of eloquence which immediately succeeded the American Revolution, and which may be said to have been quickened into life by the warm breath of that memorable period. From this source, a speaker who is desirous of adding fresh resources of music to his voice, by exercises in declamation, may select speeches remarkable both for the fervency of their language and the brevity of their sentences.

The speeches delivered about the time to which we have just referred, by that imperishable ornament of the eloquence of Virginia, Patrick Henry, occupy a conspicuous place among the intellectual memorials of the past. They are uniformly pervaded by an impassioned glow, by a strength and point of language, and by a convenient structure of the sentences, which fit them for easy declamation. It is true that the language of that celebrated man, like his character, is marked by a massive solidity, which renders the words which were used by him too ponderous in many instances for easy declamation. But this impediment may be vanquished where it occurs, by a frequent repetition of the particular sentences.

The speeches of Fisher Ames are also characterized by a felicity and smoothness of expression, and by a well-tempered animation, which adapt them, in a very peculiar degree, to the exercise of being declaimed. They are perhaps smoother and more flexible in their diction than those of Patrick Henry, though greatly inferior in strength.

The speeches of William B. Giles are also stamped in a very remarkable degree with the impress of those remarkable traits which figured so prominently in his intellectual composition. They are distinguished for versatile thought, fertile invention, ingenious reasoning, quick repartee, and for great sprightliness of diction.

There were other eminent statesmen who adorned the councils of the nation at the period which we have mentioned, and whose names perhaps fill a much more extended circle of celebrity than those which have been just submitted; but their speeches have not been introduced into a circulation so extensive, and they may not be so easily commanded by a speaker who is seeking the best productions for the exercise of the voice.

In descending to more recent times, the speaker will find that a large proportion of the speeches of the late Mr. Webster are admirably adapted to the business of declamation, especially those which were addressed to popular meetings. These are distinguished for a brevity of sentence and a vividness of spirit which could not be legitimately communicated to many grave and abstruse questions, to grapple with which successfully, required the heavier metal and munitions of reasoning. There are many of his congressional speeches too which may be very appropriately and easily declaimed by those who are seeking the improvement of their voice and manner by preliminary declamation. What is usually known as his speech on Foote's resolutions, may be regarded as being particularly suited to those exercises in reading and recitation which are practiced by public speakers for the improvement of the voice. But there are portions of that speech which may be declaimed by a pupil with infinitely greater returns of benefit than the speech would yield in that exercise, considered as a whole. The speaker or pupil will be enabled to make the proper selections from this speech by referring to those pages or paragraphs in it which may be pervaded by the largest share of animation, united with short sentences, with the frequent recurrence of interrogatories, and with the happiest combinations of soft and manageable words. The speech of Mr. Webster, delivered in the prosecution of John F. Knapp for the murder of Joseph White, is very finely adapted to the business of declamation.

The speeches of the late Mr. Calhoun, though in all the highest properties of thought and reasoning, they possess an intrinsic value which should endear them to the people of America, far beyond the purest and largest returns of gold which they have received from their newly-acquired fields of enterprize in the West, yet these productions, like the precious metal to which we have referred, are distinguished for their weight as well as for their value. That eminent statesman and almost matchless logician, estimated language, as he observed in one of his early congressional speeches, "*purely as a scaffolding for thought.*" He seemed to scorn everything which approached figurative ornament or verbal decoration, and adopted that species of language, both in regard to the words and the mass of its integral elements, in its single and in its blended terms, which promised to convey his ideas most forcibly and perspicuously to his audience. Hence the speeches of Mr. Calhoun, similar to those of Lord Brougham, and those of many other intelligences which stand like pyramids upon the plane of this world's history, are deficient in that brevity of sentence and smoothness of language which would fit them for the exercise of disciplinary declamation.

Many of the speeches of the late Mr. Clay may be very appropriately and beneficially adopted for the exercise of declamation by those who are seeking improvement in the field of popular eloquence. But with one or two exceptions, it may be very truthfully observed, that the speeches delivered by this eminent and gifted man during the progress of the war with Great Britain, were marked by a gushing fervency of spirit, by an ethereal flow of patriotic sentiment, by a musical structure of sentence, and by an impassioned glow of language, which would offer to the pupil in elocution a much more alluring field of selection than the speeches which were delivered in the more mature and advanced periods of his public life. The speech which he delivered in the Senate, in 1841, on the subject of Mr. Tyler's veto of the Bill proposing to re-charter the Bank of the United States, was regarded at the time it fell from his lips as infinitely surpassing (in point of pure and impassioned eloquence) every other effort which had been made by Mr. Clay since the period of the war discussions. And that speech would furnish a very suitable exercise for a pupil in elocution.

The speeches of the late Mr. Hayne of South Carolina, may be classed amongst the most eligible specimens of eloquence, in the business of declamatory discipline, which have ever emanated from the National Councils of America. They breathe throughout an elevation of sentiment, a purity of feeling, a perfection of principle, a grandeur of aim, a quenchless soul of patriotism, and an utter isolation from all the tainting and sordid passions of life, which impart a glow of inspiration to every susceptible heart. But when these speeches are declaimed by one who has made any proficiency in that embellishing art, the moral and intellectual ingredients which are blended in the composition of these speeches, will be found to be immensely enhanced in point of influence by the simple beauties of language in which their sentimentality and reasoning is clothed. The frequent declamation of these speeches on the collegiate stages of the United States, very clearly attests the high estimation in which these inimitable memorials of departed excellence are held by cultivated worshippers at the shrine of eloquence. For no matter how exalted the sense of morality may be, which pervades a speech of any description, and no matter how uniformly solid its intellectual merits may be the ambition of the young candidate for oratorical renown runs too high, in the matter of selecting speeches for declamation, to permit him to yield an attention to their moral and intellectual properties, so close and concentrated in its character as to avert his attention from those elements in a production, which might commend it to his regard as a suitable exercise for the production of an agreeable and musical enunciation.

The speeches of the late George McDuffie, as productions suited to the exercise of declamation, may be regarded as being rarely surpassed in this country, or on any other theatre where the blessing of speech may be prized in a special degree. They are distinguished for a nervous boldness of language, for an impetuous fervency of spirit, an intensity of devotion to the matter about which he was speaking, and by the compendious form of the sentences, which gives them a peculiar adaptation to effective declamation.

The speeches delivered by Edward Everett in the Congress of the United States which have been published, also present a very appropriate field for the selection of exercises for declamation. The language contained in them is distinguished for its classic polish and smoothness, whilst the sentences are unsurpassed in point of neatness.

But if the pupil in elocution shall venture on theological ground, in search of productions for declamation, there is nothing which has fallen either from the lips or the pen of man which will be likely to surpass the sermons which were delivered by the late Doctor Channing, of Massachusetts. There is about these sermons a tempered animation, a brevity of sentence, and a classic felicity, purity, and softness of language, which entitles them to the most devout and impassioned regard of a speaker who may be seeking the correction of his voice in delivery by the practice of declamation.

CHAPTER L.

THE HABIT OF NOTING DOWN THE POINTS ASSUMED BY A SPEAKER IN DELIVERING AN ARGUMENT WHERE THE OBSERVER MAY NOT BE CONCERNED HIMSELF.

One of the most powerful auxiliaries in training the human mind for conducting a discussion with skill, regularity, and success, will be recognized in the constant practice of observing, with a scrutinizing degree of attention, speakers of every description, as they are progressing in the delivery of an argument, speech, essay, or address. This exercise of the mental powers, with a juvenile candidate for the benefits and the honors of eloquence, will be found to rank next, in point of efficacy and importance, to the discipline involved in the actual labor of preparing a speech or argument.

The course here enjoined was a favorite resort with the celebrated William Pitt, and he acknowledged its charming efficacy in developing the irresistible powers as a debater, which he manifested even at a very early period of his life, in the Parliament of Great Britain. It was his daily habit, during his hours of leisure, to sit in the gallery of the House of Commons, to note down in his mind the points assumed by the different speakers of celebrity, to examine in silence the validity of these points, and also to reflect on the methods by which they might be improved, and how they might be answered.

It is rare that we find a person endowed with a temperament so stolid and apathetic as to be perfectly impervious to the reception of some small degree of pleasure from listening to an able and animated argument. But it is not the listless and superficial attention to an intellectual performance, which yields to the student a return of rich benefits and blessings. He must habituate himself to the practice of yielding to an argument as it unfolds itself in its various divisions, that measure of abstract and concentrated attention which an enthusiastic aspirant to perfection in any mechanical art or pursuit, gives to an accomplished artizan or mechanic, as he adds one part to another in perfecting the whole of any useful and complex piece of machinery.

With an attention of this description given to the argument of a luminous and enlightened speaker, one would be at a loss to determine why a pupil for advancement in the accomplishment of debating, should not be benefited to an extent corresponding with that which is derived by students in any of the professional departments from an intelligent and uniform attention to the lectures of their respective professors or preceptors.

When a susceptible pupil shall have received the benefit of this species of discipline from a devout and patient attention to speakers in the pulpit, at the bar, and in deliberative assemblies; when he participates in conflicts with the master minds of his country, on the various theatres of intellectual contention; he will possess the same advantage over the young debater whose faculties have not been previously practiced in this way, which the person who has long received instruction from an expert swordsman, will possess over an untutored son of the forest in any grave contention in which the sword may be appealed to as an arbiter.

CHAPTER LI.

THE IMPORTANCE OF SECURING ONE CORRECT VIEW, IDEA, OR ARGUMENT IN RELATION TO A SUBJECT ON WHICH A SPEAKER IS ABOUT TO REASON.

IT is a principle in the process of reasoning which may be legibly revealed to an intellect in the perfection of its maturity, but which may readily elude the observation of a writer or speaker of limited experience, that when a debater shall once have accomplished the preliminary point of writing down perspicuously on paper the premises on any given subject which he is about to elucidate, and even one sound argument; that he is then prepared to progress in reasoning on that subject until he reaches its close, just as a vessel is ready for being wafted with perfect facility over the surface of a smooth sea, when her canvas is fully unfurled and propelled by brisk and propitious breezes. When a speaker shall have perfected one link in the chain of reasoning, which is to be developed in the discussion of any particular subject, he may then rapidly complete other links in succession, until he has finished his web of reasoning. After this incipient step is adopted, the debater may safely lay aside his paper until some future day, if the exigencies of some approaching occasion shall not demand a more speedy arrangement of his thoughts. For a brief statement of the premises, and one pertinent and just view, lucidly drawn off on any specific subject, are seminal principles which contain all the hidden germs of reasoning on that subject, just as the acorn contains within its contracted hull the oak in the integrity of its parts.

The philosophy contained in the proposition just affirmed, has a very close affinity with a principle which discloses itself very clearly in operations in mathematical or arithmetical science, where, if one branch of a problem or sum is correctly disposed of by a student, he can easily subject the subsequent divisions in either, to the control of his under standing. This principle, too, is very closely assimilated to a fact which discloses itself in musical exercises, in which, if a beginner should succeed in sounding one note which enters into the composition of a tune, with perfect accuracy, he can then easily progress in acquiring in succession the kindred notes which enter into the formation of the same tune.

Some degree of minuteness and particularity have been used in the explanation of the principle which has been presented in this chapter, from a desire to demonstrate to the student in a lucid manner, the incalculable convenience which flows from once securing a fair start or beginning in the work of reasoning on any given subject. The accomplishment of this object secures a vast abridgment of labor, for when the student shall have succeeded in expanding the premises of any selected subject, and one idea legitimately connected with it, he has a broad aperture provided, through which he may intelligently survey the whole compass of that subject, just in the same manner that he can command a perfect survey of the whole space enclosed by a blank wall, when an ample gate at the entrance of the enclosure is thrown open to his view.

It is then a matter of incalculable moment to a writer or speaker to secure one good argument or idea on any subject which he may have under deliberation, and to write the argument or idea thus produced, immediately and perspicuously off on paper. For other arguments and ideas will continue to come within the reach of his intellectual vision on the same subject, if he continues to reflect on it, as naturally as it is when he looks in at the window or door of a room to see a friend who is setting in that chamber, to perceive at the same time the chair in which that friend is sitting, the table before which he is seated, and every other visible object within the bounds of the cham ber.

There is an invisible charm connected with the birth of one full, healthy, and perfect view of a subject, which com municates a surprising degree of fecundity to the mind of a reasoner. His thoughts may be rambling over the theme before him, like a shipwrecked mariner over a dark and dreary waste, without a gleam of light to cheer the heart, and without a patch of verdure to refresh the eye. But once let the light of one clear view of the subject beam upon the mind, and the mists of darkness will vanish before the luminous rays thus let in, like the shades of night before the dawning radiance of the rising sun, and the light will continue to grow brighter and clearer, under the influence of reflection, until he may survey the subject in all its relations and bearings.

CHAPTER LII.

WHEN A SPEAKER SHALL HAVE ONCE INDICATED BY THE COURSE OF HIS REMARKS THAT HE IS ABOUT BRINGING AN ARGUMENT TO A CLOSE, HE SHOULD NEVER TAKE A FRESH START IN SPEAKING ON THE OCCURRENCE OF A NEW IDEA OR FACT TO HIS MIND.

THERE is some peculiarity connected with the manner of every one who participates in the labor of speaking, which clearly indicates to intelligent observation when he is verging to the close of his remarks. And when an intimation of this kind is once given to his audience by a speaker, as they will prove as exacting as death in expecting a rigid share of fidelity to it on his part, he should never disappoint them by taking a fresh start in the business of speaking, should a new idea occur to his mind or an omitted fact rise to his recollection. For unless he should be a speaker of uncommon fascination, who has only consumed a moiety of that space which is usually occupied by speakers distinguished for the moderate length of their discourses, his audience will certainly look for his conclusion with some degree of impatience, when he has once manifested to them an intention to close. And an addendum which he may annex to a discourse, or argument which may be predicated on freshly-discovered lights, will not only be labor lost, but it will be calculated to invest with dark hues, in the mind of an audience, the anterior part of the argument or discourse, which, but for the after-piece, might have left a fine impression.

The body of men which is addressed by any person is impressed with the belief that it has rights as well as the speaker; and when he has once prescribed, by his manner, where the terminus of his discourse shall be located, his hearers will regard that indication as a tacit specification on his part of the amount of time they shall expend with him in the capacity of listeners. And if he shall blaze up, like a half-extinguished flame, after having reached what his audience would suppose to be his closing point, they will regard this commencement *de novo* as a gratuitous enlargement of authority on his part. A person who, as an act of grace and accommodation, authorizes another to draw upon him for a sum of money which has been previously specified to the drawee by the drawer himself, will feel somewhat irritated at finding that double the amount of what was originally requested by the drawer himself is finally inserted in the draft actually drawn. An audience will consider a fresh start on the part of the speaker, after he has once indicated that his discourse is coming to a close, an innovation on the original implied contract, existing between him and his hearers, pretty much after the same fashion with the hypothetical case between the drawer and the drawee. They will view it as an attempt to shoot two balls at one load out of a gun which was made for chambering one.

The proposition has all the truth of an axiom, that every advocate or speaker who habitually indulges in annexing addendas, postscripts, codicils, or after-thoughts, to speeches already concluded, or starts as it were on a newly-discovered trail, when his argument has previously given symptoms of a dying struggle, will certainly disarm of its power the particular argument in which the enlargement of original boundaries ensues, and an habitual practice of the kind will shed an incurable blight on his influence and acceptancy.

CHAPTER LIII

THE PRACTICE OF NOTING DOWN IN SUCCESSION THE PROMINENT POINTS WHICH MAY BE INVOLVED IN A CASE AT LAW, OR ON A SUBJECT WHICH HAS BEEN SET FOR DEBATE.

It should prove an inflexible rule of action with every speaker, when a subject is presented to his attention, in the discussion of which he must necessarily participate at any future day, to fix at once in his mind the prominent points that will naturally and legitimately arise in the progress of the coming debate.

The most compendious and convenient mode by which to accomplish this object, is after having maturely considered the facts blended with the case or proposition to be debated, to note down in the smallest conceivable number of words, the leading points which must inevitably pertain to his side of the question. These points may be inscribed on the page of a commonplace book, or the speaker may take one-half of a sheet of paper, and having folded it in such a manner as to assume the form of an entire sheet, he may inscribe his heads for debate for the sake of convenience on each of its outer sides.

These heads, as they are noted down in order, should be marked with the figures 1, 2, 3, 4, and so on in succession, or they may have prefixed to them the different letters of the alphabet, commencing with A, to denote the order in which he intends to discuss them. These heads or points will usually be imprinted upon the mind and memory of an experienced speaker by the time the ink used in writing them is dry upon the surface of the paper. But for the purpose of placing this matter beyond all contingency or doubt, he should concentrate his powers of thought on each of these heads in succession, immediately after they have been noted down, until he shall be satisfied that they are perfectly fixed in his memory. And he should continue to glance at them and to reflect on them for the purpose of rendering them familiar to his mind, until the question in which he is interested shall be finally disposed of.

These heads or points noted down, are to a debater what stage-houses or mile-posts on a public highway are to a traveller. They serve to give some conception of distance, progress, and termination. If a traveller should once pass along a public road, at the end of successive divisions of which houses occurred, at which the horses were changed, or at which he stopped to take some refreshment himself; when he might go over the same road again, his apprehension of the progress he was making would be greatly assisted by the presentation, as he was prosecuting his journey, of the same houses at which he formerly stopped. If, on the contrary, the road, instead of being enlivened at each of its sides by dwellings of any description, should present in this respect a cheerless blank, a person who had once travelled over it would be presented with no memorials to fix its identity in his mind; and when he passed over it a second time, he would possess but an obscure perception both of the identity of the country through which he had formerly passed, and of the progress he would be making at the time.

Thus it is with the points comprehended in a subject set

apart for debate, which are noted down in regular order, even on a small slip of paper; they serve as relief points to indicate the space over which a debater is to travel, what he is to do at each division of his journey, and when he is to consummate it. These points in reality constitute the case or subject itself in its broadest latitude, and no speaker who cherishes a just regard for his reputation, should ever omit the making them. For notwithstanding he may study profoundly and laboriously authors which may have a bearing on the subject on which the notes have been taken; and although he may write closely and voluminously on the subject, independent of the notes; yet the authorities which he collects from the books, and the views which he has copiously written out on the subject; should be arranged in such a manner in his mind and memory, as to be used in the delivery of them under those heads to which the authorities and written arguments bear a particular relation, and with which they may correspond in nature and in character.

But the student or speaker will be far from the point of having completed the labors devolving upon him, in noting down on paper the leading points connected with a subject. He must revolve these heads over and over again in his mind, with the view of collecting the best resources, in the shape of facts and arguments, with which to fortify his points when he shall reach them in regular succession. If he has at command any amusing incident, any historical fact, or any apposite fragment of poetry, which has an application to the subject, he should so arrange the incident, fact, or quotation in his mind as to be able to bring it to bear under its appropriate head.

In addition to these preliminary cautions, he should earnestly reflect on the species of artillery with which his adversary will probably assail the points on which he bases the security of his cause, and he should provide a corps of reserve, with which he may either destroy his opponent by anticipation, or with which he may come back at any time, in the event of his having the privilege of a reply.

And it also devolves on a judicious speaker, in addition to noting down his own leading points or propositions, to write down very briefly the points which may be in all probability assumed by an opposing counsel or debater. Those points he should be prepared to weaken or overthrow by arguments advanced in anticipation of their coming up, or by replying to them when once they shall have been regularly argued.

The process of noting down on a slip of paper the points or propositions which must legitimately arise in the discussion of any question which is to be debated, is very different from what is usually denominated a lawyer's brief, though it may accomplish in effect the same objects. What is commonly termed a brief, comprehends in a succinct form all the authorities which a lawyer intends to bring to bear on the points involved in his cause, together with a compendious presentation of his own views annexed to each of the authorities and points. The process of noting down the heads of a discourse or argument, here suggested, is much more simple in its character, for only the heads or points are written down in succession themselves, in as few words as a due regard to perspicuity will permit. The process is so very brief, that one word is sometimes used to express the nature or character of a single head.

CHAPTER LIV.

WRITING OUT COPIOUS NOTES ON A SUBJECT WHICH IS TO BE DISCUSSED.

For the purpose of securing an ample supply of materials to be used in an approaching debate, the speaker can rarely resort to a more useful or prolific expedient than that of previously writing out copious notes on the subject which is to be discussed. This preliminary exercise clears that rubbish from a question which obscures its aspect when first presented for consideration, familiarizes the mind with both its proximate and remote bearings, and places the speaker in possession of an adequate fund of original views with which to fortify his own side of a subject.

It has been frequently urged as an invincible objection to this practice, that it grafts upon the intellect of him who imbibes it a slavish dependence upon written memorials; and that when he has once slided into the habit of writing out a discourse or argument, that he can never afterwards dispense with his written fortifications, or make what is usually termed an off-hand or extempore speech. This proposition receives a triumphant refutation from the most en lightened experience which illumines the path of modern research, and from the authority of the most illustrious intellects which beam in splendor from the shades of the past. It might be as appropriately alleged that a person who had learned to swim by the use of corks or buoys could never afterwards dispense with the assistance of these artificial aids.

It is somewhat a hackneyed usage to reap counsel in a matter of intellectual exploration, from the most distinguished actors in the drama of antiquity. But the early wor shippers at the classic shrines of Rome and Greece are familiar with the fact, that those who stood at the apex of the pyramid of renown in those celebrated fields of human action, as orators and writers, not only explicitly ascribed their eminence and success to the early adoption of the discipline now under consideration, but also earnestly enjoined it on their successors in the race of glory. These sages, too, prosecuted this discipline not merely as an appliance which would serve to impart strength to the pinions of the juvenile orator in his earliest flight, but they commended it as a perennial spring from which the speaker may imbibe health, vigor, and power even to the gates of death.

It is unnecessary to mention names, but it is a matter of authentic tradition that many of those who reached a colossal elevation as debaters in this country, not only drew the elements of their power from this resource at the commencement of their labors as speakers, but even to the close of their career as public or professional men.

It is not true that a servile adherence to this practice through life, flows as a necessary result from the fact of writing out an argument at length, at the commencement of one's labors as a speaker. The adoption of this preliminary caution by a speaker, when his faculties are yet untrained by the labors of debate, puts him fully in possession of the subject, and he will not enter the arena of contention destitute of arms for the conflict. But when he shall have frequently repeated this mode of framing a speech or argument, he will be enabled to discard his ink and paper entirely, if he chooses, and he may rely with security upon the acquired creativeness and promptitude of his own mind, amidst the sternest exigencies of debate. For when the intellectual faculties have been trained for a considerable time, by the severities of the discipline which is involved in the act of writing out an argument methodically and closely, the mind will silently contract the mode of thinking in such a way as to frame and elaborate the whole of an argument, internally and invisibly, without a resort to written memorials. This is the infallible and inevitable result of the discipline in question, and the love of ease and repose will soon reveal to a student the particular point at which he may safely secure his independence of this support.

At the commencement of public or professional life, when the young mind has not been much practised in the trials of controversial skill, it may require a liberal expenditure of labor and thought to commit previously-written arguments to memory, and to render them completely available in debate. But the necessity for this labor and reflection will gradually wear away under the influence of practice, until it totally disappears. And it is the acknowledged experience of debaters of extended celebrity, who have devoted themselves to this mode of preparation through life, that the act of treasuring up in remembrance a written speech required no application of thought whatever, inasmuch as the written production would imprint itself on the tablets of the memory by the time it was fairly written out on the surface of the paper.

But independent of the invaluable assistance derived from this auxiliary to a speaker, as a purveyor and conservator of sound views and cogent arguments, to meet the exigencies of any particular occasion, it may be regarded as an exercise of almost incalculable importance, from the salutary discipline which it yields to the mental faculties. In every instance in which a speaker writes out methodically and at length any production whatever, which is the fruit of close and severe thought, he effects infinitely more in training his mind to regularity and closeness of thought, and to reasoning in connection, than he would accomplish by devoting the space of time to a satisfactory solution of the most abstruse problem in mathematical science. The habits of thought are as severely taxed in the one case as in the other, with this advantage superadded to the practice of writing, if it should be properly conducted, that it accelerates the approaches of him who labors in that way to a perfection in practical reasoning, which is at once applicable to the highest duties of life; whereas the other exercise, though highly beneficial in its influence, is speculative in its character, pointing to invisible and perhaps remote results.

In addition to the beneficent results flowing from this discipline, which have been already suggested, it blends with the intellectual treasures of the student an accomplishment of immense power and value, which is collateral to the profession in which he labors, and which may be exerted for the benefit of his fame and for the good of his race, on every field of human exertion.

CHAPTER LV.

A SPEAKER SHOULD NOT REPLY TO EVERY POSITION ASSUMED BY AN OPPONENT IN DEBATE.

There is a class of speakers who consider it obligatory upon them to reply to everything which has been advanced by an opponent who may have preceded them in debate. They consequently take up the positions advanced by an adversary, without the slightest shade of discrimination, the weak as well as the strong, and make a Quixotic effort to see what wild havoc they can produce amongst them. This very comprehensive performance of duty is dictated by the stimulus of two very frivolous motives—the desire to appear expert in the matter of making a replication, combined with the ambition to exhibit an uncommon fertility of resources in the exercise of speech-making; for the work of replying to everything which is said by a competitor in debate, will enable a speaker who has not one original idea of his own to advance on a subject, to weave out a speech of interminable length.

This mode of conducting a discussion is productive of some very serious and visible disadvantages. It gives an undue and irksome degree of extension to a speech, which includes in its limits so much irrelevant lumber. It produces in the mind of the assembly which is addressed, from the multiplication of unnecessary points and impertinent issues, an obscure and confused conception of the grounds of the speaker's defence, who adopts this very injudicious and exceptionable course; and by fixing the attention of the speaker almost exclusively on the points assumed in the argument of his opponent, it leaves the available positions which ought to be pressed on his own side of a question, unfortified and completely exposed.

This course of conduct in a debater bears a very strong similitude to the military policy of a general who would visit fire and sword upon the country of the enemy, whilst he left his own encampment without a single gun to defend it; or it may be compared to a wanton system of butchery by a commander, who, on capturing a city of the enemy, puts to the sword both women and children, both the sick and the disabled.

A large proportion of the positions assumed by an adversary in debate, may be permitted to stand untouched and unmolested by a speaker on the opposite side, who succeeds him in the discussion, without injury to the cause of the latter. The most of the points taken in debate are perfectly indifferent and harmless, and the labor expended in assailing them, is worse than a useless consumption of time.

It should be the chief aim of a debater to fortify the prominent positions pertaining to his own side of a cause, in such a manner as to render them impregnable, and to select two or three of the most plausible points assumed by his opponent, and to attack them with brevity, point, and spirit, and to close his case.

CHAPTER LVI.

THE ORDER IN WHICH A SPEAKER SHOULD DISCUSS THE POINTS OR PROPOSITIONS WHICH MUST NATURALLY ARISE IN A TRIAL AT LAW OR IN A QUESTION WHICH MAY BE IN THE PROGRESS OF BEING DEBATED.

It was the uniform practice of Lord Erskine, in arguing a case to a jury, to seize what he conceived to be the strong point in the cause, and to bring all his resources of thought and of argument to bear upon that particular point, to the almost entire exclusion of everything else. The example of a jurist of such high and merited celebrity, addresses itself to the judgment with a very impressive share of weight, the more particularly as it has been said that he rarely lost a client who confided a cause to his care. But the justness of the course pursued by him in this respect, considered as a universal practice, may be justly questioned; for men are so organized, both in their moral and mental constitutions, as to be conducted to the point of conviction by processes and influences widely variant in their nature. On conferring with a jury subsequent to the rendition of a verdict in Court, we will find that some of its members have been determined to the conclusion which they reached, by one fact or point which arose in the trial of the cause, and another portion of the panel by other circumstances, perhaps differing widely from each other, whilst a third division of the same body may profess to have been influenced by the force of facts which were not presented for the consideration of the jury, either by the court or the counsel employed. This is pre-eminently the case with those who constitute the voters in deliberative and popular assemblies—the judgment and feelings of one part of such assemblies will be borne away by one consideration, and another part by influences and facts as widely opposed to each other as the poles.

The facts just submitted present to the mind as broadly as a pyramid in the sun, the imperious necessity which devolves on every debater, of pressing into the service of the proposition before him every resource in the shape either of reasons or facts which may justly pertain to it. What is denominated the strong point in a cause or proposition, should be allotted a measure of space in a discussion commensurate with its importance—it should be, in truth, the axis around which the minor points in the question should be made to revolve; but a speaker should never omit the smallest circumstance which may possibly tell for the side he is advocating; but, on the contrary, should adopt for his guiding star, in conducting a discussion, the celebrated observation of Napoleon Bonaparte respecting himself, "that he never felt acquitted, after an action had terminated, if he was sensible of having omitted any resource of defence which was clearly within his reach."

But whether the prominent point in a cause or proposition should be presented in the middle of an argument, supported on each of its sides by propositions of inferior strength, like the centre of an army with the two wings auxiliary to its support, or whether it should occupy the position of a *corps de reserve*, or rear guard, coming up at the last of the fight, is a question which cannot be so easily determined. The object here aimed at will be to present a double aspect of the case, that is, the advantages and disadvantages resulting from each mode of discussing a proposition, and leave the matter to the choice of the speaker himself.

If a debater or advocate, in the early stages of his address to a jury or legislative assembly, shall have presented the subordinate points in his proposition with a superior share of ingenuity and power, he will have thus made a lodgment in the hearts and minds of his audience, which will cause the strong point to be more highly appreciated when that is reached; and if he should touch the leading point itself with a herculean degree of power, a more welcome reception will be apt to be secured for such other points as he may choose to present in the closing portion of his argument. The proposition last affirmed, is founded on the philosophy of our nature, for it is an exceedingly obvious principle in the constitution of man, that when a pre-existing prejudice is removed from his breast, or his sympathies are strongly enlisted, by the relation of circumstances which weigh strongly in favor of an individual or a doctrine, that his faith will then be placed in a condition to yield an assent more readily than it would have previously rendered to anything plausible which may be advanced in favor of the individual or doctrine in question.

The sense of the foregoing proposition, when reduced to its simplest elements, is this; that if a speaker in the opening part of an address, shall prepossess the feelings of his audience by the masterly discussion of preliminary points of subordinate strength, that a more easy access to its judgment will be provided for the strong point when that shall be brought up; and that then if the strong point itself should be urged with such effective ability as to weaken or destroy prejudices or adverse opinions previously formed, that an easy credence will probably be yielded to propositions and arguments subsequently submitted.

A question is frequently argued with a vastly effective degree of power, by presenting the points involved in it in a succession or order to be regulated by the comparative strength of these points, reserving the strongest of all for the conclusion of the argument. If a series of propositions should be presented in succession to an audience, each flowing from one leading question, and each augmenting in force and influence, as it arose in its order of succession, it must be naturally presumed that the last of this series when reached, if argued with signal perspicuity and force, will descend upon the mind with a decisive degree of weight.

We feel somewhat inclined to prefer the mode of discussing a question which has been last submitted for the consideration of the pupil. For the obvious reason, that if he should marshal the points disclosed in his argument, in such a way as to present each with a very perceptible increase of force as it arises, he can hardly fail to inspire convictions favorable to his own side of a question, by the time he shall have properly disposed of the last and most potential point of all.

But it may sometimes happen that time and circumstances will not admit of either of the preceding comprehensive modes of debating a question. A court or deliberative assembly may be approaching the close of its labors, or a jury may be rendered weary and impatient by the protracted nature of the discussion. In either of these cases a speaker, let the theatre of his labors be what it may; should seize the strongest point in the subject before him at once, and having pressed it with all the resources within his reach, and in the most animated style, should drop the subject.

To demonstrate clearly to the mind of the speaker the magical influence which is exerted at times by presenting points or propositions in the order of their strength, we will appeal to a living exemplification of the matter. It frequently happens in the courts of criminal jurisdiction, that two or more persons are charged with a murder in one indictment, and that they are tried without a severance in the defence. Now if the counsel for the prosecution, in presenting his argument to the jury, shall argue the evidence applicable to the case of that prisoner who ought evidently to be acquitted (from a deficiency of proof), with such marked ability as to inspire the mind of the jury with even a slight suspicion of his guilt, when he reaches the evidence applicable to the most guilty culprit, the mind of the jury will be in the most aus picious of all conditions to pronounce his conviction from the effect of comparison.

So it is in the defence of a number of prisoners. If the counsel in the defence shall in the first part of his argument take up the evidence applicable to the case of the guiltiest client, and succeed in raising in the minds of the jury even a bare doubt of his guilt, the proofs adduced against those on trial whose guilt has been made least apparent, may be blown away in many instances by the vacant breath of declamation.

CHAPTER LVII.

THE PREPARATORY PROCESS TO BE ADOPTED WHEN A STUDENT IS ABOUT TO PREPARE A WRITTEN PRODUCTION OF ANY DESCRIPTION.

There are many judicious thinkers who regard it as a beneficent precaution in every writer who is about to present his views to the world in any document or production, whether of transient or enduring importance, to adopt some process by which to provoke the powers of thought into spirited and productive action. For fervency of feeling and fertility of invention, though they may exist in a latent form in the intellectual constitution of their possessor, will not uniformly yield a spontaneous tribute to his demands. To secure a copious harvest from these precious properties, they must be frequently stimulated by appliances congenial to the nature of the mind.

There are many, who, for the purpose of securing the possession of their best thoughts on any subject on which they are to write, will lock themselves up in a chamber to the exclusion of all company, and will reflect intensely upon the matter under consideration, until they have painted on the tablets of the mind a complete outline or diagram of it, in all its bearings and relations. They then emerge from their state of seclusion, and write out their views at some subsequent period. There are others who retire to the shades of some sequestered spot, where they may revolve a subject in their minds, free from every species of interruption. There is another class of thinkers who take a seat at a table with paper and ink before them, and who note down as they arise in their minds, the brightest and most valuable thoughts which occur to them on a subject, and who, after having perfected a skeleton of the subject in this mode, will then commence the secondary labor of embodying their views in suitable language.

It is said to have been the usual practice of Alexander Hamilton, who was one of the most original and prolific thinkers who has enlightened the world in modern times, when he had an important subject under deliberation, to concentrate his thoughts upon it in the silence of night, then to retire to rest, and immediately on awaking from sleep, to inscribe his views on paper. Apart from the encouragement which is presented for the adoption of this mode of procedure in an example so attractive and impressive as that of Hamilton, there is a sort of invisible charm or magical influence associated with nocturnal meditation on a subject, which powerfully commends it to the young mind. This species of mental labor may be assimilated to the act of sowing seeds which are to vegetate during the indulgence of sleep, and to exhibit with the light of the morning sun, the plant fully developed both in its stem and leaves. Those who have had difficult exercises assigned them to be committed to memory during the period of juvenile instruction, will remember with delight how vividly some portion of an author was painted on the page of memory in the morning, which they had carefully studied on the preceding night. The success connected with this specific mode of reflection may be traced to the principle or fact that the last thoughts which hang on the mind, previous to a temporary suspension of the functions of nature, will be the first to visit it when that suspension shall have been removed. The repose of sleep may be regarded in the light of an Isthmus intervening between two seasons of labor, and the images or objects which were most carefully observed and cultivated on the commencing side of that Isthmus, will certainly be the first to accost the memory at its terminating boundary.

With the view of rousing the mind to a spirit of invention and a free flow of diction in the investigation of any particular subject, no method is preferable to the act of reading, preparatory to commencing a production of any kind, an author, the pages of which breathe throughout a glowing spirit of invention. If any one had in contemplation the act of writing an essay or address on any branch of religious duty, it would be a difficult matter for him to give his days and nights to the gorgeous pages of Chalmers, without catching in some small degree the fervid spirit of inspiration by which they are pervaded. If he should be engaged in writing an essay on any topic of a literary nature, it would be difficult for a writer to refrain from contracting some portion of the classic elegance which beams in every line of Channing, and of Washington Irving, if he should previously read their inimitable works. And if any production of a political tendency should be contemplated, it would be almost impracticable for the writer to yield a liberal share of attention to the numbers of the Federalist, or to Say, or to Montesquieu, without imparting some hues of the coloring of those works to his own composition.

But the author from which a student may seek the spirit of invention, or inspiration, in this way, should possess a direct relation, in regard to the subjects which it treats, to the topic on which he is about to write. For the benefit which he must reap from the perusal of any particular work, in prosecuting the labors of an intellectual production, will be proportioned to the closeness of the relation which exists between that work and the subject which he may be investigating.

And if the student should not be able to command an author identical in principles and in theory with the views which he designs presenting in his own production, let him procure some book which bears the nearest imaginable affinities with the subject which he intends to elucidate. For instance, he may be on the point of writing a speech or essay on some political topic, concerning which not a single word may be uttered in the numbers of the Federalist. But inasmuch as political topics are treated at large in those papers, and that with a measure of unrivalled strength and spirit, he will by the careful study of these papers be enabled to augment his own intellectual power in discussing any question which may fall legitimately within the department of politics.

After the student shall have yielded his reflections to an appropriate author, in the mode heretofore pointed out, the next question to be disposed of, is the manner in which he shall render these preliminary devotions available in the matter of preparing a production of any kind. On this branch of the subject, we have only to suggest to him, that whenever he finds his mind teeming with the subject which he is engaged in studying, let him take his seat and commence the labor of writing out his views on that subject, until he shall have exhausted the supply of materials he has in possession at the time. For when the fervor of invention shall have once deserted him, it may not return to him again in the exuberance of its vein.

CHAPTER LVIII.

THE PRACTICE OF NOTING PASSAGES OF PECULIAR EXCELLENCE WHICH OCCUR IN VARIOUS AUTHORS.

There are very few intellectual habits which a worshipper at the shrine of eloquence may contract, which will yield a larger return of improvement to his style both in writing and in speaking, than the constant practice of observing, with the most fixed and deliberate attention, those passages in the authors which he reads which are rendered attractive either by their peculiar strength, brilliancy, wit, perspicuity, smoothness, elegance, or for the luminous and practical exposition they afford of the principles and character of man.

This was a practice to which Richard Brinsley Sheridan perseveringly and tenaciously adhered during a large portion of his eventful life, as was abundantly attested by an examination of the works which he was in the habit of perusing. It has been affirmed, by those who possessed the fairest opportunities of knowing his intellectual habits, that every passage in the authors which he read which was stamped by any peculiar excellence, was marked where it occurred in the page of the book. And though he was unquestionably endowed by nature in her beneficence with a fine intellect and a prolific imagination; yet he has bequeathed to his country shining and imperishable memorials to demonstrate the magical influence which was exerted over his mental productions by this practice; in the almost matchless gorgeousness of his eloquence, in his unfailing promptness in apposite and beautiful quotations, and in the electric flashes of wit which so frequently communicated an unspeakable charm both to the social circles and to the legislative counsels of Britain.

To the fertilizing influence of this practice, too, many of

those whose names cluster around the apex of the pyramid of American renown, were indebted in a high degree for the splendor of their diction and the pungency of their wit. Amongst these may be appropriately numbered, William Pinkney, William Wirt, John Randolph, and Daniel Webster, the fame of whom is co-extensive with the surface of the globe. When living, their conversation, from abounding in classic embellishments of the most exquisite beauty and finish, gave conclusive evidence that they had appealed to the practice now under consideration, in the work of magnifying their intellectual resources; and they left behind them, on their departure from the world, indelible traces of its effect in the unsurpassed brilliancy of their political and forensic efforts.

A reference has been made to the preceding illustrious names for the purpose of affording to the pupil some shining proofs of the immense practical benefit which may be derived from a persevering use of the particular appliance which has been suggested in this chapter. But its use and application is enjoined and enforced by an intelligent observation of the nature and structure of the intellect of man. That human being must be afflicted with a hopeless and incurable imperviousness of mind, who can yield his days and his nights to any book conspicuous for the superlative excellence of its language, without imbibing some traces of the spirit and the language of the author.

Works which glitter with the gems of human thought in every page and line, like those of Gibbon, Burke, Hume, Chalmers, Channing, and Macaulay, cannot be perused by one endowed with a susceptible mind, without the style of the reader contracting in some degree the glow and the tinge of classic elegance which breathes in every passage of these caskets of classic treasure. So powerful and palpable is the influence wielded by the perusal of such authors over the style and language of some readers endowed with an exuberant flow of fancy, that they are compelled to abstain from the study of such works entirely, and to tie themselves down to writers of a sterner and less gorgeous character, otherwise their productions would teem with the flowers of fancy without being commended to a sufficient extent by any of the solid and available fruits of mental culture.

If, then, the bare perusal of authors highly imaginative in their character, is calculated to enrich the human fancy, and prompt it too frequently to ethereal flights, how vastly greater in point of specific influence and value, must be the daily habit of plucking the purest and most precious gems from such authors as Bacon, Milton, Dryden and Shakspeare, and depositing them for safe keeping in the mental treasury of the student.

This judicious and discriminating choice of the brightest portions of an author, is widely variant too in its results from that promiscuous absorption of all the gorgeous properties of a writer which has been referred to in the preceding lines. It is similar to the process by which an alchemist separates the particles of pure ore from the mass of worthless tinsel with which it is incorporated, or like taking the nutritious pulp of any species of fruit whilst the exterior coating or husk is discarded.

But the precious and crowning benefit which flows from the preceding practice, consists in the fact of storing the memory with a rich supply of beautiful expressions, which serve as models from which the mind of the pupil may spontaneously create and cast off rare and captivating images of its own. It is not exclusively for the purpose of being used in the character of quotations in writing and speaking, that the collation of sentences of rare excellence from various authors is advised. They supply a very precious treasure of ornamental decorations regarded as quotations. But that is not their principal value. When these expressions are thrown into the cabinet of an inventive mind, they become incorporated with its native and acquired resources, in such a manner as to form a part of its essence. When the person who treasures them up may be engaged in speaking or writing at a period long subsequent to that at which he collated the expressions, they will fall from his lips or his pen in a costume so perfectly new, that he will not know that the intellectual property of another is entering as an integral portion into the composition of his own intellectual creations. Without having aimed at any such blending of separate intellectual emanations, he will find on a cool survey of some of his most beautiful expressions, both in speaking and in writing, after they have been given to the world, that he has merely united some new beauty with a gem of thought which had been long previously thrown into circulation by some other writer or speaker.

In instances of the preceding description, the speaker or orator is only entitled to a right of property in the images of rare beauty which he exhibits in a discourse, on the same principle precisely with that on which a person receives a patent from the government for having added a fresh improvement to a machine which had long previously been in operation. But it discloses a high quality of mental combination in a speaker whose mind may be competent to throw out compound gems of thought in the structure, of which fragmentary portions of foreign gems are distinctly visible. One of the principal charms of this particular mental process, consists in the fact of the person who thus draws on the resources of others not being conscious of the fact when he is engaged in it. And probably he may never be apprized of his obligations to another intellect, for some of the most beautiful mental creations which sparkle in the casket of his spoken and written productions, until he shall have critically analyzed them and traced them to their source. It is highly probable, too, that the world may never recognize in this case a re-enactment of that legal sort of admixture which is sometimes referred to in the law books, where the goods of one individual are so intermingled with those of another, that they cannot be apportioned to their respective owners. It is fortunate, too, for the compounder of intellectual commodities, that he does not, like a jumbler in law, incur an entire forfeiture of his portion of the goods, in consequence of their being mixed with those of another.

Whilst alluding to the intellectual creations, in which the elegant expressions of some other person may be involuntarily and unconsciously blended with the frame-work of a speech, when it is in the progress of being delivered by a speaker, it may be appropriately suggested that some of the most celebrated oratorical productions which are now extant in the world, are visibly marked with the traces of that mingled or compound beauty, concerning which we are now discoursing. And it may so happen that a person will subject some of these productions to repeated perusals, and arise from each successive perusal with a fresh glow of admiration for some highly sentimental and glittering figures which they contain, without the faintest suspicion that these ornamental beauties are invested with the smallest share of borrowed lustre. And perhaps, at last, when this splendid union of separate beauties is detected by the eye of a reader, he will be indebted for the discovery to a perusal of the works of Shakspeare, of Milton, of Dryden, or those of some other renowned genius, in which some shining particles of the expression he originally admired in a speech of recent times, will broadly assert their presence.

But the practice of collating rich and beautiful expressions from the authors he reads, may be tributary to the improvement of a speaker, not only in the fact of supplying him with choice materials which may be advantageously blended with his own creations. The rare expressions which he thus collects, will serve as models or types from which he may form, in rapid succession and in rich profusion, splendid creations of his own. If a painter who is animated with a passionate devotion to floral beauties, should pass through a vale which was robed in beautiful flowers, he might contract images of beauty from the flowers which then charmed him, which would arise in new forms of beauty on the surface of the canvas adorned by his pencil at the termination of years afterwards. An artist catches some of his choicest conceptions of that beauty which graces the productions of his chisel, from observations of statuary which float amongst the dreamy shadows which have long passed away.

Thus it is with the speaker or writer who may be blessed in possessing a cabinet which is well supplied with the brighter mental creations which have been charming the world through a series of years. Each of these glittering passages will probably serve as a model or image, in the mind of the person who treasures them up, to suggest the formation of other charming expressions, which may add to the elevation of his own fame, and enhance the resources of his country's entertainment.

CHAPTER LIX.

A SPEAKER SHOULD ALWAYS MAINTAIN THE MOST PERFECT GOOD HUMOR IN ADDRESSING AN AUDIENCE OF ANY DESCRIPTION.

WHEN a person has no special or desirable object before him which is to be accomplished in a short time, if it should be his inclination to fret and get angry, he may indulge in that vein according to the measure of his largest desires; for he will have the whole term of his existence before him as a season in which to cool, and he will not incur any loss or inconvenience which will flow as a necessary consequence from the particular flush of irritation.

But if an applicant should be seeking an office from any

appointing power, or if he should be courting a bright and benignant glance from the eye of beauty, or if he should be soliciting the interest of a voter in any pending election, he should refrain from the slightest exhibition of ill-temper, as cautiously as he would from drinking a beverage which he knew to be strongly impregnated with arsenic. For the persons at whose hands a favor is sought, from the very nature of man, will scrutinize the person who seeks the favor with a more jealous and critical eye than they would if he had no object to accomplish with them. They become much more accessible to distorted views of slight passages in the demeanor and person of the applicant, which may not be positively agreeable, than they ever were before; and it becomes one in this situation, if he has not determined to acquire the coveted object, according to the most approved *Bonapartean* method, by force of arms, or to adopt the expedient which is sometimes resorted to by despairing lovers and lasses, that of proud disdain; to carry about him, in their fullest measure of perfection, all the fascinations of manner, appearance, and disposition which he may be able to muster.

It is thus with one who may be engaged in addressing a jury, or any assembly upon whose suffrages an important decision may be suspended. Because persons in this situation, from the very fact of holding a specific measure of power, in which the person addressing them is interested, are temporarily inflated with the pride of power, or infected with what may be termed a punctilious or exacting spirit. They have at the time the appetite of a famished wolf for all the fascinations which the speaker can pour out before them, merely because they are the dispensers and he the applicant for a favor. Or it may be that they are peculiarly sensitive to any apparent withholding of incense and fascination on the part of the speaker, because it is the custom of the country to play the courtier on such occasions, and they may conceive that they are grossly slighted when there is any lurking suspicion afloat that they are not honored with the same gales of perfume which have feasted the senses of all other persons and voters.

That sagacious observer, as well as accomplished actor, Julius Cæsar, made it one of the inflexible rules of his personal code never to be angry, for he knew how like a malignant star the baleful spirit of anger shone upon all the precious enterprises of life. And it has been remarked by Lord Chesterfield, that the illustrious Duke of Marlborough had been more indebted for his unrivalled success in life to the commanding elegance of his person and the winning grace of his manners, than to any other qualities he possessed. It might, perhaps, seem to be a very broad and extravagant assumption, to affirm that these renowned captains, whose mere attempts were the precursors of accomplishment, had been much reinforced by the insinuating graces of mere good humor, in capturing a besieged city or in vanquishing an opposing army. But the universal cultivation and preservation of the spirit of suavity and courtesy, may have in the first instance raised them to that eminence of promotion which invested them with the opportunity of taking cities and of defeating armies. But there are two propositions which, if the pen of history has been faithful to its sacred trust, are incontrovertibly true, and these are, that each of these celebrated men were unsurpassed in courtesy and good temper, and that they also enjoyed a measure of success in all their enterprises which has been seldom reached by the strength of any human arm.

In relation to the preservation of good humor by speakers, when engaged in delivering an argument or address, it will occur to every observer of the active scenes of life, with what a gracious welcome an advocate or politician, who may be indifferent in other respects, but who presents himself before the body he may be addressing with perfect good humor, is universally received. A jury or popular assembly will not only yield to a speaker of this description a very evident share of their attention, but they also indicate by their good-natured smiles that they are willing to meet him more than half way to gratify his wishes. And if they should not be borne away by the charge of a judge, or by some circumstance which exerts an imperative control over their judgments, the jury will yield their verdict, and the popular assembly will render their votes to the good-humored speaker.

It is observable, too, how quickly an assembly of any description contracts the dark hues which are painted on the surface of the manners and character of a speaker, who exhibits either anger or a peevish humor when he rises to speak. They feel almost as adverse to his interests and wishes as if he was angry with them, and instead of indulging any wish to oblige him, they feel a disposition to punish him for his implied aggression on good manners and good feelings, by sternly withholding the benefit he seeks. Advocates and politicians of this description may succeed, but their success will prove the fruit of accident, perseverance, or of some peculiar impediment in the opposing side; it will not certainly be the legitimate or necessary result of their displays of bad temper, for these are calculated to darken the prospects of success in all the enterprises of life, which possess any claims to intrinsic value.

CHAPTER LX.

A SPEAKER SHOULD NEVER BE DISCOURAGED BY AN EARLY FAILURE IN AN ORATORICAL ATTEMPT.

It has been the frequent experience of beginners in oratory to be embarrassed at the very threshold of their public career, by a signal failure in their earliest attempts to mingle in debate. But so far from being depressed or paralyzed by an incident apparently so discouraging in its character, the young heart should extract an exhilarating influence from that soothing declaration of an ancient sage, "that it is more glorious to rise with grace, than not to have fallen at all." When such an occurrence shall not, like a chilling frost, communicate a freezing influence to the fervid blood which flows through the veins of young ambition, it will serve as a passage of shade at the entrance of the great expanse of life, to enhance, by the effect of contrast, the splendor of its subsequent brightness, or as a superficial execresence or dimple on the cheek of some lovely fair one, serves to improve the bloom of her surrounding beauty.

If it was the necessary or even the usual result of a failure in early attempts, to quench the glow of ambition in the bosom of the young candidate for renown, some of the most radiant names which shine on the catalogue of the world's benefactors would have been doomed to everlasting obscurity. For the forensic and professional records of every enlightened nation on earth abound in memorials to show how often the brightest ornaments of our race, in arms, in art, and in civil polity, stumbled in passing through the porch of entry to the temple of fame. It is in many instances the direct tendency of beneficent intellectual endowments to inspire such an eager and intense desire for absolute perfection in execution, as to prevent and suppress any performance at all; just as an exquisite performer in music may have all his capabilities palsied, in the very outset of a performance, by a failure to produce some note or tone, in a favorite piece of music, in that perfection of elegance and sweetness which he had long anticipated with delight.

It would present an anomalous feature in the intellectual economy of our race, if the divine property of genius should prove inadequate to the task of improving upon its early miscarriage, when persevering stupidity has rarely ever failed to cover the shame of its first ignoble efforts by ultimate success. There is a sterling share of efficacy associated with an unshrinking spirit of hardihood and a brazen front, which enables mediocrity to pass unscathed over the most mortifying failures in early efforts at oratory. And it is certain, that should a speaker of moderate endowments, instead of quailing under the disheartening influence of an early failure, keep straightforward in his course, without exhibiting the slightest apparent sensibility to the ridicule and sneers which may be supposed to flow as a legitimate consequence from an explosive attempt at an oratorical display in the presence of the world, that the public itself will become tired of a contest with a determined spirit, and will ground its arms of opposition to his success. With how much greater certainty will liberal attainments and well-directed genius or talent be enabled to overcome an early failure in speaking?

CHAPTER LXI.

WHICH PLACE OR POSITION IN ARRANGING THE ORDER OF A DISCUSSION A DEBATER SHOULD PREFER.

To deliver the concluding speech in a discussion, is the prize of ambition to which every advocate aspires. And where this desire is prompted by any other considerations than those of utility to a particular principle or cause, it cannot be regarded as the fruit of an elevated or sound ambition. It is right that a speaker should covet the concluding speech in a debate, when, from his superior adroitness in making a reply, and from his larger experience in covering the weak points which may be presented on his side of a question, he will be enabled to render the most effective service for the side he advocates, in that particular position.

But a debater should never contend for the concluding speech for the gratification of feelings of personal vanity, such as desiring to appear to the bystanders as the speaker in chief of the occasion, unless it be his clear right from priority of appointment, or from some special authority his client may have vested in him on that particular subject. But even in the case of being entitled to the concluding place in a discussion, from the technical right of the earliest appointment, a counsellor or speaker, if guided by the dictates of even a moderate share of wisdom, will surrender the post to abler and more experienced counsel. For a juvenile or inefficient debater, particularly at the bar, will cover himself with a merited share of derision, by affecting to lead abler and wiser men.

The only personal advantages which an advocate derives from the concluding speech at the bar, may be summed up in very few words. If he enjoys but an imperfect acquaintance with the merits of a cause from the fact of having been but recently employed in it, he will be enabled to have his path blazed in advance of him, both by the light emanating from the counsel associated with him, and those opposed to him. His power of argumentation will be impelled into vigorous motion, by hearing the arguments on the opposite side, for every one of these, as it makes its appearance, will suggest what may be said in reply to it. He will have the credit of filling up every chasm in the defence on his side which may have been omitted by associate counsel who preceded him. He will be afforded an opportunity of expending his resources of wit and repartee, if he should possess them, on the opposite counsel. If he should surpass his brethren who are associated with him, in the work of making a reply, it will enable him to display his powers in that exercise of talent to some advantage; and this point in the debate will cause the gaping outsiders, who know nothing of these things, to believe that the concluding speaker has been placed at that particular point because he is the great man of his side.

The advantages which result to a cause from placing any particular speaker at the concluding point in a debate, are referable purely to his quickness of apprehension in discovering the weak points of an adversary, his power and address in assailing such points, his dexterity in repairing the intrinsic flaws of his cause, and in filling up such chasms as have been produced in the defence by the oversight of associate counsel, and to his general agreeableness and ability as a speaker.

There are a few very glaring disadvantages which may accrue to a speaker from the fact of reserving his resources for the conclusion of a debate. In most cases, he will find himself anticipated in all his favorite points by the speakers who precede him, and in repeating the arguments previously used by them, he will present himself in the attitude of a copyist, though his arguments may be the creations of his own ingenuity. If he should succeed immediately, in the progress of a discussion, a speaker of superior ability, whose positions he may not be able to shake or overturn, he will be temporarily injured by the contrast. He will be held responsible, by those interested in the issues of the cause on his side, for every omission on his part to use the materials of defence before him. And if the cause is a complex one, involving a great variety of principles, a mass of conflicting testimony, and a number of speeches to answer, his powers of attention will be painfully taxed in the work of separating the pure ore from the dross, in the elements of defence and assault, which may be spread before him.

Although the opening speech in a cause is in most instances shunned, like the fang of a deadly serpent, by all ambitious members of the bar, yet it is a locality in debate which may not be entirely destitute of attraction to a mind of comprehensive grasp. A mind of the preceding description, exerted in all its vigor on the elements of a cause, in advance of all other speakers, will be apt to leave traces in its progress which cannot be obliterated by adverse counsel, and having pre-occupied the ground, will frequently have exhausted all the best defences and points disclosed by a case before the debate reaches the concluding counsel on the same side. He will thus make impressions for his own side of a question by speaking first, which his adversaries will not be competent to efface; and he will present the counsel associated with him in the light of copyists, in pressing into their service precisely the same arguments and points which he may have already totally exhausted.

If, in the trial of a cause, the argument should be opened on one side and concluded on that side, and two or more counsel on the opposite side of such cause should present their arguments to the jury, between the counsel on that side which had both the opening and the conclusion, the counsel among that number which argues in the central position, who opens on his side, will possess the advantage of both an opening speech, and of a concluding one, in some respects. The opening counsel of the two or three who argue in the middle and between two speakers on the opposite side, will have the advantage of anticipating his associates in all their available points of defence, and he will have, equally with those who succeed him on his side, the benefit of replying to the positions which may have been assumed by the opening counsel on the adverse side of the question.

The question has been frequently propounded, without any satisfactory or positive solution, as to which formed the most eligible position in a controversy where there were but two contestants. This question must be settled with a due regard to the relative ability of two antagonists in debate. If there are but two speeches to be made on any given occasion, and one of the speakers is endowed with but moderate powers, a prudent opponent would decide that a speaker of such moderate abilities should precede him in debate, for the obvious reason that a feeble speaker will make no impression which a gifted one will find it difficult to destroy; whilst the latter, in destroying the positions of his adversary, will be prêsented with an open and fair field in which to exert his own reasoning faculties, without any sort of obstruction.

If, however, there are but two contestants in any given case, and they should both prove to be men of extraordinary endowments in debate, a prudent debater would, in most cases, concede the concluding speech to an opponent of extraordinary ability, where there are but two speeches to be made. Because, if a speaker of the character just mentioned should engrave upon the mind of a jury, or any other assembly, the first impressions which are made concerning a cause or question, it will be very difficult for a conclusion of the most masterly ability completely to remove impressions thus early and powerfully imprinted.

In deliberative assemblies, a speaker may glean large supplies of information and of reasoning both, from other speakers, by postponing his remarks until towards the close of a pending discussion. But he may also lose in this way by having all the grounds or positions which he might wish to take when he debates the question himself, previously assumed by others. And in addition to this disadvantage resulting from the practice of reserving one's remarks until late in a debate, the debate itself may be entirely divested of its power to interest the attention long before it reaches a pro crastinating speaker. And if the interest connected with the question under discussion should unfortunately evaporate be fore it reaches him who speaks at or near its concluding point, all his efforts to gain an appreciating attention from his audience will be futile and vain. In a deliberative assembly, a participation in debate about midway in its progress will prove in most cases the most eligible point for a speaker, because, when he shall appear on the stage as a participant at that point, he will then have been able to observe the question at issue in all its bearings and relations, from the course pursued by the speakers on both sides of the subject, and in addition to this, he will not at this point of the debate have lost the ear of the body he is connected with, for the matter in debate will about this time have reached the acme of its interest.

The man in the reply usually thinks he must reply to everything which has been said by the speakers adverse to himself, no matter how minute and innoxious the particles of proposition may be. And this course he indulges in from the united force of vanity and weakness. Considerations of personal vanity stimulate him to reply to every proposition of an adversary, for the sake of acquiring the reputation of being expert in a reply. Imperfection of ability prompts him to this course, because with the assistance of the pegs or pins to hang arguments upon, which are presented to view in the points presented by opposing counsel, he may appear to be making a respectable argument; without such aids he would not even enjoy the benefit of appearing to make a tolerable argument.

But this device of weakness and vanity should be studiously and sedulously avoided by every speaker who feels any concern for the success of his cause, or any regard for his own convenience. For by promiscuously answering all the positions of an adversary, the speaker will conceal the meritorious and available points in his cause, by burying them beneath a mass of rubbish of his own creation, and will render his own labors much more irksome and fatiguing by unnecessarily magnifying their amount.

A speaker should reply to as few points of an adversary as possible, and these points should be selected with masterly discretion. For by noticing everything which has been said by an opponent, the impression may be imparted to the minds of those in whose opinions a speaker is interested, that a great deal may be said on the opposite side; and that it yields a large supply of materials for defence. And another objection to this indiscriminate mode of replying to arguments already made, may be found in the fact that in thus multiplying the opposing points which he is to touch, a speaker must inevitably have his attention diverted from the points of intrinsic strength on his own side, in such a way that he will touch them but feebly.

A speaker may at times acquire some appearance of strength for a cause which is utterly destitute of intrinsic resources of virtue and merit itself, by declaiming terribly on the defects and demerits of an adversary's cause, but this is a work which must be conducted with great address and expertness to insure its success.

CHAPTER LXII.

THE INTRODUCTION OF ANECDOTES INTO A DISCOURSE OR ARGUMENT.

The introduction of an amusing anecdote or incident at the opening, and even at other points of a discourse during the progress of its delivery, may produce a felicitous effect in placing the opposing counsel or his client, and perhaps both, in a ludicrous position. Or it may have a tendency to inspire a jury or an audience with prepossessions in favor of the speaker himself, just as a pleasant remark by one on being introduced to a stranger, disarms the latter at once of all reserve, and gives an animating touch to his social and colloquial qualities.

Those who have enjoyed the benefit of an enlarged con verse with the world, have experienced the genial and charming influence of a single kind or spicy remark uttered to them by a stranger, in relation to whom they had maintained an icy deportment at the same table for weeks, and to whom they had, perhaps, resolved never to speak a single word. Thus it is with an amusing anecdote drawn from the familiar scenes of life. when appropriately introduced into an address, speech, or argument. It presents the speaker in the light of an acquaintance to the body he is addressing, the wall of separation between him and his hearers is removed, and they feel as if they could afford to join with him in the recreations of a familiar old-fashioned conversation.

The relation of an anecdote, too, at the commencement of a speech, has the effect of placing the speaker himself at ease, especially if he should be encumbered with an unusual amount of diffidence; for when he succeeds in eliciting symptoms of pleasure and of mirthfulness from those to whom he is speaking, at the very threshold of his observations, these lively sensations, by the process of reflection, are transfused into his own bosom, and he proceeds through the whole tenor of his disconrse with a light heart and with an easy and elastic pace. An exhibition of amusement thus produced, is calculated to enliven the path of the most assured speaker; but on the breast of one who is in some degree paralyzed by timidity, it pours the same measure of relief which is imparted to the feelings of an urchin who whistles or sings when passing at night through the solitude of a thicket which he imagines to be infested with ghosts and hobgoblins. When the little fellow discovers that he is not immediately captured by evil spirits, after having indulged himself in a bravado so presumptuous as that of having rendered the woods vocal with his own music, or shrill with his own breath, his heart becomes lighted up with the warm flushes of heroism, and proceeding with a light tread, he tacitly bids the dreaded fiends to advance at their peril. The diffident speaker becomes emboldened pretty much after the same fashion, when, instead of being coldly repulsed by an au-audience, for a display of so much impudence as he imagines to be embraced in the narration of a joke, he feels himself honored by a benevolent smile or by electric peals of laughter. He becomes at once inspired with the confident assurance, that if he has been able to pass unscathed through such a perilous attempt as that, he is competent to stand all other dangers which beset his path on the occasion. The caution which has been adopted in explaining this principle in our nature, as applicable to speakers, may be regarded as culpable particularity; but having frequently observed the value of this expedient to debaters of shrinking modesty, it has been thought that no expenditure of words could be too extravagant, which might serve to portray its effect to the young and inexperienced.

The chief end to be accomplished by the use of anecdotes, in their application to the opposing counsel or his client, is to divest the defence they have presented of their cause of its gravity and solidity, by the effect of a ludicrous image. If the positions assumed and the arguments made by counsel are covered with ridicule, they will prove like shots discharged from a fowling-piece, which have merely penetrated the surface of the skin, and which may be easily extracted. If the counsel himself should be temporarily thrown into a droll or grotesque position, by the relation of an apposite and felicitous anecdote, what he has said will contract in some degree the hues of that drollery, and it will form a difficult task for the body which has been addressed, to regard, with proper seriousness, the strongest points submitted by him. If the client should become the victim of derision, the whole merits of his cause will frequently catch a taint from the farcical levity which surrounds his own person, and it will be difficult for the jury to believe, during the time, "that any good thing can emanate from Nazareth." Ridicule was an efficient and sometimes a deadly weapon in the hands of the ancient Greeks, when they wished to blast an obnoxious individual; and its fatality, in its application to prominent and hated persons, was experienced during the progress of the French Revolution.

But there is yet another use of anecdotes which is commended, perhaps, by a larger yield of practical good, and sanctified by a purer morality, than any appropriation of them which has been thus far submitted. They serve, when related occasionally during the delivery of a protracted discourse of any description, to disarm it of its monotony and tediousness, and to refresh the wearied attention of an audience. They answer, in this aspect of their use, the same purpose which is accomplished by relief posts along a lengthened and dreary frontier. When the audience have been enlivened by one or two amusing anecdotes in an argument, they will be looking ahead, with pleasurable anticipation, for other contributions of a similar character.

But there are certain rules to be applied to the introduction of anecdotes, of such stern obligation, that they should never be relaxed. They never should be of such a character as to invade the sanctity of religion, the precepts of sound morality, or the decencies of life. For, independent of the prohibition of such anecdotes by the dictates of true propriety, they are most explicitly proscribed by the personal interest of the speaker himself. For the fact of interweaving with a public address of any kind, an anecdote impregnated with smut, immorality, or irreligion, will certainly, to some extent, reflect an injury on his own reputation, and this no matter how vociferous the shouts of merriment he produces at the time.

There are other rules connected with the use of anecdotes, which pertain more particularly to considerations of success. The speaker should submit an anecdote with the most imperturbable good humor, and he should never be lured into an extravagant use of them, except perhaps on the hustings; when he has struck a mirthful vein in a promiscuous assembly, towards the conclusion of his address, when the appetite of the audience may be insatiable in its demand for nutriment of that kind; when no ill consequence will be apt to result from an overcharge of that sort of ammunition; when, too, in addition to these considerations, the speaker may be enabled by a recourse of the sort to overwhelm an opponent, or relieve himself from the crushing weight of some pre-existing prejudice, by putting his audience into a fine state of feeling towards him.

Many persons cautiously abstain from the introduction of anecdotes into a discourse, because, as they allege themselves, they possess no turn for that sort of embellishment. There may be exhibited in this exercise, as there is in all others pertaining to the condition of man, very broad shades of difference in the respective talents of individuals. But every person who can intelligibly relate a simple fact, can also relate an anecdote, if he only remembers the facts embraced in it. Those who have reached unrivalled success in this department by practice, were not experts in the business when they first commenced, and have been stimulated to a more extended reach of improvement than they originally possessed, by the rewards of merriment which were meted out to their earliest efforts.

The speaker should studiously guard against ushering in his anecdotes with too much pomp and parade of manner; for the feelings of the audience may be chilled by an icy shower in the shape "of a terrible to do," in advance of the arrival of the anecdote. The most successful mode by which to secure a graceful reception for an anecdote, is to take due precautions in the first place, that it shall apply to the subject, and in the next place, that it shall be submitted in the simplest manner. And if a speaker should be diffident of his powers in this respect, he has only to interweave his anecdote carelessly as he proceeds with the thread of his discourse, and if it should prove spicy in its character, it will provoke feelings of mirthfulness in an audience, without regard to the deficiency of manner; and if it does not inspire merriment, it will pass for a part of the speech, and not recoil on the speaker, inasmuch as he has not previously heralded its coming by fixing his feet and by making his bow.

CHAPTER LXIII.

A SPEAKER SHOULD NEVER BE RESTRAINED FROM THE PERFORMANCE OF DUTY BY THE INFLUENCE OF DIFFIDENCE.

There is a clog in the shape of diffidence which encumbers the young energies of life, to as great an extent as the movements of a convict are cramped by a ball and chain appended to his person. But the juvenile aspirant to oratorical renown should cast aside this blighting principle from his composition, just with the same degree of impetuous determination that he would hurl a viper from his bosom. It will never contribute the most inconsiderable pebble to the elevation of his pyramid of personal renown, whilst it will meet him like a grim spectre, at the entrance of every field of exertion or enterprise he intends to explore, with the picture of dark bodings in its grasp, of defeat, disappointment, mortification, and disaster.

Every passing acquaintance professes to cherish the most amiable and tender sympathies with the young attorney whose diffidence pins him to his seat, or if he rises to speak, which causes his utterance to falter and stick in his throat. But no kind messenger of comfort strays across his path to dry up, by the application of sanative words, this copious spring of disaster which perpetually flows in his bosom; and no good Samaritan intervenes to remove a single impediment which this doleful defect drops upon his professional path.

This sensation of diffidence is inspired, not so much by an under estimate of his own capabilities, by a debater, as it is by an over estimate of what is due in the shape of perfect execution to the world. As the timid hare apprehends the tread of an enemy in the sound of every rustling leaf, so the diffident young speaker imagines a stern and inexorable critic in every auditor, the glance of whose eye he chances to meet, when in the act of commencing a speech. But if intelligent youth, in pluming its early wings for oratorical flights, could only be apprized of the fact, it is in nine instances out of ten, much better qualified to meet the world in an exhibition of the reasoning faculties, than the world is to meet it. And a display of confidence by a speaker at the commencement of an effort, if it should be fortified only by a few grains of intelligence, will put the critical propensities of his audience to flight, and will reduce his hearers to that pliancy of disposition which may enable him to lead them captive at his will.

If one who is constitutionally pusillanimous can cause a perennial spring of heroism to rise in his bosom, by resolutely meeting every peril which arises to his view in the journey of life; and if the individual whose bosom from infancy to manhood has been vividly tortured by the fear of ghosts, hobgoblins and fiends, can so effectually vanquish this defect of character; by marching up to every grim-looking death's-head which he spies in the distance, in moon-light travel, as to be able to sleep with composure in grave-yards and charnel-houses; most certainly the intelligent but bashful young speaker will be competent to triumph over the principle of diffidence in his own constitution; when he sees how much of mediocrity there is which not only passes with impunity in its efforts before the public, but also flourishes in the complacent sunshine of its favor; when he discovers, in addition to this, how small a portion of wisdom it requires to propel the ordinary machinery of life in its operations.

Persons, into the business of whose life, speaking must necessarily enter as a large component element, should make it a duty of imperative obligation, never to be re strained from speaking by the influence of diffidence, when they shall feel it incumbent upon them to take part in a discussion. They should give vent to the expression of their views on such occasions, even if they should experience all the nervous sensibility, in rising to speak, which they would feel if they were in the act of applying a match to the world that would blow it into atoms. This inordinate diffidence must be vanquished by a speaker in the commencement of life, for the act of being silenced and kept back by this principle, at length becomes habitual, and the privations in the shape of usefulness and fame to which a speaker may be subjected by its supervening force, whilst it does endure, are of too grave a character to be lightly encountered. The practice of overcoming it after frequent repetitions, becomes habitual, like every other adventure long persisted in, and it will become so much a matter-of-course with a speaker to repress this feeling, after he has often slighted its damping admonitions, that he will eventually wonder that he ever should have yielded to it.

CHAPTER LXIV.

REASONING BY THE ADDUCTION OF A SINGLE FACT OR PRINCIPLE IN DEBATE.

The world is so greatly addicted to reasoning by the wholesale measure at the present stage of its history, that any expedient which promises to narrow the field of inquiry in debate, to strip the process of reasoning of all superfluous drapery, and to reduce it to its essential properties, will be received by the speaking portion of mankind like an uninvited guest at a feast, with a chilling and repulsive coldness. Every attempt to contract the area of discussion, similar to the legislative guards which have been recently thrown around the freedom of traffic in the matter of spirituous liquors, is denounced by the venders of windy rhetoric as a positive encroachment on the freedom of the citizen. Every debater of superficial education or feeble powers, cherishes an unrestricted latitude in debate as his most precious privilege. Because, to such speakers, a long and verbose speech, similar to the fancy-colored kerchief which trails from the pocket of a country buck, constitutes their proudest badge of distinction. If the privilege of vociferating empty and insipid verbosity for five hours at a stretch, should be abstracted from such men, they would be deprived of their only certain ladder of promotion. For these tedious and senseless exhibitions of loquacity, similar to the foam on the fountain and the froth on the syllabub, exert a powerful share of fascination over superficial and illiterate minds. For the sound and the stuff present themselves in unmeasured quantities to the view, and it is a matter of but little concern to the unreflecting crowd, whether under this gay and bubbling surface there be any sound nutriment or healthful liquid or not. It would consequently prove as severe a measure of retrenchment to windy orators, to engraft any restriction upon the usages of the times which would bring interminable speeches into disrepute, as it would be to snatch from the grasp of a noisy urchin his favorite rattle, and to cast it in the depths of the sea.

But all judicious and practical men, in an age which is ever on the wing in search of utility, will hail with delight the advent of any improvement which may gild the prospects of the future with the auspicious hope of expelling forever, from human society, that perpetual and insatiate absorbent of time, the *mania loquendi.* For speeches of indefinite length stand in the same relation to the business of the world with copper and other base metals which encumber its circulating medium. It requires such an extended volume of such matter to effect any beneficent object, that these speeches, like the coins in question, should be driven to take their position exclusively at the rear of the oyster-carts and other ignoble stands for business.

There is one mode of approaching a subject under discussion, which commends itself to the favor of the passing age, not only from the immense saving of time which it secures to the hearers of speeches, but also from the vast economy in the expenditure of labor which it effects for those whose business it is to make speeches. The method of debating, to which reference has been made, is that of reasoning by the introduction of a single fact or principle, which may be decisive of the fate of a measure, either in securing its adoption or producing its defeat. This mode of reasoning has been sanctified by the example of the principal architect of the temple of American freedom, and by that of Benjamin Franklin, one of the great apostles of liberty, whose fame shines in the same constellation with that of Washington, and who was guiding his country to safety in the counsels of peaceful wisdom by his experience, whilst the Father of his Country was conducting her forces to victory and glory by his heroism and discretion in the field. Washington spoke but seldom in the convention which adopted the Federal Constitution, as will appear by consulting the journal of that body, but when he did rise from his seat, it was almost universally to state some decisive fact or principle which bore immediately upon the subject, and he was certain to exert a formidable influence on the fate of the question pending before the house, by the pertinent character of the fact or principle adduced by him, as well as by the unrivalled weight of his character. Franklin generally reasoned by the introduction of practical principles and examples drawn from the ample records of nature and from the great volume of life, and he frequently put to flight a bevy of prolix speakers.

If any member of a legislative assembly, opposed to some commercial measure that might be under discussion in the house to which he belonged, should produce a passage of political history which would prove, with incontrovertible clearness, that the same measure, when adopted on a former occasion, had scattered bankruptcy and ruin in its train, wherever it had been acted on, it would prove exceedingly difficult for the supporters of such a measure to overcome the effect of this authority against it.

If a candidate before the people for some highly-attractive station, should proclaim from the hustings the prodigious sacrifices he had made for his country during the last war with Britain, or with Mexico, the charm of his vaunted services would vanish into mist and vapor, if an opponent should reply to him by the production of resolutions which had been offered by the boasting member at some public meeting years before, strongly condemnatory of either of the wars in question.

If the payee of a note of hand, should institute suit against the ostensible drawer of the note, for the amount purporting to be due on the face of the instrument, it would interpose an unsuperable bar to the recovery of the claim, if the defendant should produce positive proof that he was in a foreign country concurrently with the date of the note.

Facts like the preceding stand immovable to the sternest pressure which may be brought to bear upon them by the resources of argument and eloquence. The only way of obtaining relief from the influence of such facts, is to introduce countervailing testimony to disprove them, for they cannot be reasoned down.

This mode of arguing a question, suits beyond all others a modest attorney or legislator, who entertains an invincible aversion to making speeches, for whilst it saves him the physical exertion and the trial of sensibility incident to the delivery of a long argument, it at the same time renders the person who adduces such facts more formidable in debate, if it should be his fortune to submit them with frequency, than the most eloquent and elaborate speakers.

It is not in the discussion of every question that facts of such crushing weight can be produced. But research and perseverance will enable a statesman or an attorney to produce them much oftener than is generally apprehended. And all that the legislator or lawyer has to do, in submitting such fact to a court or a deliberative assembly, is simply to introduce the fact, and to propound the inquiry, "if this fact be true, how can the gentleman's doctrines or proposition prevail?" The fact itself, fortified by this simple question, will ordinarily produce an effect which it would require oceans of ink and ages of ingenious reasoning to destroy.

CHAPTER LXV.

HE POLICY OF RESERVING PARTICULAR FACTS BY A SPEAKER TO BE DISCLOSED BY HIM IN THE DELIVERY OF AN ARGUMENT.

It may prove an available resource to a debater on many occasions, to keep in reserve until some very suitable point for its disclosure shall be reached in the progress of his argument, any very startling or important fact which may be in his possession, unknown to his opponents, and which may possibly have a direct tendency to settle the question in controversy directly against them.

A controversialist in any department of life, whether it be in Politics, Law, Science, or Literature, will in most cases be enabled to determine with a very near approach to accuracy, the auspicious moment in the speech he is delivering, for popping upon his adversary a fact or circumstance, the force of which cannot be easily counteracted.

In a trial at law, a receipt for the specific sum concerning which the suit on trial was instituted, some fact which is utterly inconsistent with a date which constitutes the main hinge of the opposite party's case, or any passage of information, the sudden revelation of which may take an adversary by surprise, or impart to the matter in controversy an entirely new complexion in the estimation of a Court and Jury, are specimens of the controversial tact to which we have referred in the commencement of this chapter.

In every species of discussion which is known to mankind, whether it pertains to politics, literature, or general science, a debater may with peculiar advantage to his cause, preserve until the audience shall be completely ripe for its reception, any fact which may be perfectly inconsistent with the propositions, doctrines, or principles affirmed by an opponent.

It may serve his interests to approach the delivery of the momentous fact with the stealthy tread of one of the feline race, and watching the feelings of the body to whom his remarks are addressed, together with the peculiar adaptation of some particular point or passage in his argument to the discharge of the shot which he wishes to be fatal, he should let it descend on his adversary like a thunderbolt from a serene and clear sky.

If a debater should have in his possession any historical fact of incontestible authenticity, the production of which may be absolutely fatal to his adversary's assumptions, he may in the course of his remarks submit such opposing fact to his audience, with the simple interrogatory, How can the gentleman's proposition be valid if the fact in question be true? And if the fact thus introduced be not utterly disproved, it will stand against all opposing assaults, like an immovable rock in the ocean when lashed by the surrounding billows.

If a debater should obtain a passage of personal history in the life of his opponent which is utterly antagonistic to the positions assumed and the professions made by him in the course of the debate then in progress, he may very quietly and carelessly in the course of his remarks, bring the piece of history in question to the notice of his audience, prefacing the introduction of the matter at the same time with the intimation of a doubt as to the identity of his opponent then before the assembly, with the one associated with the personal incident submitted.

CHAPTER LXVI.

THE PROPRIETY OF ABUSIVE LANGUAGE BEING APPLIED TO PARTIES AND WITNESSES BY ADVOCATES, CONSIDERED.

A LARGE proportion of professional men, in the morning of their career at the bar, conceive it to be an act fraught with chivalry and daring, to load with opprobrious epithets and abuse clients and witnesses on the opposite side to themselves. This is a mistaken and perverted view of qualities and effects. This practice wears the semblance of intrepidity, because, in the act of abusing a rational being endowed with the usual share of sensibility and resentment, an advocate is sure to incur the anger and hatred of the object of his abuse. And these emotions of the human heart, when fortified by the power to requite retribution, and a parity of rank with the offending individual, may by possibility produce some mischief to him. But in the case now under consideration, the resemblance to heroism and daring, is purely a counterfeit similitude.

The suitor or witness possesses no privileges within the

circle of the bar as a speaker, and here there is a glaring disparity presented in the respective conditions of the aggressive attorney and the aggrieved suitor. But even if suitors and witnesses should be clothed with every privilege of speaking within the bar which pertains to a licensed practitioner, it would be a privilege perfectly barren of useful results to them in resenting the abuse of a member of the bar—for not having been regularly bred and trained to the practice of speaking, there are but few suitors or witnesses who could use the privilege of speaking with much advantage to themselves in retorting on an attorney.

There is another consideration, too, which has a powerful tendency to deter suitors and witnesses, especially those of a moderate share of elevation and influence in society, from resenting the abuse heaped upon them in the trial of a cause, by advocates and attorneys. Parties bearing this relation to an attorney, are sure to imbibe the impression, in some degree of strength, that the lawyer inflicts this gross aggression on the rights of his fellow men, under the robe of his office; in other words, they think his abuse has been officially applied to them. And this consideration is sure to repress wrath, except in those volcanic bosoms from which the flame of resentment bursts forth like an impetuous torrent, sweeping before it in its progress every impediment and mound of opposition which may be interposed either by law or usage.

Adopting the preceding views of the subject as being correct, the practice of assailing suitors and witnesses with bitter asperity, so far from constituting a brave or a chivalrous act, verges very strongly to the opposite property of cowardice, for it is a responsibility assumed for the purpose of acquiring the reputation of intrepidity, when, in most cases, there is no real peril encountered. But whether an advocate indulges himself in a vein of abuse, from a desire to earn a character for bravery on cheap and easy terms, or whether he adopts this unworthy expedient as a lure to suitors who may be stimulated to employ him in the management of their business, with the hope of procuring a suitable vehicle through which to convey their malice to the objects of their hatred, merits the severest reprehension.

For humanity is a virtue which is imperiously enjoined, not only by the precepts of our eternal system of faith, but which is also explicitly prescribed by every sound system of social ethics. And its application has not been limited, by these high depositories of human duty, to rational nature, but its extension to the brute creation has not only been sternly enjoined, but the injunction is supported in many enlightened nations by the severest penal enactments.

But if cruelty and ruggedness shall be practiced on that theatre of action where intelligence and gentleness might naturally be expected to reign supreme, what are we to expect amidst the rougher and less cultivated pursuits of life? For when we speak of cruelty, we do not confine our remarks to those exhibitions of the vice which are executed through the medium of torture, stripes, and burning ploughshares; but we also refer to that butchery of human feelings which may be perfected through the use of brutal and ferocious language, and unkind and demoniac looks.

And the evil results of this revolting practice, do not terminate in the infliction of pain on the feelings of helpless and defenceless suitors. By long perseverance in it, a mind constitutionally kind and gentle will contract an artificial tendency to coarseness, harshness, and cruelty.

CHAPTER LXVII.

A DEBATER SHOULD NEVER, WHILST ENGAGED IN SPEAKING, SINGLE OUT ANY MEMBER OF A JURY OR PERSON IN ANY OTHER ASSEMBLY, AND ADDRESS HIS REMARKS DIRECTLY TO THAT PERSON.

It is a proposition which is fortified by the best experience of the world, that a person engaged in addressing a jury or any other assembly of persons, should never designate by name, any particular individual in the assembly to which he is speaking, and direct his remarks personally to him. This expedient is frequently adopted for the purpose of engrossing, through the medium of personal vanity, the good opinion of the person thus made the subject of special attention, and also his influence over his associates. For it is supposed that the self-esteem of the person thus singled out from amongst his fellows, will be so much soothed by the transient distinction he thus enjoys, that he will be willing to go even to the gates of death to oblige the lawyer or politician who thus flatters him. But the attempt to which we have referred, is founded almost universally on a gross misconception of the principles of human nature. The person who receives this very ephemeral and worthless badge of distinction, although not by any means wounded by it, will suppose that he has received no more than his just deserts or dues in being thus addressed, and will not feel disposed to make any large surrender of convenience to the speaker who has paid him the compliment. But there is another circumstance in addition to this, which will prevent him from manifesting his devotion to the complimentary speaker at the time his devotion is wanted, and in the particular way in which it is wanted. He has become a marked man by the very complimentary notice which was intended to buy him;

his liberty of action is fettered and circumscribed by the verbal pittance which was intended as a trap to extract golden opinions from him. The complimented voter or juror cannot display much enthusiasm in supporting the speaker who has catered to his vanity in this way, without having the act of support ascribed by his brother jurors and voters to the specific matter of homage. Persons thus situated are frequently sneered at and ridiculed by their associates for giving their verdict or suffrage to the person who has thus made them the subject of adulation.

But whilst the person specially addressed on a jury or in any promiscuous assembly may not be surely won by the act of being singled out by the speaker, yet the remnant of the body to which the designated individual belongs, will in almost every instance be alienated to some extent from the speaker. If the juror or voter who happens to be thus selected as a mark of temporary distinction should be above his fellows in influence and in prominence, they will feel themselves a little hurt and aggrieved at the speaker for holding up to the public view and rendering more conspicuous that very superiority of a neighbor, in the favor and good things of the world, which has perhaps, previous to their getting on a jury, annoyed them at every step they took in the daily walks and intercourse of life. If the person singled out by a speaker should enjoy a parity of rank and fortune with his associates, having nothing more and nothing less to boast of in the way of fortune, talent, or distinction than they, why then they will fire up in some degree, because the speaker has committed an act of positive injustice in fixing a temporary badge of distinction on their brother instead of them. If the person on a jury or in an assembly who is addressed in the mode referred to in the preceding lines, should be greatly inferior to his neighbors in point of respectability, they will consider the speaker himself as stupid as an oyster, in annexing so false an appreciation to an undeserving man, or as unprincipled as a knave in meting out to him the meed of personal homage, in direct contradiction to his own better knowledge, whilst the poor fellow himself acquires temporarily a comfortless and unenviable celebrity, which makes him the subject of sneers and derision for having had timelessly and injudiciously thrust upon him an honor which he did not covet.

The preceding practice, considered in any conceivable light, can effect no good for the advocate or speaker who resorts to it, and it is sure to militate against his cause in some slight degree on every occasion. Perhaps a punctilious regard to truth may require one exception to be reserved, where this designation of persons will not injure the cause of an advocate or the popularity of a speaker, and that is, where he addresses himself to some venerable father in Israel, who, by tacit consent, is raised several cubits above every person in the society in which he moves, and is the recipient of universal homage.

It is not a safe or legitimate procedure, either to address adulatory observations to members of juries or popular assemblies, according to the countries they emanate from. If there should be a large proportion of Irish or Germans on any particular jury, or in any given popular assembly, it is the fruit of a very low and grovelling ingenuity to discourse eulogies on the excellent traits of the German or Irish nations, in order to catch the few individuals whose opinions may be a matter of interest at the time. And the expedient is attended with this peculiar disadvantage, that whilst from the grossness and staleness of its character, it rarely ever wins for the speaker the favor of the persons who are courted at the time, it is sure to repel from him the esteem and kind regards of persons on a jury who may not belong to either of the nations which may have been referred to. There was an orator of unsurpassed celebrity in this country, whose speeches, from the commencement to the close of his public career, are blazoned over with high-wrought encomiums on the Germans and the Irish, and yet the music never charmed, for the proportion of either of these nations is small indeed that ever darkened a slip of paper with his name in exerting the right of suffrage.

But however injudicious it may be in a speaker to address individuals by name, on a jury or in a popular assembly, with a view of engaging their partialities in his behalf, yet he may study the predilections and antipathies of men, and shape his discourses in such a way as to insinuate a predilection in behalf of himself into the breast of every member of a jury invisibly to the world. Being previously apprized of some practice, theory, or principle, that an individual in the assembly before him cherishes a profound devotion to, he may applaud that particular principle, theory, or practice, in such a dexterous manner, as to make the votary of them his own impassioned friend, without offending the complacency or taste of any one else. If he knows, on the other hand, any particular subject to which any person in the assembly he is addressing indulges a very lively antipathy, he may take occasion to express, in the course of his remarks, if he may do so without infringing his moral integrity, a lively abhorrence to the subject in question. He may take occasion to eulogize, in glowing terms, qualities of character in which certain persons before him are known to abound, without seeming to have the remotest reference at the time to the persons who possess those qualities. In addition to this, he may speak slightly and disparagingly of properties of mind or character in which he is certain that other persons in an assembly before him are known to be deficient, and may build up such persons in their own esteem, by holding up for the public admiration high endowments of character, to which these persons may possess some slight pretension, without being martyrs in support of the particular excellence. These keys in the human machine must be touched under the control of a sound morality on the part of the speaker, and always with a due regard to the relation which things may bear to each other.

Whilst speaking of the possibility of rendering available, for one's own benefit or advancement, the antipathies of other parties, it may not be regarded as a culpable departure from the path of our present explorations, to introduce an illustration of the ready use which may be made of this principle, drawn from the page of practical life. There was a politician in one of the Western States, more noted for his expertness as an electioneerer than for his wisdom as an architect of laws. He had two neighbors who were bitter and implacable foes. Whilst an election was pending, in which every individual vote enjoyed a high appreciation in the estimation of the expert electioneerer, (owing to the closeness of the contest,) one of these neighbors came to his house. The first had not been there very long, before the other neighbor, to whom he was so odious (and whose vote was yet trembling in doubt) was seen approaching the house in the distance. "Now," said the artful electioneerer, to the neighbor who was sitting with him in the piazza, "you are my friend, and it is very doubtful whether Mr. B——, who is now coming to the house, will vote for me or not. But as he hates you very much, if, just as he is getting pretty near the house, and in hearing, you will let me take you by the collar and kick you out of the house, it will make him my everlasting friend." The first neighbor did as he was bidden, and the prize was accordingly secured.

CHAPTER LXVIII.

NO SPEECH OF ANY DESCRIPTION SHOULD ABOUND IN ALLUSIONS TO THE SPEAKER HIMSELF.

A MUSICIAN, when discoursing the divinest melodies from an instrument, cannot draw a large share of the attention of his auditors to the machine itself, without abating the charm which the music has shed upon their feelings; neither can the gorgeous tints in pictures and flowers be held up to the admiration of the persons who survey them, with a persevering share of success, without impairing a higher sense of enjoyment which might be derived from a due concentration of the attention on the fragrance emitted by the flower, and the perfection of the sentiment or resemblance conveyed by the picture.

Thus it is with the frequent introduction of the speaker himself upon the stage, when he is engaged in addressing an audience. He cannot indulge in allusions to himself, in the progress of an intellectual performance, without detracting from the weight of what he says. He must appear to be spoken through, and not make his own person the star of attraction by discoursing about himself. If he does, he disparages the subject about which he is speaking. An instrument derives some degree of sacredness in the estimation of those who behold it, from a vivid association constantly preserved in the mind between the material frame of the instrument and the delicious notes which it breathes when controlled by a master's hand. So it is with an orator of celebrity, a charm for the popular mind hangs upon his person wherever he may present himself. For the glory of the effect produced is traced back to him as the cause wherever he appears. But this result is realized when he appears in the character of a man. When he appears before his fellow-beings as an orator, he must keep his individuality off the stage as much as possible. Because, except in the case of an address which is made in vindication of the speaker's own character, or which may be purely personal to him, on any other ground, whenever he dips into his own personal concerns, or makes free reference to his own person, the discourse he is making at the time will assume the badge of frivolity, and be divested of its intellectual influence. Instead of the subject being grasped with tenacious attention by his hearers, the speaker in his every-day capacity and identity is presented to their minds, and they feel as if they were assembled to converse with him about the last quadrille, the last entertainment at the theatre, or a late joyous fishing excursion, instead of being enlightened by sage instructions reflected from his mind.

A celebrated cotemporary of Lord Chatham once remarked, that he never observed that great man when speaking, but he was struck with the fact, "how much greater the man was than the orator." This was truly an enviable compliment, paid by intelligent lips, to the exalted personal character of the prince of modern eloquence. But the phrase in which the commendation was expressed, shows that it was paid to Lord Chatham utterly abstracted from the work he was then performing. But if, at the time the sentiment here expressed was inspired, Lord Chatham, instead of keeping his own person in the background of contemplation, and his subject at a front view to his auditors, had burst from behind the scenes and commenced talking familiarly about his own concerns, a letting down of the augustness of the scene would have occurred with the celerity of lightning, and his auditors would have felt that they were addressed by an ordinary piece of humanity.

A tendency to egotism impairs the appreciation of one's social qualities in the daily intercourse of life; but it inflicts a much more perceptible injury on the influence of a person, when blended in a glaring manner with a performance of any of the intellectual duties of life. For, apart from the fact that the revelation of personal vanity, in very broad lines, in the character of any individual, inspires strong prepossessions against him, wherever it makes its appearance, there is yet another feeling incorporated with frail humanity, which prohibits the indulgence of egotism in a speaker. And this is that imperishable and unquenchable spirit of self-esteem which glows in the breast of every respectable human being, and which causes him to rebel and revolt whenever and wherever a member of our race attempts obviously to grasp more than his appropriate share of honor and consideration.

CHAPTER LXIX.

A DEBATER SHOULD GIVE COURTEOUS REPLIES TO QUESTIONS PROPOUNDED TO HIM WHEN SPEAKING.

It is not unfrequently the case that persons who are participating in debate, become flushed with irritation, and render ill-natured and splenetic replies to questions which may be propounded to them by a debater on the opposite side of a question to themselves. This is exceedingly impolitic. If a speaker cannot preserve his composure, when such interrogatories are put to him, he ought to refrain from any replication to them whatever. For a mere ebullition of bad-temper, without being armed with the property of superior wit or repartee, places the speaker himself in a disadvantageous point of view before his audience, and sheds an enervating influence on his cause. And an angry reply, seasoned with the spiciest degree of wit, whilst it may extend the circle of the debater's fame, simply as a wit, and magnify the terrors of his name to those who come in contact with him in public or professional life, yet such replies impart a dark hue to the estimate of his disposition in the public mind; he makes many personal enemies of the most implacable character; infuses the same dread into the society in which he moves, which is created by the presence of some animal of untameable ferocity, and is certain to produce invincible prepossessions against his cause.

It is by no means a novel or anomalous doctrine, that splendid reputations are formed by the presentation of auspicious opportunities. It is an incontestible proposition, that repeated interrogatories, propounded to a debater whilst he is in the act of speaking, are so many occasions which may be crowned with solid and enduring benefits to him, should he conduct himself under such circumstances with a proper share of tact and address.

Every reply rendered by a speaker on such occasions, which may be marked by the blandishments of a graceful amiableness, or brightened by a spirit of benevolent and playful humor, communicates a charm to the popular mind which does infinitely more for the speaker and his cause than the most brilliant flashes of ill-natured wit.

The preceding reprobation of replies, on the part of a debater, which are impregnated with asperity and anger, has been designed chiefly to apply to the habitual indulgence in a practice of the sort. For grossly offensive questions put to a speaker by any one, may merit the most fatal bolt in the shape of a replication, and a pertinacious persistence in impertinent questions, may also justify the pouring out of a vindictive retribution.

CHAPTER LXX.

A SPEAKER SHOULD NEVER CONDUCT AN ARGUMENT IN SUCH A WAY AS NECESSARILY TO COMMUNICATE PAIN TO THE FEELINGS OF ANY CLASS OF PERSONS.

It is a duty of high obligation on every citizen of the country when engaged in the delivery of a public address of any description, to avoid giving pain to any body of men. This is a duty dictated by the imperishable principles of morality, which should certainly preside in full force and supremacy over the actions of every intelligent being. But a faithful observance of this duty is encouraged by considerations which address themselves much more directly to the personal and temporal interests of a speaker, than those derived from either the published or the traditional systems of moral ethics which prevail in society. He is stimulated to the rigid performance of this duty by a very persuasive appeal which it addresses to his own durable comfort and acceptancy amongst his fellow beings.

It is not an act which will be likely to prove exceedingly productive of benefits to a speaker, to indulge in the gross and wanton abuse of any single individual when delivering a public address. For he will thus be certain to produce a jarring string in the composition of the person who may be touched by his shot, which perhaps may never be composed during the life of the wounded party.

But the act of wounding the feelings of an entire class of men is attended with indefinitely greater disadvantages. For these bodies of men when compacted together by the bonds of religion, of politics, of profession, of country, of trade, of States, or of counties, will be competent to the work of inflicting a very serious annoyance, both in their individual and aggregate character, upon an individual who may thus become obnoxious to them.

And notwithstanding many integral members of these bodies may be hateful to each other in their individual capacity, yet when wounded in their associate character, the sting which is thus imparted, will arouse them in such a manner as to cause every personal interest and animosity to merge at once in a general grievance, and will band them together by the firmest bonds of union in visiting retribution upon a ruthless invader of the general hive.

If a speaker in the course of an address should take occasion to speak contemptuously of any denomination of Christians, of any nation of people, of any party in politics, of any mechanical occupation, or of any professional pursuit, he will most certainly let fly a shaft which will pierce to the quick the sensibilities of the mass of persons which may be united by any of these ties. And it will require all the soothing appliances which the offending speaker may be enabled to collect, blended with a long application of the lenient hand of time, to assuage the pangs of injury which are thus conveyed.

In the previous strain of remarks presented in this chapter, reference has been made exclusively to wanton and unjustified assaults upon persons in their aggregate capacity—remarks which may be dictated by the personal, political, or professional spleen of the speaker. But animosities may be infused into the bosom of societies of men, by a speaker in the discharge of his duties, when he may be as guiltless of any intention to communicate pain, or to give offence, as a mouldering tenant of the tomb. This may be effected in the discharge either of political, professional, or personal duties, by a speaker. He may animadvert with peculiar asperity and bitterness in the course of a public address, upon a particular individual for the exhibition of some principle, or the adoption of some particular practice which may be, not only openly ratified by the opinion of some sect of Christians, some body of mechanics, some nation of people, or some party in politics, but which has also been enthusiastically supported and daily sanctified by the practice of that party.

The offence here would be very innocently given, but the attack upon a particular principle which may be cherished by any particular body of men, will be recognized as a corporate wrong, and will send a vibration of revengeful feeling through the whole body, which will be acutely felt in its extremest and remotest nerves.

A wise and intelligent speaker may be enabled to conduct an argument or address with a degree of prudence and discretion which will prevent a mass of persons from regarding the denunciation of a principle in its individual manifestation as an impeachment of the entire body. A speaker blessed with a respectable share of discrimination and address, may preserve his personal independence in the perfection of its integrity, in discharging his duties, without imparting offence even by implication to any body of men who may be identified with the obnoxious principle against which he shall be declaiming. He may visit the fullest reprehension on the individual offence which may comprehend in its moral composition the principle which is cherished by any particular class of men. But he may adopt the precaution, at the same time, to reserve the body itself out of the pale of the general anathema. It would appear, on a superficial contemplation of the matter, to be an impracticable attempt to shield the feelings of an oppressive dealer in money from injury, where the business of exacting an exorbitant percentage on loans might be denounced, and it would seem equally difficult to deliver an argument which would waft very fragrant incense to the senses of a Mussulman, that would present an explicit and harsh condemnation of the principles of the Koran. But such achievements constantly grace the political and professional reputations of a large number of persons who ascend the rostrum. They immolate the individual depository of the principle, and give his bones to the dogs, whilst they burn incense in a supply of grateful and redundant profusion, at the shrine of the nation or the party to which he belongs.

CHAPTER LXXI.

THE ELEMENTS OF EUCLID AND THE INTELLECTUAL SYSTEM OF ARITHMETIC, CONSIDERED AS PRELIMINARY AIDS TO THE REASONING FACULTIES.

A BRIEF exposition has been afforded, in another portion of these commentaries, of those exercises which may be judiciously adopted by a speaker or writer, for the discipline of the mental faculties, when the preparation of an intellectual production might be under consideration. And in extension of the suggestions which were then imparted to the speaker or pupil, it may be here added, that fragments of wisdom, collated from the best sources of human experience, justify the conviction that the study of a portion of Euclid's Elements, as a preliminary measure to the preparation of an argument or essay, is an invaluable auxiliary. This proposition is based upon the solemnly-declared opinions of men of the most exalted professional eminence who have now passed from the public stage.*

But the advantages blended with an habitual resort to the discipline afforded by Euclid, are attested by the nature of the exercise itself. Geometrical science has been justly pronounced the perfection of logic, and the train of reasoning is there presented in a state of such pure abstraction from all extraneous matter, and all superfluous verbiage, each link in the chain of geometrical ratiocination is so perfectly consecutive in its character, is so dependent on precedent links and propositions, that the mind of a reasoner, by studying one of these propositions closely, previous

* Governor Iredell and the late Gavins Hogg Esq. of North Carolina.

to the investigation of any abstruse question in legal or political science, is prepared for the work of searching after the pure ore of truth. The mind of a reasoner, by this preliminary training, is narrowed down to a specific point in an inquiry, instead of rambling over the indefinite field of speculative reasoning. It has a measure of ballast imparted to it, which renders it firm and stable in its operations, instead of being inflated with that passion for ethereal soaring which is frequently created by the perusal of highly-imaginative authors.

The great anchor of confidence which a reasoning mind eagerly covets when approaching the investigation of any complex and important question, is the ability to tie down the faculties to some specific or isolated point, and to retain them there until the light of truth shall beam in splendor upon the dark and chaotic concave which is shadowed forth to the mental contemplation anterior to the process of severe reflection. This potent auxiliary is supplied by an intense application of the powers of thought to Euclid's propositions.

No definite amount of the exercise now under consideration has ever been prescribed. The only object in resorting to this discipline, is that of putting the faculties in tune for reasoning in consecutive order or in continued series. And the speaker or pupil will have performed this duty when he shall have achieved this object, whether he has read one proposition in Euclid or more.

Another invaluable auxiliary to the reflective faculties, is the study of what has usually been denominated the intellectual system of arithmetic. The founder and original introducer of that system, we believe, was Pestallozzi; and it has frequently received a titular appellation correspondent with the name of its author. But others have followed in his train, and have presented plans of mental arithmetic to the world which have been simplified to such an extent as to square with the accelerated advances of the age in the march of improvement. Colburn prepared a work of the kind, which was honored with a large share of acceptancy at the period of its introduction. And the process of rigid thought which was cultivated in connection with the study of that work, may be regarded as an inestimable source of power to a reasoner. For in perusing a chapter in that work which may be marked by any complexity, the mental faculties are kept on what may be termed a stretch, until every sum or proposition in the chapter shall be completely solved or worked out by the head, without an appeal either to the hand or the pencil. It may be regarded as almost impossible for a mind, which possesses any share of innate power, any grasp of thought, to devote itself for the space of half an hour intensely to the perusal of intellectual arithmetic, without finding the reasoning powers perceptibly strengthened at the close of the labor.

It is the fact of dispensing with all artificial or material props to the mind and memory, which constitutes the spring of efficacy in this exercise. It is like compelling a traveller to estimate his progress in a journey, by a vigilant observation of the native features of the country through which he may be passing, instead of falling back upon the assistance of mile-marks. And when the mind shall be thus inducted into a logical frame or spirit, this condition of mind may be transferred and appropriated to other subjects of thought entirely distinct from the arithmetic; just as when the temper is thrown into an irascible state by a provocation received from one person, it may not be regarded as a very difficult operation to apply the feeling of irritation thus inspired to other individuals who may cross the path of the provoked party at the time, and who may be perfectly guiltless of all offence towards him.

CHAPTER LXXII.

THE PRACTICE OF OBSERVING THE MOST BRILLIANT PASSAGES OF WIT WHICH OCCUR IN AUTHORS, AND ALSO THOSE WHICH ENLIVEN DEBATE AND CONVERSATION.

The proposition has a prevalence as extensive as the domain of letters, that the principle of poetic inspiration is a beneficent endowment of nature, isolated in its essence, and having but few affinities with any other distinguishing quality of the mind or imagination. The same theory also has been so habitually applied to the property of wit by a large proportion of mankind, as to receive that tacit sort of acquiescence which is yielded to an axiom.

With the origin of poetical gifts we have nothing to do in this connection, but we feel very great sincerity in expressing an entire dissent from the application of the foregoing theory to the principle of wit. That some members of the family of man may be more favorably organized by providence for the felicitous and ample display of this quality than others, it would be a futile attempt to deny. Human beings occupy precisely the same situation in regard to this subject, that they do in relation to all the other faculties and functions which pertain to the organization of the intellectual system. One person may display an unusual facility in the acquisition of mathematical science. Another may exhibit more promptness in the apprehension of philosophical verities. Another may astonish the world by his expertness in translating the pages of recondite literature. Whilst a third appears to possess no organ of perception for the beauties which bloom and perfect in the foregoing fields of intellectual exploration, but gives his heart in the plenitude and fervency of its devotion, to the province of mechanics. But that either of these fields of acquisition is hopelessly barred to the entrance of those candidates for intellectual renown, who may exhibit an original obtuseness of intellect in regard to the particular subject of mental speculation, included in any one field, is a proposition which cannot be maintained. By the use of persevering labor, minds of the most unpromising early developments in reference to some particular subjects, may possibly grasp with distinguishing success and thrilling delight, the most precious treasures which are attainable within those particular tracts of thought.

The property of wit may, with a very ample measure of justice, be included within the range of the proposition affirmed in the preceding paragraph. Persons who may have never exhibited the faintest gleam or scintillation to attest its presence in their mental composition, by yielding a heartfelt devotion to a few disciplinary measures, may enrol their names amongst the most formidable wits of the period in which they live. Some of those orators who have instructed and charmed the world by the splendid fascinations of their eloquence, were once almost incurable sceptics on the subject of their possessing in their intellectual organization the minutest ingredient of eloquence, and in their earliest advent on the public stage were harshly repulsed by hissing crowds, in consequence of their apparently nonsensical and incoherent babblings. Many of those who have discoursed the divinest melodies to enraptured assemblies, in the department of music, were actually terrified at the grating dissonance and discord of their earliest performances.

If a student should be desirous of registering his name amongst the wits of his country, he will be infallibly gratified in having his aspirations crowned with success by submitting to the essential expenditure of toil and pains.

When he is engaged in perusing an author which abounds in striking passages of wit, let him note each passage as it presents itself to his mind, and having dwelt upon it for some time, let him survey it in all its varied bearings and relations, to see in what respect it might be improved; and if the witticism has been perpetrated at the expense of any particular individual, let him see what reply could have been aptly made to it by the individual whose feelings may have been punctured by letting it off.

But the most successful and productive manner in which the attention of a student can be exercised in this sphere of discipline, is to watch the progress of discussions in the halls of legislation, in the courts of justice, and on the hustings, and when an effective witticism or pungent retort falls from the lips of any speaker in his hearing, he should take it right up, and scan it in his mind, with the view of satisfying himself as to the most appropriate and happy replication which might have been given to it by the person upon whose shoulders the squib has descended.

The student may also profit in this sphere of mental exertion, by observing the course of conversations in the sprightly and cultivated circles of life, and whenever a fragment of spicy repartee or a well-timed and appropriate retort, or a witty expression, drops from the lips of any one present, he should subject it at once to the searching operations of his mental crucible, with the desire to test its genuineness, to ascertain in what respect the particular effusion might be improved, and what reply might have been effectively given to it.

Even when the student has been the subject of a witty or cutting remark himself, and the occasion for visiting retribution on the author of the witticism has passed by without any retort from the injured party, yet he may nevertheless turn this failure to his future advantage, in taking up the shot which hit him, and after having examined it at his leisure; by settling in his mind the most suitable reply which might have been given to it at the time the squib was discharged.

These exercises, though silent in their progress, and unobserved by the world, train the human mind for the exhibition of that species of mental adroitness which has been the subject of this chapter, as infallibly as shooting habitually at a mark trains the hand and the eye of a practitioner for shooting successfully at living objects.

CHAPTER LXXIII.

THE EXPEDIENCY OF QUESTIONS BEING OCCASIONALLY PROPOUNDED BY A SPEAKER, IN THE COURSE OF AN ARGUMENT OR ADDRESS, TO OPPOSING DEBATERS, OR TO PERSONS SYMPATHIZING WITH SUCH DEBATERS IN OPINION.

It frequently happens that questions may be propounded with a singular share of advantage by a speaker, whilst progressing in the delivery of an argument, to an opponent in debate, or to persons sympathizing with that opponent in opinion and in feeling.

But the speaker, previous to putting a question of this kind to an opposing party of any description, should be perfectly convinced that the interrogated party will not yield an answer adverse to the propounder's interests. For such an answer will recoil upon his person with all the stunning fatality of a rebounding shot.

The way in which this passage of policy is to be conducted is very simple in its character, and only requires the application of some nice observation and acute sagacity on the part of a debater to know when to adopt it. In politics and in law, the party who is principally interested in a pending controversy may be supposed to have performed some act which, in the event of its being known to the world, would exert a blasting influence on the prospective interests of such party. It may be also presumed, without at all straining the belief to take in the proposition, that the parties chiefly concerned in a pending political or legal controversy may be possessed of some information which, in the event of its being promulgated, would crush their hopes of success in the bud.

It is unnecessary to define the mode in which a process of this description should be conducted by an advocate, when managing a cause, for this is a matter of daily repetition in court. But whilst we concede to debaters on other fields of discussion as large and enlightened an acquaintance with the matter under consideration as their most grasping desires would demand, we do not regard that as a superfluous expenditure of time and of language which may be employed in explaining an operation which may be productive of very conspicuous and enduring advantages to the young and inexperienced in debate.

When a candidate for any public situation shall be impressed with the conviction that an opponent has been connected with some public enterprise, measure, or principle which is exceedingly obnoxious to the public taste and fancy, as he progresses in his argument, when he reaches an eligible point for doing so, he has only to propound the question to his opponent, whether or not he has ever been a supporter of such measure, enterprise, or principle, or whether he has been openly or covertly interested in or identified with it. This question may be presented with all that placidity, good humor, and grace which marks the intercourse of the most elegant and courtly persons in the social exchanges of life.

If in a question of the kind supposed, the opposing candidate should answer in the affirmative, when charged with some act or identity which may be considered a digression from the path of sound political principles or pure morals, then, of course, the interrogator has secured his object, in casting an effectual blight on the interests of his opponent. If the question propounded should convey the charge of a dereliction of duty or nonfeasance, in not giving support to some wholesome and just enterprise or measure, of course if the interrogated candidate or member admits that he did not yield to the measure or enterprise in question his support, the answer may be fatal to his prospects, if the matter concerning which the interrogatory was propounded was itself a thing of any intrinsic importance, and concerning which the public feelings were greatly enlisted.

But the benefit usually sought in propounding questions to opponents, either in deliberative bodies or in discussions before popular assemblies, does not consist in extracting substantial and responsive answers from opposing candidates or their friends, which will exert a deadly influence over their interests. The object sought is not so much a specific answer of any sort, but to get them to floundering and fluttering to avoid coming to the point, or to sit with sealed lips under the interrogatory.

If a question shall be propounded in a deliberative assembly to the advocate of some measure before that body, which conveys the charge of having been implicated in some other measure or identified with some particular principle which may be exceedingly odious to the Legislature or to the people, or to both, then, if the interrogated member should yield no answer, it may be assumed to be a confession of the charge conveyed; and if he should flounder, and wince, and yield a very incoherent answer, it will injure his cause to a still greater extent.

There are two principles at work, in a case of this sort, to render these interrogatories in a high degree operative for the production of injury to the person to whom the interrogatories may be propounded. Whenever a question shall be propounded by a dexterous debater, with a good deal of dramatic skill and in a very portentous manner, the information which is sought by the question or the charge which it conveys, contracts a fictitious valuation and importance from the way in which it is frequently propounded; for an audience will suppose that the question would not be put if it should not be considered by the debater who asks the question a matter of very great importance. And if an answer is totally withheld, or a bungling and incoherent one given, the persons who may be present will immediately attach additional importance to the matter, simply because the information is not given. And in addition to the foregoing inference, the persons who compose an assembly where a scene like that just mentioned occurs, take a refusal to answer, or an imperfect answer, equivalent to a confession—for why, say they, does the man refuse to answer if he be not guilty?

The expediency of asking questions to an opponent in debate, is based upon the same species of policy precisely, which dictates the act of pressing questions upon a witness, which the attorney propounding the questions well knows, anterior to asking them, that the witness will refuse to answer. It matters but little, as far as the cause of the attorney propounding the question is involved, whether a witness thus refusing to answer, is restrained from giving an answer by a tacit knowledge on his part, that a truthful answer will be fatal to the party to whose success he may be devoted, or whether he is prevented from giving an answer by the interposition of the Court, which may instruct him not to yield an answer, on the ground of personal privilege, or because an answer might injuriously affect his own personal interests. The proper object of inquiry in regard to the matter, with every one who may be desirous to analyze the moral ingredients comprehended in the act of keeping in reserve any information which may be sought, is to this effect; Why should the party refuse to answer the question propounded, unless he is aware that a just and true answer will be fatal to the interests of his friend, or fatal to his own character? Under such circumstances, a refusal to answer is equivalent to an answer favorable to the interests of the party asking the question.

The same unfavorable inference attaches directly to a respondent in equity, who refuses to answer a question which is propounded to him in a bill of complaint, because it is believed that he would have no objection to answering an interrogatory respectfully propounded, and which suggested no species of criminality on the part of the respondent, unless he knew that a true response to the question would exert a blasting influence over his own interests.

This is the object sought when a skilful debater, either in a deliberative assembly, or in a popular meeting, or on the hustings, propounds a question to an opponent, or one sympathizing with that opponent. The speaker asking the question may not entertain the faintest expectation of receiving an answer. But he asks the question with the view of putting his adversary to some extent in a suspicious attitude. And notwithstanding the specific question propounded may not of itself, and independent of assisting circumstances, come with a crushing degree of weight on the interests of the party interrogated, in any aspect of the case. Yet, as a combination of very minute circumstances of a suspicious character, may exert a blighting influence over the interests of a party, in a case where one isolated fact might effect nothing, an expert debater in politics may regard it as the supreme point of wisdom and policy to crush an adversary by causing an avalanche of minute particles of odium to descend upon his person, when each of the facts or particles in the combination, taken separately, would be as light and harmless as the dew-drop which descends on the mountain summit.

CHAPTER LXXIV.

IT WILL PROVE AN INJUDICIOUS COURSE, IN ANY MEMBER OF A DELIBERATIVE ASSEMBLY, TO PARTICIPATE IN DEBATE WITH UNDUE FREQUENCY.

MAN is so constituted by nature that his taste becomes immediately revolted whenever the supply of any object of gratification passes beyond the limit of the natural demands of his appetite. Even the most delicious and captivating strains of music, when presented to the ear day after day in long succession, under the modification of one isolated tune, will at length fatigue the patience of the hearer. It is exceedingly difficult to define the exact boundary at which sufficiency becomes complete and satiety commences. But the principle is as broadly revealed in humanity as the faculty of reason itself, that interest and inclination lag when any indulgence shared by the senses passes beyond the limit of sufficiency.

In no exhibition or recreation which is tributary to the rational enjoyment of man, does this principle assert its presence more visibly than in connection with an undue frequency of participation in debate by any particular individual. A voice of eloquence, which may touch the feelings of a deliberative assembly at its opening scenes, similar to a wand of magic, will, when frequently sounded in its hearing, fall not only in futile and unheeded strains to the earth, but will also, in the course of time, if unduly pressed upon the attention of any body of men, assume the grating harshness of the screech of some bird of ill-omen.

The most profound and varied attainments, the most enlightened and comprehensive experience, the most insinuating blandishments of manner, the most matchless sweetness of tone in utterance, and the most lovely and immaculate purity of life, all united in the person of one particular speaker, will not secure a grateful reception for his remarks when he shall have already appeared with a proverbial degree of frequency on the floor of a deliberative assembly.

The speaker himself will usually have his perceptive faculties so completely obscured by the measure of homage which was paid to his earliest efforts by his hearers, as not to observe the dawning symptoms of their disinclination to hear him when he rises. But his disinterested fellow-members will notice the budding evidences of discontent and impatience excited by the sound of his voice when thrust upon the house with undue frequency, with as much certainty as a practiced physician will detect an eruption which may be thrown out upon the surface of the skin by any familiar disease.

The first indications of the declining acceptancy of any particular speaker which will present themselves to the view of intelligent observation, may be recognized when he arises to speak, in the scarcely audible buzz, shuffling, and restlessness which will seem to pervade the entire body of which he is a member. This is merely in the green tree of his decay; when the leaves of his popularity assume a sere and yellow hue, the members will begin to abandon their seats in groups, and when the dry leaf of his decline makes its appearance, his advocacy of any measure will prove as fatal to its prospects as the poison of the asp to animal life.

This repugnance to hearing any one speaker with unusual frequency, is founded upon two principles which are very broadly and palpably interwoven with the nature of man. The first is the disposition to revolt at an over-expanded supply of any earthly gratification which may be ministered to the taste; and the second is that almost universal distaste which is inspired by the disclosure of a disposition in any person to grasp a lion's share of any privilege, benefit, or emolument, in the use and enjoyment of which others are entitled to an equal dividend with himself.

And whilst even a patriarchal sanctity and weight of character will rarely secure to a legislator a gratifying possession of the floor, when he has occupied it with inappropriate frequency already, it may safely be alleged that those who are regarded as the plainer members of a deliberative assembly usually conceive that they can pay no higher compliment to a fellow member than to say of him, "that he never speaks except when his business calls him to do so." And it is equally certain that the member of any business assembly cannot select a path which leads with more infallible certainty to the hearts of his associates, than a sparing use of the privileges of debate.

It may so happen in the course of legislative service, that a member may be summoned from some peculiar position he holds to address the house with uncommon frequency. He may occupy the post of Chairman to some committee to whose care and management a large portion of the business of the house may be confided. In this connection, it may necessarily devolve upon him to explain and defend the action of his committee on particular subjects. But he should take especial pains to perform this duty in few words and in a business-like manner.

It may be regarded as an almost impracticable task to specify the number of times in which a member may be indulged in appearing upon the floor, when no special obligation may render it obligatory upon him to participate in the discussions of the house. On this subject a speaker must himself exert a large share of wise discretion. It may be suggested, however, that three regular set speeches is about the maximum of a member's privilege during any one session. He may at the same time properly indulge in pointed suggestions, and in brief discussions on points of order and of business.

CHAPTER LXXV.

THE IMPORTANCE OF MAKING AMPLE PREPARATION FOR THE DISCUSSION OF ANY QUESTION LONG PREVIOUS TO THE PERIOD AT WHICH IT IS TO BE DISPOSED OF.

A STATESMAN who once constituted one of the brightest political stars that ever shone in the firmament of America, being asked by a friend how he managed to be so perfectly at home on every measure which was debated in Congress, replied, "because I universally make it a duty of indispensable obligation, to inform myself thoroughly concerning every measure of the slightest importance, which has the least complexity about it, on which I shall be called to vote." The adoption and faithful observance of the foregoing rule of practice, would light up in the varied counsels of this country many resplendent luminaries which, from a tame surrender to the charms of indolent repose, may never cast even a twinkling beam on the sphere of the public service.

A large proportion of those who are chosen to fill seats in the legislative assemblies of the United States, are perfectly content to give their judgments and their consciences in charge to associates in counsel, whom they may esteem to be more experienced, enlightened, or industrious than themselves. They depute others to think for them, in deciding on the course they shall pursue in voting on any measure of a dubious character, that may be pending in the body to which they belong.

They can peruse with patient industry and attention the most ponderous volumes of history, which shed light upon the manners, customs, and policy of nations which lived and flourished in the night of past ages, but they are unable to yield a few transient moments to the consideration of measures which are closely associated with the glory and prosperity of their own country. They can devour with ecstatic sensations of delight mountains in the shape of fiction, which are as light as the foam which floats upon the surface of the waters, but they do not in many instances possess the industry and research to devote a few hours daily to the investigation of authors, an acquaintance with which might enrol them amongst the brightest benefactors of their country, and which would probably light up the pathway which would conduct them to a height of imperishable glory.

Every member of a deliberative assembly, who may not possess the insensibility of a stone to what is passing around him, must necessarily be apprized of the measures which will naturally be disposed of during the term for which he shall be elected. And it will cost him but a small expenditure of labor to devote an interval of meditation daily to measures of the most critical importance, on which it will be his duty to vote, and to note down in a commonplace book, separately and distinctly, the result of his reflections on each. He should carefully read the authors within his reach, or those portions of them which may apply in a special manner to the measures on which he is to act in future; and he should be careful to classify and arrange any established principles or incontestable authorities he may collate from the authors he reads, in such a manner as to correspond with the order in which he may marshal for discussion the different branches or divisions of the subjects on which he shall either speak or vote. He should make it his business to ascertain the assailable points of a measure as well as those which are indisputably valid and tenable, and should provide himself, where he is favorable to any particular measure, with resources of defence which will enable him to repel with efficiency the thrusts which may be made at the vulnerable parts of his argument by an opposing member. By adopting the course here suggested, a speaker may render services of durable importance to his country. He will store his intellectual treasury with information of incalculable value, and he may earn for himself a reputation which will survive the granite walls which may reverberate with the sound of his voice.

CHAPTER LXXVI.

A LEGISLATOR SHOULD NEVER PARTICIPATE IN DEBATE EXCLUSIVELY FOR THE APPLAUSE OF THE GALLERY.

When it shall once become evident to the world that any member of a legislative assembly is induced to participate in debate merely to earn the applause of the gallery, no matter how potent the fascinations of his eloquence may be, this discovery at once impairs his influence as a legislator, and imparts a tinge of levity and frivolity to his reputation as a public man. He stands revealed to the public eye with the same badges of imputed vanity clinging to his character, which cluster upon the person of a city *belle* who perpetually glitters in jewels and silks to attract the admiring gaze of the thoughtless thousands that throng the most frequented thoroughfares of a large commercial emporium. As the fragrant incense of that admiration which is inspired by the belle, as she passes along the streets arrayed in the splendors of oriental life, is wafted to her senses, blended with a large admixture of ridicule and sneer, so the trumpet which sounds to the world the praises of the gallery-worshipping orator, uniformly sends abroad a mingled strain of applause and contempt.

When any member of human society, it matters not what his vocation may be, inscribes upon his daily walk of life in characters as legible as if it was written in sunbeams, a fervid aspiration to popular admiration, the soothing appliance will be administered in frugal supplies as certainly as the light of parting day is succeeded by the shadows of twilight. And even when the sparing contribution is rendered, it almost invariably comes scented by some ingredient which renders it nauseating to the taste of the recipient. There seems to be an inherent propensity in the human race, to withhold golden opinions from those who obviously covet them with a spirit of impassioned devotion. The more especially is mankind disposed to deny the gilded lure to those who are willing to convert the gravest duties of life into instruments of service to their own childish personal vanity.

The contrast which is presented between the usual demeanor of a sensible and discreet legislator, and that of the gallery-worshipping orator, is too glaring to have eluded the observation of any sagacious and attentive observer of deliberative assemblies. The former, when about to participate in the discussions of the house, glides into the performance of the duty as quietly and as free from observation, as it may be practicable for him to do. The latter, when about to deliver a speech, sits as restlessly on his seat as a nervous culprit in the criminal's dock. He at one time adjusts his cravat, at another he trails his fingers through his hair, he paces the aisles of the house with as much vivid concern painted upon his countenance and manner as if some mighty and crushing calamity was suspended over his head. His eyes are directed first to the gallery and then to the floor, to ascertain whether there be a fair prospect of having a brilliant array of visitors to grace the advent of his coming speech; and when the hour arrives for the assumption of his place on the floor, the chances greatly preponderate in favor of his proposing a motion to the house to postpone the debate until a future day, if the gallery does not present to his view a blazing front of the most fascinating beauties of the city. If such a speaker should discourse with the ravishing eloquence of a seraph, he might engross a munificent harvest of the world's admiration, but he never could engage a large portion of its enduring and solid esteem, he never could secure for his name and reputation a welcome and fond abode in the hearts of his countrymen.

CHAPTER LXXVII.

THE GREAT ADVANTAGE TO A SPEAKER OF PRESERVING A PERFECT DEGREE OF SERENITY AND COOLNESS WHEN THE ASSEMBLY OF WHICH HE IS A MEMBER MAY BE THROWN INTO A STATE OF EXCITEMENT, TUMULT, AND CONFUSION.

THE speaker who is adequate to the preservation of unmingled serenity and composure, in the act of addressing an assembly which is itself thrown into a state of tumult by heat and excitement, considered in the light of a broad and attractive mark to public admiration, stands next in rank to a soldier who, with the most undisturbed calmness, performs prodigies of valor amidst the din, smoke, and carnage of the battle-field.

And in proportion as those who recognize this coolness in a speaker, may be overcome on such occasions by a nervous sensibility themselves, in the same proportion will their admiration of his self-possession glow with intensity. For it is not the natural course of things, when a multitudinous body of men is agitated and torn by a conflict of the fierce and impetuous passions, for any portion of those united with it by the bonds of duty, or who are observing its proceedings from the pure impulses of curiosity, to remain like statues, completely impervious to the surrounding heat.

A display of coolness in one who may be speaking, when the body which he is addressing is itself calm as a summer's evening, does not attract much observation or inure perceptibly to the advantage of a debater. For it is a spectacle of daily occurrence, to witness self-possession when there is no supervening cause to disturb it. It is the self-control which enables a speaker to maintain the equal balance of his feelings under the stern pressure of surrounding elements of commotion, which supplies the food for public admiration. For the world is certain to imagine that there is some inherent property of excellence in the composition of such speakers, which renders them vastly superior to the bulk of mankind.

The influence exerted by this coolness commands a higher class of benefits, however, than that of causing the esteem and respect of the world to centre upon the person of a collected speaker. It frequently lulls the waves of commotion into a quiet state of repose in emergencies of incalculable interest to the country. For the voice of a debater of this description strikes an assembly tossed by the billows of passion, with a force which may at times be entirely disproportioned to the intrinsic value of what he utters in the way of instruction and argument. The most commonplace truths delivered to an excited assembly with a degree of imposing coolness, will descend upon its ear with the gravity and weight of the sagest counsels of wisdom, if the speaker himself should possess an ordinary share of respectability.

Such exhibitions of coolness reflect still greater lustre upon the reputation of a speaker, when he maintains his equilibrium under the pressure of an assault made upon him in debate, which may be marked by a singular degree of asperity and personal bitterness. The world regards a calm and collected manner in replying to assaults of a fierce and pungent character, as nearly allied to heroism.

The speaker, too, who disciplines his feelings in such a way as uniformly to sustain this admirable degree of coolness on exciting occasions, will not only possess the advantage of appearing to be cool, but what is preferable to appearances, he will be actually and intrinsically as he seems to be. And his entire freedom from heat and excitement will enable him to survey minutely the whole surface of the ground of debate which is spread before him. He will thus be competent to impart judicious counsel to the house of which he is a member, at points which the body itself may have entirely overlooked, from the intensity of its heat. He will also perceive with perfect clearness the vulnerable points which have been assumed in debate by speakers opposed to his views of the subject under discussion, and he may descend upon them if he possesses even an ordinary share of intellectual power, with the irresistible power of an avalanche.

The question may be propounded, "is this self-possession attainable by men of an unusual degree of nervous irritability?" There is nothing more certain than that it is attainable by every human being who possesses the share of reason and mental power which has been appropriated to the great mass of mankind. Persons who were constitutionally cowards of the most hopeless stamp, have been converted into heroes at times by the effect of discipline accidentally thrown upon them, and at others, by a determined resolution on their part, to encounter with firmness every peril and emergency which might cross their pathway in the journey of life. It may be regarded as a far more practicable attempt to brace a person's nerves to meet in a collected manner heat and excitement which produce showers of words, than to replenish a deficient supply of courage in such a manner as to be enabled to face enemies in battle, whose wrath rains bomb-shells and bullets. There is one encouraging circumstance which should stimulate every speaker of peculiar nervous sensibilities to make an effort to overcome his constitutional tendencies in this respect, and this is, that no speaker has ever been mortified by a failure, in an enterprise of the kind, who has perseveringly endeavored to acquire coolness and self-possession in debate.

CHAPTER LXXVIII.

THE AUTHORS WHICH A SPEAKER SHOULD HABITUALLY REAI WITH THE VIEW OF IMPROVING HIS DICTION IN SPEAKING.

It may constitute the perfection of wisdom and discretion on the part of a student in elocution, to yield his fervid devotions, both by day and by night, to authors which are utterly foreign to the profession of which he is a member, when the object he seeks is that of becoming thoroughly imbued with some peculiar excellencies of style which they contain.

The illustrious Earl of Chatham, with the fervent and self-devoting spirit of a votary at some saintly shrine, yielded his devotions to the sermons of Doctor Isaac Barrow, because they abounded in words distinguished for their electric strength and energy. Whether the great Colossus of British eloquence derived his magic powers in debate from the reverential homage which he paid to this author or not, it is certain that he distanced all other men who flourished in his era, in the matchless felicity, fervor, and force of his language.

The voice of tradition has conveyed to times more recent than those in which he figured upon the stage, that Lord Mansfield was a warm admirer of the writings of Chillingworth, from the acute and methodical system of logic which they presented, and that he enjoined the reading of that work most earnestly on all beginners in the legal profession, concerning whose interest he cherished any spirited share of concern.

The advice has been given by Doctor Samuel Johnson, who was generally revered as the brightest ornament which adorned the literature of England in the eighteenth century, "that a person who might be anxious to acquire an easy and flowing style in writing, should yield his days and nights to the pages of the Spectator."

That eminent expounder of the Gospel, Doctor Chalmers, from the lofty strain of panegyric on the writings of Edmund Burke with which his prolific pen continually teemed, blended with the vivid resemblance which is presented in his own writings to the philosophic productions of the great Commoner, both in solidity and gorgeousness, must have given no stinted share of his time and attention to the pages of that engaging ornament of British eloquence and learning.

There are conclusive memorials scattered in profusion over the bright expanse which is adorned by the speeches of Daniel Webster, to attest the fact, that in the path of his literary labors and researches, he drank in copiously the spirit of Milton, Dryden, and Shakspeare.

Whether President Jefferson imbibed from a frequent perusal of the works of Livy, the compendious brevity of the speeches which he acquired the reputation of having made in his professional and public career, or whether it was the native tendency of his intellect and taste to make such speeches, independent of any impulse derived from the influence of particular authors, the proposition is undoubtedly true, that he warmly eulogized the speeches of Livy as appropriate models for debaters, from their uncommon briefness.

John C. Calhoun was a fervent admirer of the works of that great light of Theology, Jonathan Edwards, on account of the extreme severity and closeness of his logic. And there is a traditional report abroad, that in the early portion of his public career, he made these works his pole star in the style of debating.

There was an intellectual star which shone with a conspicuous share of splendor in the revolutionary service of America, both in the sphere of belligerent strife, and in the counsels of peaceful deliberation, which is reputed to have drawn a large proportion of its brightness from a constant devotion to the pages of Bolingbroke. That star was General William R. Davie, and his own flowing and lofty style in speaking, gave confirmation to the rumor.

There was another ornament of the revolution, whose talents and learning reflected an attractive measure of lustre upon the highest judicial tribunal of this country, and who was an ardent and unceasing votary of the writings of Jonathan Swift. And the remarkable acumen, point, and brevity of his own style as a debater, shows that he did not employ his time in that species of devotion, without the production of a decided and visible effect.*

John Randolph, who conclusively showed both in his speeches and writings, that he was as thoroughly imbued with the spirit of the English classics as any person who figured on the political stage of America in his day, expressed the opinion in one of his excursive speeches, once delivered on the floor of Congress, that Gil Blas, Roderick Random, and Fielding's works, contained a larger supply of the philosophy of human nature, than the whole mass of current literature besides. And there was one who, when living, reflected an uncommon share of lustre, both on the path of letters and jurisprudence, that affirmed in a literary production of some celebrity, that Milton's Paradise Lost, Shakspeare's works, and Don Quixote, would reward a student for a faithful devotion to them, with a larger return of precious benefits, than would the perusal of countless volumes of mediocre literature.†

These examples have not been introduced for the purpose of arbitrarily binding down the student to the insertion of these works in his code of disciplinary reading, but to show that the practice of selecting certain authors with a view to specific mental adaptations possessed by them, has been sanctioned by the authority of some of the brightest names which shine in the pages of human history.

* Judge Moore, of North Carolina. † Judge Murphy, of North Carolina.

And whilst it must be conceded that the preceding authors might at all times prove highly efficacious in producing the desired result at those intellectual points at which they have been hitherto applied, when the mind of a student might be inspired with a firm conviction of their importance. Yet so much depends in the choice of works for the creation of any particular mental quality or function, upon the congeniality of the style and spirit of the works themselves to the taste and feelings of the reader of them, that a very broad field of discretion must be left, in the choice of these disciplinary authors, to the enlightened experience and judgment of the student himself.

The same principle sometimes presents itself in the literary experience of a human being, which occurs at times, in the physical history of our race, that a literary work which may prove a charming antidote to the mental infirmities or defects of one reader, may prove the pernicious bane of the intellectual interests of another. In this aspect of the case, it may be the judicious course to apply the same rule in the work of admonition and suggestion here, that might be adopted by a conscientious locksmith, when applied to for a key to unlock a door by a person who may have incurred the misfortune of losing his own. That is, to give him a huge bunch suited to the opening of every variety of locks, and to instruct him to try them all in succession until he found one that would open the door, and that would be infallibly the right key. Different authors are here adduced, which have been used by a portion of the most celebrated men in modern times for the production of specific mental results, and the discretion is reserved to the student of selecting those particular works which he will find on an intelligent inspection to be best suited to his taste.

That class of pupils who may cherish a higher degree of admiration for bold and confident assertion, than for a conscientious and salutary degree of caution in an adviser, may regard the suggestions presented in the preceding lines as being impressed with the brand of a very indefinite character. But if a diseased individual should apply for a remedy to a physician who had no acquaintance with his constitutional peculiarities, and under whose supervision the patient was not going to remain even a single hour; the physician could not be blamed for indefiniteness in his in structions, in delivering to the applicant a list of all the innocent remedies which had proved successful in curing such diseases in the published cases; and in leaving it to the discretion of the patient himself to try them all in succession until he should strike upon the right one. The same rule has been applied here in suggesting those particular works to the student in elocution, which have heretofore administered strength and regularity to mental operations, and in leaving him, on a fair experiment of the matter, to determine which author is best adapted to the production of a desired result.

And the proposition is here respectfully but confidently advanced, that a sagacious and intelligent reader of literary works, can by the assistance of even a slender stock of experience in matters of the kind, decide with as infallible certainty what authors will prove most conducive to the augmentation of his intellectual power and fertility, as a person of acute perceptions and close observation can pronounce what articles of food shall best correspond with his physical health and constitution.

It is only necessary that the student should read a sufficient number of pages in any particular author, to procure a taste of the spirit which pervades its pages, to enable him to apprehend with clearness whether it will enhance the vigor and fertility of his mind or not.

It may usually be assumed as a rational inference, when a student is found engaged in preparing himself for entering so ostensible a department of the broad field of practical life as that of public speaking, that he has described as the course of his preliminary reading, that entire circle of ancient historical literature, which has been generally prescribed to enlightened students as a porch of entry to either of the liberal professions. And if not the whole circle, that he has acquired a respectable knowledge of those historical works which every substantial farmer puts into the hands of his children when they attain the age of fifteen years.

For the sake of preserving prominently in the remembrance certain authors which will be derided by the vaporing pretenders to an exquisite degree of taste and refinement, because these works have become hackneyed and profaned as they will naturally suppose by vulgar use; it is deemed proper to suggest that too large a share of attention cannot be assigned by the student to Rollin's History and Plutarch's Lives, on the field of ancient history, and to Hume's History of England, Robertson's History of Scotland, and Voltaire's Life of Charles XIIth, among modern historians and authors of celebrity. The information conveyed by these works is exceedingly precious in its character, but it is not so much on account of the value possessed by the literary lore contained in them that they are commended to the attention of the student, for that might probably be extracted as abundantly from the leaves of other authors. It is for the rich spirit of philosophy which is imbibed from the pages of some of these authors, and the deep tincture of classic elegance, which is imparted by others amongst them, that this selection of very familiar works has been made to the pupil.

There have been so many pens which have become nimble in sounding the praises of "Gibbon's History of the Decline and Fall of the Roman Empire," that it seems to constitute almost a profanation of literary sanctity, to dissent from the proposition, that this eloquent embodiment of historical truth constitutes one of the best authors to place in the hands of a student for perusal. But its style is ornamented with such a cumbrous weight of magnificence, that it is almost impossible for a student of any ordinary share of susceptibility, to pass over its glittering pages without finding his own phrase marked for a considerable time by a redundant floridity of verbiage. The juvenile reader passes from page to page of this splendid work, with the same feelings that he would pass through an extended grove, painted with beautiful flowers, robed in refreshing verdure, and scented with fragrant odors, but at the terminus of which he finds that he has gathered no solid nutriment to compensate him for his rambles. And independent of its prodigal display of decoration, it presents in its incidents, its scenes, its nomenclature, and its characters, such a mournful transition from that splendid era in which Rome was an exuberant spring of glory in learning, in eloquence, in arms, and in arts, that the student must inevitably turn with the languor of unrewarded expectation, from an expanse which is decked with so much bloom, but which yields such a stinted supply of fruit.

There is no class of authors which, from the great variety of interesting subjects disposed of in them, and from the sprightly and racy manner in which they are written, which may be more eminently calculated to enrich the social casket of the student with a copious supply of colloquial embellishments, or to communicate a high seasoning to his style in speaking and writing, than the most approved and celebrated works in natural history. In this very inviting catalogue may be included Buffon, Cuvier, Goldsmith, Godman, Audubon, and Willson, a perusal of either of which, in addition to the fine literary culture they afford, will certainly charm away the languor and tediousness of the dullest hour.

There is another class of authors which a student in elocution should read with a share of true and sincere devotion. The works to which reference is made, are the standard works in political economy. He should study these with peculiar care, regardless of the political bearing and complexion of their doctrinal tenets on particular topics; for they shed a broader and clearer blaze of light upon varied topics of a political nature which enter into the aggregate of human business, and they imbue the human mind with a more astonishing versatility of thought and power, in discussing subjects of a political nature, than the whole range of human literature besides. It is almost impossible for a mind in any degree susceptible, to give its thoughts to the best works of this description, without receiving from their inflnence an admirable training for the duties and discussions of political life. We refer to the most approved authors which have enlightened the world on the subject of political economy, among which may be included the works of Adam Smith, Say, and Wayland.

Another department of literature which is calculated to re quite a student for its perusal with rich and varied supplies of ornamental and useful instruction, comprehends the ablest and most enlightened works in medical science, the more especially those which have been devoted to physiology and medical jurisprudence. It cannot be expected from the student of a profession altogether distinct from that of medical science, to study the whole circle of medical authors; but he may very profitably yield a portion of his leisure moments to the most instructive and celebrated works in that interesting field of science, under the guidance and instruction of a practical and enlightened member of the medical profession.

Within the circle of clerical literature, it may redound largely to the benefit of a student in elocution, to read the sermons of Dr. Robert South, on account of the massive solidity and strength of the language which they contain, as well as for the muscular power and robustness of intellect which is displayed in every argument and thought he advances. He should read with delight the sermons of Archbishop Tillotson, on account of the beautiful simplicity and perspicuity of his style. The sermons of Dr. Thomas Chalmers merit a large share of his devotions, owing both to the almost unfathomable depth of his researches on topics of theological and general science, and the luminous elegance with which he imparts the fruit of his speculations to the world. On the American side of the Atlantic, there is scarcely any production which has emanated from the pen of man, the perusal of which would communicate brighter hues of elegance, or a more graceful and attractive finish, in the shape of ornament to the style of a gifted speaker or writer, than the theological and miscellaneous works of the late Dr. Channing.

When authors which pertain to the department of legal science are submitted to the consideration of the student of elocution in this chapter, it is not with the view of enhancing his attainments as a lawyer that these works are commended to his thoughts, but with the desire to augment the richness, beauty, and strength of his style as a speaker and writer. And it may not prove an idle expenditure of labor and thought, in this connection, to suggest that, in the region of natural and political law, no writers will reward him more richly for a few hours of reflection occasionally devoted to them, than will Grotius, Puffendorf, and Selden.

Amidst the more recent treasures of legal lore, the treatise written by Sir William Jones on the doctrine of bailments, is a clear, beautiful, and refreshing spring of instruction on the subject to which it is devoted, and will be apt to requite a careful attention to its pages, with some very precious gems both of thought and expression. The treatise of Judge Story, of this country, on the same subject, is hardly surpassed in point of beauty and elegance by the work of the great English Jurist, and will amply repay a student for its perusal, both in its contributions to the cabinet of his thoughts and language. The productions also of the same accomplished Jurist, the one of which has been devoted to an exposition of the Federal Constitution, and the other to a consideration of the conflicts which occur between the laws of different States, will also form highly judicious elements in a course of reading which may be adopted by a student in elocution. The Commentaries of Chancellor Kent have presented some of the most complex and useful topics comprehended within the boundaries of legal science, in a style so familiar, luminous, and instructive, that they cannot be considerately read without leaving in their train benefits of rare value for the use and enjoyment of a susceptible mind. The Commentaries of Sir William Blackstone have heretofore chiefly attracted the attention of the reading world almost exclusively as a professional work. But there is scarcely any author within the comprehensive circle of English literature which deserves to be more highly prized by a student in elocution, for the quiet and graceful beauty which breathes in every page which it contains, than this celebrated production. They are worth far more as a model of style in composition than the productions of his bitter and memorable assailant, Junius, which have been so liberally, enthusiastically, and variously applauded by mankind.

It is impossible to enumerate all the authors which a student may peruse, with the experience of large and conspicuous returns of advantage to himself. All that can be attained in a work of this description, is to suggest a few of those which have received the approving stamp of the best experience of the world—works which he cannot fail to read without reaping at least some partial degree of service from them; and to leave to his own discretion such other works as may be commended to his homage by their acknowledged intrinsic value. It would constitute a culpable omission of duty, if this chapter should be brought to a close without pressing upon his attention, as an American citizen, in the most fervent and earnest manner, the numbers of the Federalist. They will enlighten him in regard to the institutions of his country; they will be calculated to impart to his style, both in writing and speaking, a large accession of fervency and vigor; and they will certainly have a tendency to imbue his mind with very intense powers of thought on all subjects of a political nature. Locke's essays will also constitute a highly valuable discipline for his intellectual powers, in writing or speaking on political topics of the most elevated grade, as well as a very rich repository of instruction in metaphysical and political science. A large portion of the philosophical and literary works of the celebrated Lord Bacon will, from their uncommon originality and richness, have a very direct tendency to invigorate and adorn, in a very high degree, the language and thoughts of an intelligent and considerate reader of them.

CHAPTER LXXIX.

THE INTRODUCTION OF BIBLICAL QUOTATIONS INTO SECULAR SPEECHES.

There is no field of literary exploration which is enriched with such a precious and abundant harvest of beautiful and instructive allusions and illustrations as the sacred pages of divine revelation. And these gems of thought are not found in scattered patches in the grand repository of human duty, like solitary pearls upon a bleak and sterile coast; but the whole path of revelation, from the early dawn of creation down to the closing sentence of the Bible, is luminous with these resplendent passages of wisdom; which shed a glory on the department of letters, which is only surpassed by the enduring and priceless benefits which they convey to our fallen race, for its deliverance from ruin and for its guidance to felicity. The beautiful in the Bible is not monotonous in its character from being applicable alone to some particular interest or concern within the range of human duty. Endowed with a universality of elegance, and an unfathomable profundity of richness, it may be used as successfully to impart a fragrance to every page of classic literature, as it is to pour the radiance of unerring wisdom on the darkened understanding. The beautiful passages have not lost their zest, like withered flowers, from the long and hackneyed use of them in the way of quotation; partaking, in some degree, of the ever-freshening and ever-renovating happiness which flows from the faithful service of their author, these passages may be applied by different writers, to subjects differing as widely as the poles, with some new apparition of beauty arising to the view in every successive use of them.

As an embellishment to true eloquence, no extract from the choicest page of secular literature, can approximate in point of elegance and effect a happy selection from the Scriptures, when appropriately introduced and applied. The works of Shakspeare have constituted a standing and exhaustless treasury, from which pure gold has been drawn to gild with brighter beams of attraction both the dull and the attractive page. But it forms the glory of Shakspeare, that the productions of his prolific pen rank next to the Holy Scriptures in point of beauty and originality of thought, with a chasm intervening between the merits of the two, as wide as that between the heavens and the earth. The conceptions of Milton are drawn directly from the opening scene of revelation, and the very gorgeousness of his drapery only serves to disclose the necessity which exists in all human imitations of celestial sublimity for artificial appliances to supply the place of that uncreated fervor which glows in every syllable of the Bible.

But whilst an intelligent survey of the Scriptures will extort from the most reluctant lips the spontaneous confession, that in whatever is sublime in conception, grand in imagery, luminous in thought, and beautiful in language, it surpasses indefinitely the most precious treasures amongst the printed wisdom of the world, yet these sacred maxims of wisdom are not to be desecrated by an application of them to the furtherance of a frivolous sentiment, or to the accomplishment of light and commonplace objects. The authority and beauty of quotations from the Scriptures should be invoked in illustration of a noble and virtuous sentimentality, or to fortify a high and pure morality. It not only detracts from the solemnity of these holy truths, to drag them down from their high mission, to be mixed up with the petty pursuits of life, but it also sheds a blighting contempt on the enterprise of the writer or speaker who may prove so presumptuous as to profane sacred things by draggling them in the trail of his own puny aspirations.

Many of the most eminent speakers and writers both living and dead, whose fame graces the history of this country, frequently enhanced the power and the beauty of their productions by the felicitous introduction of Scripture quotations. Amongst these, John Quincy Adams, John Randolph, and Sergeant S. Prentiss, are now remembered to have held a very conspicuous rank.

But though the pure and ample field of divine revelation is open to the secular speaker and writer for the purposes of embellishment and illustration, it will be conforming to the principles of sound taste, that speakers and writers of the character referred to, should not wield the truths of the Gospel with ministerial authority. That is, they should not use these truths (in matters of temporal speaking and writing) in persuading their hearers to religion by the attraction of the promises of the Gospel, nor should they endeavor to deter men from vice and iniquity by parading before their minds the penal terrors of the divine law. They would be thus usurping a duty which pertains exclusively to the sacred desk, and whilst the practice would bring no accession of strength to the cause of religion, it almost unfailingly attracts invidious remarks to the speaker or writer who indulges himself in this habit.

CHAPTER LXXX.

A SPEAKER SHOULD ABSTAIN FROM LATIN AND GREEK QUOTATIONS, AND FROM HABITUAL ALLUSIONS TO GREECE AND ROME.

The act of interspersing a speech or argument with fragmentary portions of Latin and Greek, except where the production may be delivered in the presence of an audience distinguished for its literary culture, involves a very broad infraction both of the code of just taste and of sound breeding. The act in question comprehends a violation of good taste, because it is the invariable resort of superficial smatterers, who, having never drank from the pure original fountains of classic erudition, take sedulous care to collate a few stale and worn out scraps from the rudimental authors in the law, and ring them in the ears of the ignorant; just as men on the borrow in the pecuniary market collect a few silver pence, and jingle them on the exchanges, to create the impression with the bystanders, that they are men of a *million.*

An indulgence in quotations from the ancient classics, except in the instance already reserved, conveys an implied assumption from the speaker to his hearers, that he is himself enriched with the classic gems of every age, and that they an ignorant set of boobies, must sit with gaping mouths and greedy throats, and be stuffed by him with recondite lore, just as starving pigeons are crammed with food by the maternal bill.

A passage from the ancient classics nicely interwoven with

the web of a discourse which is spoken before an enlightened audience that may be presumed to know something about Latin and Greek, as well as the speaker, and which is introduced without parade or ostentation, may serve both as a graceful and instructive ornament. But the gross profanation of the sanctity of *classical* learning, of which fustian speakers are constantly guilty in introducing their *rectus in curiams, coram non judices, res adjudicatas*, and other withered flowers plucked from the rudimental expounders of the law, before illiterate juries in the courts, and before promiscuous assemblies from the hustings; is sufficient to loathe the almost impalpable particles of delicacy which cling to the intellectual constitution of a drayman or a chimney sweep. This practice has now taken up its refuge, so exclusively, however, amongst the rear-guard of the profession, that it is almost unnecessary to brand it with reprehension.

But there is another defective trait found amongst speakers which frequently casts a blur upon some of the most finished productions which bless and adorn our country by their presence. The imperfection to which reference is now made, is the habitual tendency of a large number of American speakers to be eternally dipping into the history of Greece and Rome in the delivery of an intellectual production. A fact of very decisive weight on any subject, or a very novel and beautiful illustration drawn from the leaves of these ancient repositories of human wisdom, will never descend with grating harshness on the ear of refinement. But the continual thrumming on these hackneyed strings of oratorical music is so exclusively the perquisite of Sophomoric orators and of graduates from provincial schools, that a tingling sensation is invariably produced in the cultivated ear, whenever an allusion of the kind now under consideration may be introduced by a speaker, when the allusion itself is unblessed by the charm of novelty, or by the vividness of its applicability.

The habit of taxing the histories of Greece and Rome for supplies in the shape of embellishment, is an expedient of superficial speakers, to cover the shallowness of their classical education. They have never enjoyed an opportunity of raising that mystic veil which hides from common observation the genuine treasures of Grecian and Roman literature, and they are prone to circulate faint imitations of these precious coins, similar to shop-keepers in provincial towns, remote from the metropolis, who, not being able to procure the shadows of greatness cast in marble, are contented with busts composed of stucco, plaster of Paris, and other frail and perishable materials.

Whilst speakers of profound and varied acquisition in the realms of ancient lore, repair at once to the unadulterated pages of Homer, Xenophon, and Longinus, amongst the Greeks, and of Cicero, Horace, and Virgil amongst the Romans, those who have taken their Academic degree on closing the lids of Corderi and Viri Romæ, draw their ornamental gilding from Gibbon, Rollin, Plutarch, and works of that description. Works, it must be acknowledged, of transcendent merit in their place, but not sufficient for imparting the consecrating touch of classic learning to every vaporing orator who draws beauty or inspiration from their much-ad mired and instructive pages.

CHAPTER LXXXI.

THE ADVANTAGE WHICH A SPEAKER DERIVES FROM POSSESSING A FINE PERSON, CONSIDERED.

The proposition that a speaker can accomplish but little by his powers of eloquence, unaided by the advantage of a fine person, is coëval with the business of speaking itself. That a tall, commanding, and symmetrical form, assisted by the graces of manner and the elegancies of motion, may earn for the possessor of these personal advantages an abstract or speculative appreciation of the most extravagant kind in the sphere of courtly fashion and romantic taste, we do not pretend to deny. But that there is any necessary determination to success which is blended with the possession of an attractive person, we regard as an assumption which is exceedingly problematical.

As far as public speaking is identified with the proposition under consideration, our past observation induces us to believe that the sympathies of mankind generally take very much the same direction, where two persons are controverting a point in debate with each other, the one of whom may be lofty, and the other diminutive in stature, that it generally assumes when a large man and a small one are engaged in a personal combat. The good wishes of the spectators almost universally cluster around the person of the *petit* champion. A large proportion of mankind, where there is no supervening circumstance blended with their lives to determine them to a contrary state of feeling, generally sympathize with those who present no prominent personal traits superior to their own. Those who exhibit persons eminently endowed with elevation, grace, and beauty, are in that enviable condition, as far as attractions purely personal are considered, that the mass of mankind may not hope even to approximate them—to reach their level would be an impracticable attempt.

Persons, on the contrary, who may be diminutive and ungainly in person, present no characteristics in the matter of appearance to excite envy in the bosoms of their neighbors; and if such persons should aspire to any object which requires the application of intellectual power to command its possession, the world will be apt to prove exceedingly quick in its impulses to yield them a munificent appreciation of their merits. If an aspirant to renown, in any department of human excellence, has a face and form which excite commiseration rather than envy, his personal appearance does not inflict a wound on the self-esteem of his neighbors wherever he meets them. An aspirant of a commanding and beautiful person, does impart a sort of standing rebuke to his acquaintances of indifferent appearance wherever he meets them. A large portion of mankind cannot endure or tolerate those perfections of person or character, which no art, perseverance, or address, which they may employ, will enable them to command.

The preceding strain of remark, then, must invincibly conduct every contemplative mind to the conclusion that the public speaker, and every person else, who covets the golden prizes which hang on popular opinion, presents a barrier to the genial flow of the popular kindness towards him, on every occasion in which he shall exhibit the ostensible advantages of a fine person to the gaze of the multitude. The self-esteem of mankind, does not enjoy a free circulation when a person of this description is about—his elegancies of person, like a chilling frost, freezes up their personal complacency in its channels.

This is far from being true in its application to a speaker who presents to the eye of the world a dwarfish person and an indifferent face. Mankind are well apprized of the fact, that a contrast injurious or humiliating to them can never be instituted between the personal endowments of such a man and their own. They feel so much at ease in regard to an individual of very inferior personal endowments, as far as that question is involved, that they can afford to be liberal and gracious with him at every other point at which he thirsts for applause or caresses. If he exhibits respectable powers in speaking, in the character of a candidate for public favor, they are willing to vote for him in opposition to an opponent who is rendered odious by a lofty and engaging person. If he be a legislator, the members are willing to vote for his measure, in defiance of the fine reasoning of an opposing member who has committed the unpardonable sin of being handsome. If he is advocating a cause before a jury, they will decide agreeably to his wishes, to mortify an opposing advocate, who daily wounds their self-esteem by the hateful exhibition in their presence of a person more graceful, beautiful and attractive than theirs.

For the purpose of testing the proposition before us, by a resort to the practical realities of life, let us inquire who it is that brings into intense play the sympathies of the populace, when a fight is in progress on a public square, between two antagonists, the one of whom is gigantic in his proportions, and the other very small? Why, experience with her truthful and unerring voice proclaims that it is the diminutive combatant. Who is it that inspires the multitude with a phrenzied share of enthusiasm, when a discussion is advancing on the hustings between a large and a diminutive debater? Both experience and the intuitive perceptions of nature point us to the *petit* gentleman as the engrossing mark of the public interest and favor. Which advocate is it that engages the fervent wishes of the people for his success, when a law case is in the progress of discussion in a Court of Justice, where a counsellor of commanding frame is on one side, and a second edition of *Lilliput* is on the other? A stern regard to the universal voice of precedent on the subject, would compel a jury who might be sworn and empanelled to try the question, to decide that it would be the badly-grown attorney who would bear away the palm, so far as the popular feeling would carry him forward to the point of success.

And it is not merely in pugilistic encounters, in contests for elective honors, and in trials of strength before the legislative assemblies of the country, that the *petit* competitor is fortified by the best feelings of the people, to the exclusion of his lofty and commanding rival. Where the heart of beauty is to be won, the *petit* suitor is almost certain to bear away the alluring prize over the shoulders of his tall and imposing rival.

The public theory affirms that the diminutive lover is hateful to the gentler sex. Public practice and experience proclaim that the more minute aspirant almost universally defeats a stately and ostensible rival. It may be probable, that the small aspirant in these adventures supplies in tenacity of purpose and in the spirit of perseverance what he lacks in the matter of grace and in elevation of figure. It is true to the letter, however, that the records of experience distinctly reveal the fact, that in a large proportion of the cases in which tall men and small men are brought into competition, for the attainment of any valuable object, that the small ones prevail.

What are the revelations of experience on the field of debate itself? John Wilkes, whose name and elocution both communicated an invincible charm to the populace of London, was remarkable for a face which was hideous in its character, and it has never been affirmed that he was blessed in a stature beyond the level of mediocrity. He said himself, "that he could recognize the difference only of half an hour between his own face and that of the handsomest man in England."

We have never seen any extraordinary elevation of person claimed for Mirabeau, and universal report declares that his face was amongst the ugliest that ever came from Nature's mould. Yet his voice was the soul of inspiration to the National Assembly of France in the most turbulent periods of her history. And when he happened to be absent from the deliberations of that celebrated council on any occasion when it was thrown into tumult and uproar, he would immediately exclaim, "let them only get a sight of my boar's-face once, and they will become as quiet as doves."

John Philpot Curran, who was the pride and glory of Ireland in eloquence, in letters, and in the romance of chivalry, was not only ugly in face and diminutive in person, but he was encumbered with the extremity of malformation in his limbs, and was without the faintest lineament or shadow of grace or beauty about his person except that imputed sort of grace which beamed upon his mortal vestments from an intellect and soul that arose above their earthly prison, and panted for an union with immortality. Yet with all this poverty of personal grace, with the presence of all these personal deformities, did any person ever indulge the belief that the tallest and most elegant advocate in Ireland could come within beat of drum of Curran in any contest which might be in progress before the people or the juries of Ireland?

Napoleon Bonaparte is said to have been in stature about five feet seven inches. Yet there was a majesty intrinsic to his person which humbled and overawed the proudest potentates of Europe, when they were standing in his presence. And one of the noblest and most finished specimens of Nature's workmanship which this country ever produced, in point of commanding elegance and elevation, being Minister to the Court of St. Cloud, when Bonaparte was first Consul, on his return to this country, remarked, "that he felt that he was a man of some note while he continued in the United States, but though he was nearly a foot taller (being about six feet three inches in stature himself) than Bonaparte, yet that he felt as if he had dwindled into the insignificance of a pigmy, on being introduced to that remarkable personage."

Dunning, a celebrated advocate, who figured in the palmiest and most flourishing era of the eloquence of England, is said to have been diminutive, ungainly, and very ungraceful in his personal appearance. Yet it has never been alleged that he ever had a verdict carried over his head amidst the contests of the bar, by the attractions of any competitor who was blessed with a more lofty and engaging person than his own.

Three statesmen, who have impressed their names and memory on this country, in traces so indelible as only to be surpassed in celebrity by the architect of the temple of our country's freedom, were each diminutive in person. We refer to Alexander Hamilton, James Madison, and Aaron Burr. Yet it is said of Alexander Hamilton, by his political adversaries, that there was an unaffected majesty and dignity about his person, which would form a rebuke to imperial royalty itself. Doctor Samuel Johnson remarked, concerning Edmund Burke, "that the lines of greatness were so legibly inscribed on his person, that a passenger could not take shelter from a shower of rain under a gateway with him, even for a few moments, without making the discovery that he was an extraordinary man." Such, precisely, was Aaron Burr, at the meridian of his fame and popularity, and such was he in the wane and waste of his political fortunes, when drinking the cup of bitterness to its very dregs. The most towering intellect of America could not be brought even transiently into juxtaposition to him, without catching by intuition the fact that he was in the presence of one who belonged to the royal lineage of nature; and the eagle glance of his eye could not be reflected upon the vision of the rudest peasant or boor throughout this wide-spread land, without communicating the lightning flash of conviction to his mind, that there was passing in review before him an image of faded grandeur, like that which Milton pronounced to be "*the excess of brightness obscured.*" James Madison was not only diminutive in person, but his most impassioned friends and admirers affirm that he was not peculiarly blessed in the graces of manner; yet was it the still small voice of reason, conveyed by his tongue to the councils of his country, amidst the most convulsing agitations which marked the progress of our government and free institutions to a state of consummation, which unfailingly hushed the waves of tumult into a calm.

Many of those who, when living, were the brightest ornaments of our country's fame and character, and whose memories, now that they are dead, constitute the choicest treasures in the casket of our national renown, were very small men.

Alfred Moore,* whose learning, talents, and integrity, reflected lustre on the most exalted bench of judicature in this country, about the commencement of the present century, is said to have been a gentleman of diminutive stature. Yet in the stern strifes of the bar it was his destiny to contend with many who were giants in person as well as giants in mind. But it has never been alleged that he did not tower to a sufficient elevation, by the force of his genius, eloquence, and acquirements, to attain the loftiest eminence which was occupied by the noblest of his rivals and cotemporaries.

John Sergeant was diminutive in person, yet the force of his intellect, the vigor and skill he exerted in debate, and the saintly purity of his moral character, invested his voice with a charm in the councils of his country, which was never broken or dispelled by the giant arm of those debaters he encountered, who rose in height greatly above the mediocrity of human altitude.

The late John Stanly, of North Carolina, was hardly above five feet six inches in height, yet a large proportion of the most towering debaters, both in person and in intellect, who acted on the public stage during the period in which he figured, are known to have deferred to his thrilling trump in discussion. And a gentleman whose mind has been munificently adorned by the learning of every age, on once hearing Mr. Stanly deliver a speech in the Legislature of North Carolina, which was replete with the richest decorations of a classic diction, commended by the most exquisite and insinuat-

* Hon. Alfred Moore, of North Carolina, formerly one of the Judges of the Supreme Court of the United States.

ing graces of a finished manner, and aided by the most elegant blandishments of a courtly and polished exterior, observed, "that Mr. Stanly came upon the stage as a speaker, and made his exit from it with infinitely more grace than any orator he had ever seen."

It will not be denied that when a debater, blessed in the possession of an elegant and commanding person, is discoursing in the presence of an assembly of persons, that the advantages of his person may attract to him a very special share of attention. But the attention which a speaker thus engages is not yielded to what he says, it is given to what he looks. The admiration which is attracted to a speaker is not extracted from the heart of an audience by any additional weight, persuasiveness, fascination, or power, which is communicated to his oratory by the accomplishment of a graceful and commanding exterior; the tribute of admiration is yielded to his personal appearance, considered abstractly from his speaking entirely. The same measure of admiration might have been paid to him if he had kept his tongue still, and had been simply observed by an assembly of persons, walking through the aisles of a deliberative hall, just as persons would admire a beautiful race-horse in coursing his way majestically through the streets of a town. And their admiration would be excited in a similar degree by observing the same engaging animal posting his way with the speed of thought over a race-course. But the spectators would not be so perfectly blinded by the symmetrical beauty and elegance of the race-horse, as to be beguiled into the belief, when seeing him on a race-path with a shabby and diminutive one splitting the wind a great distance ahead of him, that the latter was beating the small one.

It may be truly said that those attractions of person which draw a special share of attention to a speaker when he is discoursing, usually emanate from graces and blandishments which are thrown around his person by the cultivation of the intellect. For if you strip a very elegant and beautiful speaker of the blessing of intelligence and of that finish which art throws around the manner, and reduce him to that appearance of awkwardness and ignorance which is generally manifested by illiterate and ignorant speakers, so far from the beauty of such a speaker operating as a stimulus to admiration, it will make him an object of decided commiseration. And it is very certain that a speaker of the most diminutive and ungainly form, whose elocution breathes the soul of eloquence, and whose manner in speaking is adorned with the graces of art will attract an attention to his acquired graces, which entirely excludes the perception of his personal defects and deformities.

We believe that speakers and all other conspicuous and responsible actors on the public stage, are appreciated in their professional characters, for the positive amount of good which they may be competent to perform. And we also cherish the opinion that deformities of person by being contrasted with the transcendent powers of a speaker's intellect, may inure very greatly to his advantage in the public estimation of him. We think the truth of the preceding proposition is fully realized in some of the examples which have been presented in this chapter, and we also believe that attestations of its truthfulness are continually unfolding themselves to the public view in every successive year which is added to the history of the world.

CHAPTER LXXXII

THE BENEFIT WHICH MAY BE DERIVED FROM PRACTICING DECLAMATION BEFORE A MIRROR.

It is an encouraging fact in the philosophy of the human face divine, that there are many countenances which possess the capability of imbibing a degree of expressiveness from the reflections of a mirror, which they never reciprocate by defining beautiful images on the bright surface of the mirror in return. And there is no solid reason why this should not be so. The most fascinating expressions of loveliness which play upon the cheek of female beauty, are often transplanted from the transient shadow of sweetness which is painted upon the surface of a looking glass. And if a soul of celestial sweetness may be transfused into the countenance of a female, so as to become habitual, by practicing fine expressions of face before a mirror, it would seem inexplicable why a speaker might not extend the catalogue of his graces, both in reference to the action of the person and the expressions of the countenance, by frequently speaking before a mirror.

Any person who is fond of performing on an instrument of any description, may acquire a tune he fancies simply by a close observation of its notes when some other individual shall be playing it. One who delights in dancing, catches a graceful step from giving a few moments of attention to another who practices that step in the mazes of a dancing party. Another who becomes favorably impressed with the elegant carriage of an acquaintance, can, by practice, make the movements his own which he so much admires. Successful comedians, by persevering attention to properties of the kind, become so expert as to be able habitually to command all the droll expressions of countenance, voice, or manner, which they observe in persons who are circulating around them. And these acquisitions are made in most instances, too, without an appeal to the mirror.

It would appear exceedingly strange that a person should not be competent to paint more vividly upon his countenance, before a mirror, those engaging expressions which a large proportion of both sexes very frequently command, without any appeal whatever to glassy aids.

It is by the recognition of a beautiful expression or a graceful movement, clearly and specifically defined in the face or person of another, that the type or model of the desirable quality is provided, from a sincere devotion to which the person observing it will be enabled to acquire it and make it his own. Without having enjoyed the privilege of observing an image, a charming expression of countenance, or a graceful movement of the person, revealed to him in some form or embodiment, an actor or speaker could no more be competent to interweave such floating expressions and grades with his own countenance or person, than an artist would be adequate to the task of inseating in a picture tints and beauties which he had never conceived by the sight of the eye, and a description of which had been merely communicated to him verbally by some acquaintance of his.

The great feature of efficiency in the practice of speaking before a mirror, consists not in the simple capacity to indulge in a fascinating expression of the countenance, or to execute a graceful gesture of the hands in front of it, but in the power of maintaining the expression or gesture in a perfect condition some moments after either shall have been brought into being. For the mere fact of execution would effect nothing without an adjunct of some sort to sustain it in being. The desired gesture or expression without the benefit of some intelligible medium of observation through which to observe them, might vanish in the very act of being made, like the foam on the fountain or the ripple on the surface of the water.

But when the expression or gesture is distinctly surveyed in an accurate and faithful mirror, the speaker knows by the report of his own vision what degree of exertion and what sort of exertion to adopt, in order to sustain the expression or movement in being for a due length of time.

A person who has acquired a respectable knowledge of actions and expressions of the countenance, can benefit a practitioner in elocution very considerably, by supervising the expressions of his countenance and the action of his hands when he is speaking, and by imparting to him faithful counsels in regard to the correctness of every movement he makes, just as it may be made. By a vigilant and faithful superintendence of this sort, some of the most efficient speakers and successful dramatists known to the world, have been perfected.

If a speaker shall have acquired any conceptions of expression, time, and motion, which may even faintly approximate correctness, why may he not, by practising expression, gesticulation, and time before a mirror, so habituate himself to the production of each of these properties in the proper measure, before a mirror, as to be enabled to execute them with facility, in the course of time, without the aid of the glass.

It is said in the Bible, that a man looks in a glass and straightway forgets what kind of man he is. But if the image, defined on his memory by the glass, disappears immediately on his leaving, it is a very different thing with any determination which has been communicated to his character and manners by any course of action and expression long practised before the glass. This may adhere to him like the complexion of his skin or the color of his hair.

But the best evidence of the advantages which may be derived from the habit of practising before a mirror, may be recognized in the fact, that a very respectable proportion of those who delight and edify the world in the capacity of speakers, have magnified their influence in the exercise of that accomplishment by practising before a mirror. This fact in the history of any particular speaker, may but seldom reach the general treasury of human information. When a knowledge of this peculiar mode of exercise, in connection with any person devoted to speaking, obtains currency, it is generally introduced to the world through the medium of some person who enjoys a constant communion of friendship with the speaker, or who may accidentally discover the practice.

Without assuming to decide that the discipline imposed upon a speaker by habitually practising before a mirror, is at all essential to his perfection in oratory, the opinion may be safely advanced, that the practice may be adopted with the promise of deriving very considerable advantages from it. Persons who take much pleasure in mimicking the peculiar expressions of face which they see sometimes exhibited by their acquaintances and neighbors, by habitually indulging themselves in these particular expressions, contrary to their design, sometimes have them so inlaid and blended in their own countenances that they are never able to obtain a deliverance from them afterwards. If a person, by simply imitating the movements and expressions of countenance of another, without any chart to guide him to correctness in the operation, can succeed so effectually as to blend the expressions which he copies permanently with his own countenance; it would seem not to be very unnatural or credulous to believe that a speaker, by continually repeating before a mirror the production of certain expressions in his own countenance; and certain motions with his own hands, could succeed at length in producing these motions and expressions at pleasure. If these expressions and motions shall be produced in great frequency before a mirror, the muscles about the face will contract a mechanical tendency towards producing the same expressions and gestures on other occasions. They may perhaps make their appearance spontaneously, and when the speaker may not desire their presence.

And if a speaker is characterized by an expression of countenance which is repulsive, gloomy, or indicative of anger or ill-nature, there can be no better method adopted for the removal of these unprepossessing expressions than practising before a mirror. For if a speaker shall, in declaiming before a mirror, discipline his countenance to a frequent expression of joy and benevolence, these expressions will, in the course of time, mechanically preside over his face when engaged in the business of speaking.

CHAPTER LXXXIII.

THE DAILY PRACTICE OF WRITING AN ESSAY ON SOME SUBJECT, CONSIDERED.

It was once remarked by an enlightened expounder of the Gospel, who has long since passed from the theatre of his earthly labors to a brighter scene of existence, "that there was no duty assigned to man which was performed by him with a measure of reluctance so utterly disproportioned to the amount of labor involved in it as that of prayer." The same proposition may be justly affirmed in relation to the exercise of writing, for the labor involved in it is neither oppressive nor irksome, and yet the repugnance to its performance in most cases, is without any visible bounds.

A disrelish for that species of labor which is intimately blended with the most important duties and precious interests of man, it should be the unceasing ambition of every person to vanquish, who may covet the accomplishment of expressing himself with accuracy and neatness, both in speech and in writing. And there is no corrective for the repugnance in question, which may be resorted to with a larger measure of success or efficacy, than the daily practice of writing down on paper a person's thoughts on some subject which may have previously engrossed a portion of his reflections. No member of human society who possesses the faculty of writing, it matters not what his pursuit in life may be, should permit a day to elapse without subjecting his mind to this discipline; and an essay which may cover a half sheet of ordinary letter-paper, will accomplish the objects here aimed at, as well as one which may occupy a larger number of pages.

A frequent indulgence in the act of composing is not pressed upon the attention of the pupil simply for the purpose of placing securely within his grasp, the faculty of unusual expertness in writing. Even the consummation of that object would be of itself no trifling achievement. But important as would be the attainment of that point, it is indefinitely surpassed in intrinsic value, by that permanent habituation to mental labor, that prompt and lucid arrangement of thought, and that admirable precision and perspicuity of expression, which almost uniformly flow as legitimate fruits from the daily practice of composition to a susceptible mind.

By the constant expenditure of thought which is inevitably produced by the practice of intelligent writing, the human mind is accelerated in the flow of its thoughts, just in the same way that the human heart when long practiced in yielding its devotion to the alleviation of human suffering in the social sphere within which it throbs, is ready to cast its charities upon every other circle in which it may be startled by the wail of misery.

The principle of aversion to labor of every description will be vastly diminished by a daily participation in the practice of composition. Business in its varied forms will be more punctually and methodically performed. The interests of society will be more efficiently advocated either in speaking or in writing, by the votary of this practice, than they otherwise would have been. Many precious thoughts may glitter in the literary pages of the country, which might have been otherwise consigned to hopeless oblivion; and the general powers of the intellect will be vastly augmented.

As intellectual discipline is the object principally sought in adopting the exercise of composing as a daily practice, it matters little what the subject may be, on which the student may write an essay, so it be an innocent topic. And let him not plead in bar to the performance of this duty the usual plea of sloth, the want of opportunities, for these are never exhausted except by those disabilities which are imposed by disease or by the blighting calamities which occasionally descend like lightning on those who may be endeared to the heart by the ties of friendship or kindred blood. A determined mind will be enabled to snatch an opportunity for writing a brief essay on some familiar subject, even amidst the whiz, din, and bustle of steamboat travel, or at the stopping points on a stage road. A very small fraction of the time which may be devoted so some trashy author or expended in very unproductive conversation on board of a steamboat, would be sufficient for the composition of an essay which would preserve unbroken the chain of the student's mental discipline, and perhaps draw forth from his mind a flow of precious thoughts which he might not be willing perhaps to exchange for the wealth of the East.

CHAPTER LXXXIV.

THE INFLUENCE EXERTED BY COMPETITION ON THE ENERGIES OF A SPEAKER.

The creative influence of the principle of competition has been broadly revealed in the varied fields of human aspiration and adventure in every age of the world. It is that spring of life and of energy from which young and fervid ambition draws its strength and support, in a line of transmission just as direct as that which conveys the nutriment of life from the maternal bosom to the lips of feeble and confiding infancy. When this spring is drained of its inspiring draughts, the soaring heart of early ambition languishes and withers like the verdant leaf of spring under the influence of a nipping frost. Without the stimulus of rivalship to excite him in the path of glory, the arms of a soldier become as impotent and harmless as the birchen rods which may be wielded by some antique governor of a nursery.

Without the incentive provided by rivalship, the arm of heroism becomes relaxed, the tongue of the orator becomes stiff, the ethereal aspiration of the statesman is quenched, the enterprise of commerce is chilled, the ingenuity of mechanism is blunted, the fields of agriculture become waste, the searching vision of science becomes dim, and the inspiration of literature becomes extinct. But in the extended catalogue of human aspirations, which may be paralyzed or extinguished by an absence of the spirit of rivalship, there is not one which carries the symptoms of its fatality so visibly painted upon its progress, as the thirst for oratorical renown. It matters but little how enchanting the opening prospects of a beginner in oratory may be. It matters not how rapidly his intellectual powers may be expanding. It matters not how fervid the appeals addressed to his pride from the voice of kindred or social affection, may be: whenever the spur of competition is withdrawn from that field in which a juvenile speaker is destined to labor; from that moment he is doomed to decline in his advancement and to verge towards a changeless mediocrity in the department of eloquence.

Lord Chancellor Thurlow, being once interrogated by an honest and simple-hearted father, as to the best means of making a lawyer of his son, the Lord Chancellor replied, "Let your son, in the first place, spend his own estate, then let him get married and spend his wife's estate, and he will be certain to make a lawyer!" The philosophy contained in the reply of the Lord Chancellor was, that a beginner in the legal profession required a vigorous application of the spur of necessity to his energies to impel him to that regularly-sustained and persevering exertion, which alone would make him eminent in his profession, and that the spur in question could never be supplied so long as young members of the bar should be surrounded with an affluence of means.

The philosophy contained in the advice of Lord Thurlow, is highly applicable to cases where fame, and not money may be the coveted prize of a young man's ambition. If he may be prosecuting his professional labors in a place in which he at once takes a position greatly more elevated as a speaker than that of his brethren of the bar who move in the same circle with himself, his ambition to rise higher in the scale of excellence as a speaker will be very apt to languish and decay, from the want of that sustaining nutriment which will be unfailingly supplied by the spirit of competition. If he can, at the very starting point, master and subdue his fellow members in the contentions of debate, there is no necessity acting upon his energies to propel him forward, except the abstract fondness for excellence, and that is rather too speculative in its character to induce a very liberal yield of practical fruit. Why is this so? Simply because there is nothing in the accomplishments of those who move around him to warm his pride of intellect into brisk circulation. He is superior to them all, at the very commencement, in all those aggrandizing traits of character which chiefly attract the attention of the world, and there is no person within his reach in the department of speaking whose level as a public speaker he has either to reach or to pass beyond. He will be in the same condition within the narrow domain of his ambition, that Alexander the Great was in, on the expanded field of his aspirations, when "he grieved at having no more kingdoms to conquer." He is esteemed more highly for his powers as a speaker than other young men who come in contact with him, and he will suppose that he has nothing to contend for. He will conceive that the summit of glory in the little circle in which he lives and moves is the acme of glory throughout the world. The approbation which descends from the lips of the hoary fathers *there*, will have a solid value and a precision of accuracy which it will possess nowhere else beneath the stars. The applause of the venerable matrons will distil a soothing influence into the heart, which the same gratification could impart nowhere else, and the note of praise from the lips of virgin beauty will insinuate a music into the heart which could be afforded nowhere else under the sun.

Let other aspirants to renown, in the department of forensic eloquence, be located in the same circle with the young speaker whom we have just supposed, and if the latter should possess any latent or intrinsic powers to be unfolded, these will certainly receive an abiding impulse from the constant action of the spirit of competition, which will quicken them into a state of active progression. He may not, agreeably to Lord Thurlow's requisition (to make a lawyer), have expended his money, but the star of his intellectual ascendency has set for a term in that circle within which his pride and his hopes were accustomed to centre, and with that ascendency his soothing self-complacency has vanished like the transient dews of the morning.

Let a young aspirant to oratorical fame be placed at a locality where he will be hailed as the chief orator of a large tract of country. Let him be freed from the presence of every speaker who would constitute an irksome competitor to him on the theatre of disputation, and let him be constantly soothed by the approving smile of age, and charmed by the touching smile of beauty, and his heart will be full—his ambition will be lulled into a state of serene and quiet repose—he is presented with no fresh fields for conquest, and he would not exchange his bright and blushing honors for the diadem and the purple.

A distinguished citizen of the United States once remarked, "that great men were made by great occasions." There is nothing more true than that observation, and it included within its sweep the identical principle which we are now endeavoring to enforce. For the occasions to which the remark before us referred, were those collisions between gifted men which bring into full exercise and play the faculties of the mind; which impose upon the mental energies that sort of pressure which causes the innate principle of power, where it has a residence in any particular system, to expand and to reach an elastic sort of force which it never would attain without pressure. What destiny would Napoleon Bonaparte ever have reached in the obscure shades of Corsica? What height of elevation would Lord Mansfield ever have attained had he remained amongst the romantic hills of Scotland? What degree of space would Patrick Henry have ever earned in the world's estimation, had he remained in some obscure provincial village or neighborhood, where a thrilling blast from the trump of keen competition would never have been heard, to spur him onward in the path of exertion?

There is scarcely an instance recorded in the annals of debate, where a speaker of acknowledged celebrity, commenced and ended life in a part of the world where his energies could not receive a rousing impulse from the contact of powerful competition in the contentions of political or forensic strife. A fresh traveller in the walks of professional life, without competition, has no stern necessity imposed upon him to force him into the labors of acquisition; he has nothing to do to keep himself from being crushed by the incumbent weight of a superior mental force—he has no contentions with superior minds to engage in, which will sharpen and develop his powers of thought and of debate—he is precisely in the same condition with a swordsman, who may be destitute of the benefit of an opponent to contend with, who would both preserve the previous acquisitions of the man of steel, and extend the circle of his improvement in future. In such a situation, the progress of a speaker towards perfection must be inevitably suspended, like that of every other votary of intellectual duties, who has nothing but the abstract love of excellence to spur him onward.

The question may be asked, what course is a young man to adopt, who happens to be located in a part of the world in which he cannot receive the reviving touch of rivalry or competition to develop his powers as a debater? The answer is, let him seek some locality in which he will find competitors worthy of his steel. Let him repair to some place where he will become perfected in the art of speaking, as swordsmen are rendered expert in the sword exercise, by a constant tension of the faculties in struggles with able intelligences.

CHAPTER LXXXV.

THE INTRODUCTION OF POETICAL QUOTATIONS INTO A SPEECH.

There is in the morning of life a prevailing predilection for poetical decorations amongst speakers and essayists of every description, who possess either an exuberant fancy, or a taste for elegant literature. This is an innocent partiality wherever found, and it may be rendered, by receiving a measure of discreet indulgence, not only highly improving to the ornamental department of composition and speaking, but it may also serve to augment the utility and efficiency of the strictly practical duties of a public speaker.

A poetical fragment, rich in the philosophy of life, may secure a welcome abode in the mind of an audience for unpleasant propositions, just as the leaden messengers of death, which whistle on every breeze during an action, are frequently disarmed of their terrific influence by the animating strains of some national air. The sweet and touching inspiration of the poet takes that place in the mind of the audience which may have been previously devoted to the occupancy of truths excessively nauseating in their character, and when the spectral influences which hang upon the voice of the speaker are once expelled by the soothing charm of poetic music, they never again return in the plenitude of their supremacy.

How often has a string of sympathy been successfully touched in the hearts of an audience, by the introduction of a beautiful poetical passage, when they had been previously muttering the bitterest maledictions against the speaker, or praying for a speedy close to his address! How frequently are irksome and tedious arguments stripped of every repulsive feature, by being closed with the breath of poetic inspiration, just as the dying notes of the swan, agreeably to fabulous tradition, are said to be its sweetest!

If the poetical quotation at the close of a speech be rich in language, replete with sense, warm with the spirit of romance, and highly colored with that philosophy of nature which is certain to find a magnetic reciprocation in every human breast, the speaker and his speech will be all forgotten in the beauties of the music.

What a large number of the speeches which have been delivered on the varied stages of life, have completely faded from the memory, with the exception of some poetical decoration, which charmed the closing sentence. If, when a speech or address of any description may be in progress, the speaker shall blend with his discourse a sweet note of music, drawn from the inspiration of some poet who may be dear to the hearts of his audience, and who may also abound in sympathies with breathing flesh, the poetical passage will distil a sort of moral perfume both upon the speech, the speaker, and the occasion. The audience will, under such circumstances, feel greatly indebted to the speaker for freshening up in their minds and memories an image of a favorite poet, or a favorite image of a poet, which is perhaps rapidly fading from their recollection.

There is something infinitely dear to some hearts in the productions of particular poets. In some instances, the poem is endeared by touching associations connected with the character and life of the poet, which are vividly brought up from the scenes of the past, along with the passage which may be quoted by the speaker. On other occasions, the tenderness breathed by the fragment itself touches the heart of an audience. We find, on consulting the experience of acquaintances, in some other instances, that their hearts have been tenderly affected by a poetical quotation, when brought to their attention, in speaking or in conversation, by a recurrence to the tender emotions which were imparted to their breasts on first hearing the works of the author of the particular fragment read in their hearing early in life. They are not touched so much by the tenderness of the particular passage, as by its calling up to the memory, by its introduction, a work which had been endeared long since for some engaging features. Just as if a lovely member of the softer sex should present an ardent admirer of hers a beautiful flower on some occasion, accompanied with a most bewitching expression of the countenance; the same admirer could not behold one of the same class of flowers, at a period of time greatly removed from that at which the incident occurred, without having that scene painted afresh upon the tablets of the heart, in all its power of effect.

When a speaker is exceedingly felicitous in the choice of a poetical quotation, it may serve not only to embellish and adorn, but it may also augment the practical properties of his argument. If a speaker shall succeed in gracing his argument with one of those poetical diamonds which comprehends the very essence of the philosophy of life, the very perfection of that deep and searching penetration into the springs of human action which is possessed by some minds, it is very certain that a poetical passage of that description will descend upon the feelings and probably the judgments of an audience with more decisive weight than the most consummate argument. Because poetical quotations of the class to which we refer, may be regarded as truth in its spiritualized form. They present truth and reason to the mind, disencumbered of the material clogs and appendages, in the shape of language, through which ideas are generally conveyed to mankind. The hearer of a speech, under such circumstances, is not reduced as usual to the labor of reflecting and of examining the validity of the proposition which shall be presented to his mind. For the thought comes to him, in its poetical or spiritualized garb, with all the force and authority of an axiom.

But a speaker should use a very sound and enlightened discretion in the use of poetical quotations. For the introduction of poetical quotations which are utterly inappropriate to the occasion on which they are used, and inapplicable also to the subject presented at the time, will be received with the same degree of contempt which usually marks the use of unseasonable decorations of dress.

And the speaker should also vigilantly guard against the introduction of poetical quotations into an argument or address which have become stale and hackneyed by the long use of them in the speaking world. With an intelligent audience, quotations of this description produce very much the same sensations, when brought to its attention, which is usually produced in an intelligent congregation of persons by seeing one suddenly appear amongst them who wished to assume the air and port of a fine gentleman, and who was yet arrayed in the cast-off finery of some neighbor.

CHAPTER LXXXVI.

THE INFLUENCE EXERTED BY LOCALITY IN THE FORMATION OF SPEAKERS.

The impression very extensively prevails that every human being is rendered the architect of his fame and fortunes in life, from the force of some innate spring of energy which rises in his own system to propel him forward to ennobling and beneficent actions. That an individual is usually elevated in the scale of public consideration by the application of a well-directed energy to the business of life, is an indisputable proposition. But this energy itself must receive a creative touch from some influence or other to start it into life. For without an impetus of some kind to infuse into it vigor and animation, the most precious fund of energy that a beneficent providence ever bestowed on man, may slumber in the system of its possessor in a state of supine inaction: just as the richest treasures of the Oriental world may rust in the vault of a capitalist, from the absence of enterprises to attract them into circulation. The impulse which warms the energies of a human being into successful circulation and action, is generally imparted by some circumstance or incident which may not, in reference to the person moved by it, have been in any degree the subject of volition or control. And there is no accomplishment or endowment of man which is more largely influenced in its origin and progress by the contact of casual influences and circumstance than the faculty of public speaking.

Similar to a combustible train, which blazes into an explosion by the application of a flame to it, the principle of eloquence has the breath of life frequently infused into it by some incident of which the person affected never dreamed before its application to his fortunes. The glow of ambition is excited in the bosom of one person who ascends to oratorical renown, by casually hearing some display of eloquence in early life, at a popular meeting. Another is impelled to the cultivation of his oratorical powers by witnessing some powerful exhibition of forensic skill and eloquence, and others are fired with the thirst for oratorical fame, amidst the contentions of a juvenile debating society.

But the circumstance which lends the most potent of all incentives to the passion for oratorical fame, is the circumstance of living in a place which has acquired celebrity by possessing within its precincts a large number of persons distinguished for their eloquence. This fact of residence exerts an important share of influence over the aspirations and energies of a young speaker in three aspects of the case; he observes a practical exhibition of the consideration which is earned by the possession of speaking talents of a high order, he distinctly perceives the certainty with which perseverance may achieve for an individual the most precious acquisitions, and he also plainly recognizes the impassable gulf which will ever continue to intervene between him and the eloquent men who move in the same society with himself, unless he puts in requisition the energies of a giant and the patience of a martyr to earn the honors of that accomplishment.

And the spirit which is thus imparted to a place by the appearance of one resplendent light in it, appears in many instances to be transmitted through successive generations of men, raising up in its progress bright and benignant stars in the intellectual firmament, until its life-giving inspiration shall be finally quenched by some invisible influence.

There is scarcely a State in the American Union in which the systems of political and social organization have assumed a compact form under the maturing influence of time, but is distinguished in the presentation of localities conspicuous for the great number of gifted speakers which reside in them. Persons endowed with an ardent and susceptible mind, who may have been born and reared in places thus distinguished, are fired with ambition at the very porch of life, by beholding so many shining examples before them. And they adopt the conviction, that a principle of fidelity to the character of their native scene—a reverence for the sanctity of parental affection, and a stern principle of devotion to their own characters, enjoins upon them the duty of earning a conspicuous place for themselves in the world's estimation.

The philosophy which is comprehended in the proposition which we are now entertaining, is familiarly presented in various phases and divisions of life. The scion of some house distinguished for its revolutionary honors, conceives that the fame of his family will be tarnished in his person, unless courage and chivalry shall shine as conspicuous ingredients in the formation of his character, and he seizes the lance and becomes the Quixotic champion of every local quarrel. A stripling who feeds his father's flocks at the foot of some obscure and rural hill, deserts his cherished pursuit, seizes some tattered volume, climbs with persevering pace the steep of classic renown, and becomes the scholar of his country, on hearing the report, as it is wafted upon the breeze, that a young neighbor and associate has borne away the prize honor at some neighboring university. The soldier is inspired with the soul of heroic daring, by hearing a stirring note of the lion-hearted bravery which has been exhibited on some sanguinary field of strife by a companion of earlier years. The statesman is frequently elevated to that point where he may intelligibly read his history both in the "eyes and in the acts of a nation," by hearing a frequent recitation of the splendid conquests which have been acquired in rapid succession on the field of national debate by some friend of early life. And the individual who day by day counts his glittering millions in the solitude of the closet, was spurred on perhaps to the very pinnacle of wealth by the vivid image which was daily painted before his vision of the lordly affluence that had been suddenly reached by some fellow-laborer or school-companion.

The blast of the trumpet of fame which spreads abroad the aggrandisement of some distant stranger, usually falls in unheeded sounds upon the human ear. It is the proximity in point of origin, the identity in point of early association of him who obtains a prize in the field of enterprise or ambition, which kindles in the young heart, not that fell spirit which dragged angels down, but that ethereal and unquenchable glow which plumes the wing of ambition for immortality. Persons may hear the reported success of strangers, day after day, without being roused from a state of serene repose. But let the sudden ascension to fame of some young friend be announced, and the pulse of ambition is at once quickened into a restless state of activity, and the torpid faculties are propelled into vigorous and animated play, just as the limbs of a cripple are rendered nimble and elastic by the magic touch of some wonderful deliverer in the healing art.

It was one of the maxims of the French philosopher Rochefoucault, that the self-esteem of an individual was enhanced by the misfortunes of his friend. The morality proclaimed by the maxim of the Frenchman is very hideous in its aspect, but agreeably to opinions of our race, which prevail to a very great extent, and which are fortified both by superior experience and attainments, this declaration has some grains of truth intermingled with it.

It would be exceedingly difficult to credit the monstrous proposition that the heart of a human being could be rejoiced by the crushing calamities of a friend. But we do believe that the heart must possess a celestial purity of mould which is not inflamed with a feverish thirst for the glories of success, much more than it is expanded by the raptures of joy, by the report of a neighbor's sudden or special aggrandizement. The feeling usually communicated to the human heart by the sudden ascent of a neighbor to affluence or fame, if translated into good current English, would read thus: "*Oh, I would it were otherwise.*" "*I would it were myself rather than he.*" "*I must go and do something to distinguish myself likewise, or I shall soon lose all caste and consideration amongst my neighbors.*" And the most charming relief which flits before the imagination of one whose bosom heaves with emotions similar to those just specified, is the hope of being able to go and do likewise.

The influence which may be exerted on the ambition and energies of a beginner in life by the fact of being born and raised in a place that abounds in eloquent men, is widely different from that impetus which is frequently imparted to slumbering energies of mind by the fact of a debater being frequently or constantly brought into collision with men of sterling metal on the various theatres of intellectual contention. Competition, in the sense of the term last mentioned, may develop the mental powers of a speaker, and perfect his attractions, should it meet him on any theatre of contention afforded by the civilized world; it might stimulate him to successful exertion, should it be brought to bear on him in England or France, Germany, Australia, or any other place which might be infinitely distant and remote from the scene of his birth. This last is a competition which arises from the necessities of the case. The speaker cannot be properly appreciated in the intellectual scale, or ascend to a lofty eminence as an orator, whilst others are doing better than himself, and eclipsing him by their superior radiance. By this sort of competition, a professional man is compelled to exert himself or to sink under the pressure of opposing mental forces.

But a person whose earliest vision is greeted by the light of day, in a place where the luxuries of eloquence abound in a measure of affluent abundance, and whose ear drinks in as its earliest entertainment the music of eloquence, may have his heart fired by the glow of ambition, before he shall be released from the tender supervision of the nursery. It is the spirit of the place which penetrates the heart of a speaker and conducts his faculties to perfection in the case last mentioned. He drinks in the spirit of emulation from the mother's breast. He catches it from every note of praise bestowed on the city orator which salutes his ear. His bosom glows at every pageant in which the oratory of his native place gives its music to the world. And as he progresses towards manhood, the desire to become an orator of celebrity gradually fastens itself upon his heart so firmly and tenaciously, that when he reaches maturity, he will find himself placed among the prominent speakers of his country, from the acquired or habitual force of feeling which will have driven him invincibly and irresistibly in that special direction.

CHAPTER LXXXVII.

THE MANIA FOR SPEAKING.

THERE are many young men, endowed with fine talents and blessed with a liberal education, who imbibe the impression at the commencement of life, that they are casting away golden opportunities unless they ascend in the character of speakers every stage which may present itself to the view. On one occasion, we find a speaker of the preceding description delivering a lecture before a literary association; at another, he is contending for the palm of zeal with Father Matthew, in the cause of temperance, by addressing all the temperance societies within his reach. Then again we see him on the *Masonic* stage, addressing that accepted fraternity on the sanative principles which pertain to its organization; he then pays a quota of his respects to a Bible society, by discoursing on the precious beauties which are inclosed within the lids of the Holy Scriptures. The sunday-school does not escape his observation either, and we see him frequently enlightening the managers of that invaluable institution, together with their juvenile subjects, on the inappreciable benefits which they enjoy; and he reaches perhaps the supreme point of his earthly bliss and glory when he addresses some county political meeting on the respective merits of two candidates for promotion.

A person of the character just presented, addresses every meeting at which he may be especially invited to speak, and he would consider himself guilty of a flagrant act of infidelity to his own fame and honor, should he fail to make a profuse display of his powers, whether invited or uninvited, at every public meeting which may assemble within his reach. Such a speaker will suppose that he is rendering acceptable service to his Creator, that he is imparting choice entertainment to his neighbors, that he is elevating the standard of his country's glory, and that he is decking his own brow with laurels as unfading as the amaranth, by discoursing on every rostrum which is sufficiently stable to support the weight of his person.

In the vernal season of life, when each sound that falls on the ear breathes the music of hope, and when every opening prospect is arrayed in the bloom of coming felicity, the heart of the young speaker beats with a quickened pulsation of joy at every approaching opportunity of making a speech, which smiles in the distance, vainly imagining that the circle of his fame will be extended as the number of his speeches shall be multiplied. But this is a frothy and ephemeral bliss which tantalizes his bosom,—which *mantles high* in its inception,—which sparkles and expires, leaving a painful void in its transit. For it is an inflexible law of nature, that there is no earthly entertainment which may be ministered to the human taste too often or in a measure of unbounded profusion, without bringing the particular species of entertainment into contempt. Henry IV. of England, in the memorable rebuke which Shakspeare represents him as having given to Prince Henry, on the debasement of his person by vulgar association, and by constant exhibition, has vividly prefigured the principle which we here affirm to exist in connection with public speaking. The King says to the Prince:

> "By being seldom seen, I could not stir,
> But like a comet, I was wondered at;
> . . . . . . Not an eye,
> But is weary of thy common sight."

The preceding fragment, which presents within very narrow limits so much of the simple philosophy of life, has been distilled from the lips of a royal father of England by the monarch of the poetical world. But the existence of that principle of decay which adheres to personal advantages or accomplishments, too much used, did not die with the fourth Henry of England; it yet lives in all its original force and vigor, and clings to all earthly possessions.

The tendency of human accomplishments to depreciate, when displayed in a measure of prodigal liberality, is figured out in the rapid decline of attractions which is realized in the most interesting of all earthly objects, a female arrayed in the blended charms of beauty, grace, and loveliness, by frequenting without any visible limitation the two-penny parties which occur in the circle within which she moves.

We also observe the perceptible decline which occurs in the value of the precious metals, when a sudden augmentation of the amount in circulation occurs, in any particular State or community.

And we recognize the foregoing principle, too, in the entire evaporation of the sweets of music, which at first broke upon the ear like celestial harmony, after it has been yielded gratuitously, and unsought for days in succession at the corners of the public squares and exchanges of a city.

It is the nature of every blessing and comfort of life which may be obtained without an equivalent, and without an effort to acquire its possession on the part of a recipient, to be held in cheap estimation. And if the bloom of beauty, the preciousness of gold, the glare of royalty, and the sweetness of music, are each diminished in their power to interest by being extended in a measure of superfluous fulness, it cannot be expected that oratory will experience an immunity from the common doom which is pronounced on all sublunary accomplishments in their gratuitous extension and excessive use.

The charm fades from the hero of innumerable bloody and victorious fields, when the external badges of military life, the lace, the epaulettes, and the plumes, are continually floating before the public vision. And yet military glory is one of the most coveted possessions to which human ambition may aspire, and it is the most aggrandizing and attractive of all earthly ornaments, when once acquired.

And on contemplating this question, the public speaker will be compelled to decide on it, as it shall be presented to him in connection with the nature of man. He has either to remodel the nature of man in such a way as to incorporate with his constitution an enlargement of the affections, susceptibilities, appetites, and powers of endurance, or he has to limit the stock of oratory which he throws into circulation, to an amount sanctioned by the public taste and inclination.

The charms of oratorical entertainment will depreciate in regard to any particular person when he shall yield a superfluous supply of this entertainment to any single assembly on some particular occasion, and it depreciates vastly, certainly, visibly, rapidly, and constantly, by being dealt out with improvident frequency, either in large or in limited contributions to the people at large, at the varied points for assembling.

The elocution of any particular speaker, to be highly estimated, must be obtained with some expenditure of effort by the assemblies who are to be instructed or entertained by it. The world will not, and it cannot enjoy eloquence even of the most elevated grade of excellence, when it shall be thrust upon it, and it is certain to become satiated by its too frequent and liberal use, even when the commodity shall be demanded or invited.

Because oratorical powers of the highest order, judiciously and sparingly used, have blessed their possessor with almost divine honors, the young speaker, anterior to the maturation of his practical experience, thinks that the oftener he speaks, the more rapidly his fame will extend. But he will discover, to his intense mortification, after he shall have been discoursing to the different associations, clubs, and public meetings, which assemble within the circle of his sympathies, that an intimation that he is to speak at some particular place at a specified time, instead of operating as an engaging lure to attract the multitude to hear him in the majesty of its strength, will serve to keep them away as effectually as the death-heads and men of straw hung around a corn-field, usually serve to stay the approach of marauding birds.

CHAPTER LXXXVIII.

THE INFLUENCE OF LUXURIOUS LIVING.

It has been frequently insisted, both by students and professional men, that luxurious living and ample feeding do not operate as a clog to intellectual operations. The principle embraced in this proposition has been adopted as a shield or cover by which to protect appetite and inclination from a surrender of any of their liberties. And it approximates very closely in its nature and character two refuges which are habitually sought by a large proportion of our race, to protect them from public reprehension and from self-condemnation. The one of these refuges may be found in the habitual proneness of every youth who is indolent at college or at school, to fall back on any instance of early idleness he may find among the celebrated men of the world, and there to content himself in a soft and serene repose. The other refuge to which we have referred, is the practice so prevalent among the votaries of intemperance, of endeavoring to mitigate the enormity of their own excesses, by appealing to the authority of illustrious names which were enrolled on the catalogue of the intemperate.

But these expedients of a licentious taste are all as delusive as the maniac's vision, and must inevitably terminate, at some period or other, in landing those who adopt them, in the most dreary and unproductive wastes of life. So broad and glaring is the truth that a free indulgence in the pleasures of the table is utterly at variance with the successful prosecution of intellectual pursuits, that men habitually luxurious, who are jealous of their fame, will greatly contract the circle of their indulgence in food, when preparing a production which requires profound research and intense thought, or when about to engage in any intellectual labor of a controversial nature. With any prospective duty of a high intellectual character in contemplation, men who are habitually temperate in the use of food, grow abstemious, whilst free livers, under the same circumstances, become temperate as long as the duty is suspended over them.

The most superficial thinkers are aware of the almost invincible disinclination to mental labor, which is induced by a hearty meal at any hour of the day. Books are thrown aside as useless incumbrances upon ease and pleasure, or if they should be taken up, the student passes through them with a leaden heaviness of reflection, and with a lifeless and reluctant pace.

But even should the inclination to labor survive, in more than its wonted intensity, the influence of a hearty repast, it will be to a great extent an unproductive labor, the powers of thought under such circumstances will be usually feeble and sluggish, the perceptive faculties dim and obtuse, and the whole system of the mental faculties torpid and lethargic.

Every person who may be at all conversant with the use of books, will remember with what incredible alacrity and lightness of mind they have commenced the performance of any intellectual labor, at a late hour of the night, which appeared to them invincibly repulsive during the previous day, whilst the mind was clogged by the stupefying influence of a hearty meal.

It will also be remembered, too, by most persons, with how much vivacity of thought and feeling they have been enabled to resume any duty requiring a profound application of thought, under the weight of which they had staggered on the previous day, from a free devotion to the pleasures of the table.

There have been celebrated generals who ascribed the loss of a victory to an immoderate indulgence in the use of food immediately before going into action; and though habitually sparing in his meals, we think Napoleon Bonaparte was amongst that number. And we doubt not there have been many victories lost by this supervening impediment to clear and judicious thought, both on the field of martial strife and in the counsels of peaceful wisdom.

There are many persons who are as cautious in getting themselves in proper tune for any trial of intellectual strength in which they feel a special degree of interest, as a man of the turf usually is in training a courser of high metal for a race, on the issue of which thousands may be suspended. Men of this description relinquish the use of every gross or rich article of food, for days and sometimes weeks previous to the ostensible public performance of the duty before them, and confine themselves rigidly to the lightest articles of sustenance, and that in small quantities. And this previous surrender of all substantial food, is dictated by the blended consideration of securing the treasures of vigorous and active thought, both during the process of preparation and in the hour of performance.

But a total or partial abstinence from every rich or luxurious article of subsistence, not only confers a very signal benefit on a public speaker in promoting the strength of his reflective and inventive powers, and in heightening the acuteness of his perceptive faculties, but it also improves in a very visible degree his vocal functions or powers of delivery. Every speaker who addresses a jury or a popular assembly immediately after partaking of a hearty dinner, will find that his voice has been somewhat contracted in its compass, and that it will be also deficient in flexibility and melody. These injurious effects are wrought in the voice by that fulness and repletion of the glands and vessels about the throat and mouth which is produced by the stimulating influence of food.

If the duty of addressing a jury or other assembly should devolve on a speaker after dinner, and he is aware that this duty is in reserve for him, he may be enabled to preserve his mental and physical system both in tune for the occasion by indulging in a very sparing use of food. And he should also be careful to refrain from every article of gross food at at any hour of the day on which he is to speak, for the reason already assigned, that the mental operations are not only clogged by participating in rich food immediately before speaking, but the powers of delivery will also be impaired by the same cause.

The safest course for a student in any department of life to pursue on this subject, is to live sparingly as the daily habit of his life, and he will always be in tune for intellectual investigations. And when he is summoned by his position in life to make an argument, or to prepare a production on any subject of vital moment to his own interests, or to the interests of others, he will not find it necessary to make any considerable surrender of comfort or convenience by a large reduction of his daily allowance of food.

And whilst on this subject it may be proper to state, that one who habitually lives bountifully has no just conception of the smallness of the quantity that a human being can live comfortably upon, when he adopts the resolution of limiting the amount of his daily supplies. And the capability of man to live comfortably on an amount of food small in com parison with that which is now daily consumed by the bulk of our race, is not only revea ed in the disciplinary treatment prescribed by physicians, but also in the very limited supply of food which is daily consumed by many of the ardent votaries of science and literature.

CHAPTER LXXXIX.

A PUBLIC SPEAKER SHOULD ABSTAIN ENTIRELY FROM THE USE OF TOBACCO.

THE use of tobacco has become so pervasive in its character, as to lull almost into a state of quiet repose the spirit of speculation as to the extent of its baneful influence upon the varied interests of mankind. The specific amount of injury which is reflected by the use of this noxious weed on the health of its votaries, is a question which is not embraced within the province of this treatise. But it does fall within the pale of our present reflections to consider, to a brief extent, the amount of detriment which is communicated by the use of tobacco, to the powers of a public speaker.

And in elucidating this proposition, the mind may be accelerated in its progress to a just conclusion, without appealing to the pages of medical research. That noble and beneficent science pours a flood of light on this path of exploration, which holds up to observation as conspicuously as the brightness of a star, the various injuries which are visited upon the interests of our race by the use of tobacco. And in that enlightened classification the pernicious effect of this practice upon the human voice is included. But entirely independent of the learned deductions of the medical profession on this subject, we possess an infallible guide to accuracy of judgment, in the experience of public speakers who have habitually used tobacco in some of its varied forms, and also in the plain and legible results which must necessarily flow from pre-existing causes. Each of these auxiliaries to the spirit of inquiry affirm in characters of living and impressive light, that the voice suffers as much from the use of tobacco, as any other function of the human system.

And it is perfectly natural that the result should be so. For the voice is as dependent for its fulness, flexibility and sweetness, upon the preservation of the glands and minute vessels connected with the mouth and throat in their natural and healthful state, as is the faculty of digestion dependent for the punctual and faithful execution of its trust, upon keeping the organs about the stomach in a sound and regular condition.

The organs of speech, comprehending the mouth and throat with their varied machinery, receive those supplies of moisture, which are calculated to soften the harshness of the voice, and to give it the power of easy expansion, from an almost countless number of minute vessels or nerves which serve as conductors for the saliva. If these vessels are so stimulated by the process of chewing or smoking, as to exhaust in a given time, or even to consume a disproportionate share of those fluids, which are as essential to the facile movements of the vocal functions, as oil is to the motions of a mechanical machine, it must be perfectly evident to the reflecting mind, that the human voice cannot be as perfect and tuneable with its supply of moisture cut off or partially curtailed, as it would be with all its natural aids in full perfection. The voice is injured either by the smoking of a cigar, or by indulging in a chew of tobacco immediately precedent to the delivery of a speech; for the surplus of moisture or saliva, which would greatly assist the vocal organs in performing a specific amount of labor, will be previously drawn off by the stimulating influence of the pipe or the chew, and expended entirely in vain. But long perseverance, either in the practice of chewing, smoking, or snuffing, is calculated to impart an injury to the voice, which is more permanent in its character than the simple act of taking one chew, one cigar, or one pinch of snuff. The injurious influence exerted by one brief indulgence in this way, will be apt to expire with the act which gave it birth, whilst persisting in either of these forms of its use for a considerable length of time, not only deranges the application of the saliva, but it blunts the delicacy of the nerves and vessels about the throat, in such a way, by keeping them constantly stimulated, as to require a total surrender of the use of tobacco, united with the curative efficacy of time, to restore the voice to its original state.

There was an orator in this country, whose fame is co-extensive with the surface of the globe, who possessed a voice in speaking which was the perfection of music, and who yet was a habitual and prodigal taker of snuff. But his voice was originally so fine, and was so finely cultivated, that it preserved its silver tones in despite of a supervening encumbrance, just as some men of unusually robust constitutions, retain their health, vigor, and elasticity of frame, in defiance of the daily free use of stimulating liquids.

It is almost the certain tendency of smoking, chewing, or snuffing, to render the voice hoarse, husky, and difficult of modulation. And for the purpose of subjecting the truth of this proposition to a fair test, let a speaker who is in the habit of chewing or smoking, forego the luxury of his cigar or his chew, on the morning in which he is to deliver a speech, and he will discover a perceptible improvement in the sound and intonations of his voice, even from the influence of that brief respite.

CHAPTER XC.

A SPEAKER SHOULD NEVER RESORT TO STIMULATING LIQUIDS AS AUXILIARIES TO SUCCESSFUL SPEAKING.

A RESORT to stimulating liquids, with the view of exhilarating the feelings and warming the imagination, as a preparatory process to successful speaking, should be avoided like the fang of a viper. For even if the presence of so perilous an ally should be palpably beneficial to a speaker in the improvement of his oratorical powers, he will be greatly injured when he may not be able to command this auxiliary, in the affecting contrast which will be presented between his attractions then as a speaker, and when he has imbibed inspiration from the sparkling divinity. He will be as much incommoded, too, by his inability to grasp this baneful quiver of strength when he is about to speak, as a lame man would be at the loss of his crutches when about to start on a cruise of pleasure, in which he might feel the liveliest interest; or as a person of imperfect vision would feel at the abstraction of his spectacles when an illegible manuscript might be placed in his hands.

Another ill-consequence of momentous magnitude almost invariably flows from a servile dependence on so noxious a resource in the intellectual performances of life, and that is the deadening influence which is exerted over the reputation of a speaker by the suspicion that he is incompetent to act with success in the pure domain of intellect, without appealing to the most appalling appliance of vice. But inconceivably the most startling evil among the hated brood which springs from the practice now under consideration, may be recognized in the fact, that when a vice which pleads with the eloquence of original fascination to some minds, shall be commended to its votary by the additional charm of utility, it will most certainly seize his affections with a grasp so unrelenting and invincible, that nothing short of the power of Omnipotence can break it. Let the sparkling beverage be recommended to the lips of its already impassioned votary by the strong superadded merit of having delivered him from the clutches of some irksome disease, and it will prove miraculous if he is not placed utterly beyond the reach of moral persuasion and friendly restraint to save him.

But eloquence bears a glitter about it which shines more brightly and attractively to the human heart than even the return of blooming health to the cheek blanched with disease, and an advocate or speaker of any description who shall be allured to even the occasional use of intoxicating drinks, with the hope of grasping the prize of eloquence through its aid, will never search for any returning path to the temple of sobriety and virtue.

The path of human experience, both in this country and Britain, is strewed with mournful wrecks, in verification of the propositions which have been affirmed in this chapter. And if there be an instance on record that serves to demonstrate that there ever was a speaker who habitually resorted to stimulants to improve his elocution, who possessed any extraordinary degree of power and fascination independent of that aid; or that there ever was a speaker who was visibly improved in speaking by a recourse to stimulants, that ever was totally and completely reclaimed from the dominion of intemperance, then we are prepared to confess the revelation of a fact which has been entirely without the pale of our observation.

THE END.

Harper's Catalogue.

A New Descriptive Catalogue of Harper & Brothers' Publications, with an Index and Classified Table of Contents, is now ready for Distribution, and may be obtained gratuitously on application to the Publishers personally, or by letter inclosing Six Cents in Postage Stamps.

The attention of gentlemen, in town or country, designing to form Libraries or enrich their Literary Collections, is respectfully invited to this Catalogue, which will be found to comprise a large proportion of the standard and most esteemed works in English Literature —comprehending more than two thousand volumes — which are offered, in most instances, at less than one half the cost of similar productions in England.

To Librarians and others connected with Colleges, Schools, &c., who may not have access to a reliable guide in forming the true estimate of literary productions, it is believed this Catalogue will prove especially valuable as a manual of reference.

To prevent disappointment, it is suggested that, whenever books can not be obtained through any bookseller or local agent, applications with remittance should be addressed direct to the Publishers, which will be promptly attended to.

www.ingramcontent.com/pod-product-compliance
Lightning Source LLC
LaVergne TN
LVHW010156110826
845151LV00002B/533

* 9 7 8 1 4 2 5 5 3 7 9 1 3 *